DEDICATION

To my long-suffering, ever-loving K: without you, I wouldn't be who I am today.

And to my donor: without you I wouldn't be here at all.

CONTENTS

FOREWORD

April 2008
The New Inn, Tresco, Scilly Isles
10.15pm

"Oli are you sure we should be drinking with a load of Marines?"

"Come on, Ben, just one more Jaegerbomb!!"

Essentially that's how my relationship with Oli was cemented. We'd both taken part in the Tresco marathon in the Scilly Isles to raise money for the Cystic Fibrosis Trust. I was broken physically, having run around and around and up and down the island too many times for my liking. Oli, his then-girlfriend, now-wife Kati, along with his brother and his squad from 42 Commando Royal Marines (who had completed the 26.2 miles in full kit with 30lb packs on their backs) were slowly taking the rest of me apart. We've been mates ever since.

Oli is one of a number of friends I've been lucky enough to meet as a patron for the CF Trust. There is something remarkable about the people with CF I've met; despite the condition they have to endure day in day out, the endless rigmarole of tablets, nebulisers, and physio, the fact that they face a dauntingly uncertain future, I have never, ever, heard one of them so much as complain or ask for sympathy. And as such I certainly wasn't going to receive any in that pub on Tresco!

It would have been very easy for him post-transplant to take things easy, settle down to a calm, steady future with nothing overly challenging, nothing beyond his capabilities, nothing that could overly jeopardise his health. No one could have blamed him for that.

However, he did quite the opposite. He has embraced this second chance he's been given. He's grabbed the opportunity to really live with both hands, both feet, and a massive grin. Setting himself new challenges, giving himself new goals, ensuring the priceless gift he was entrusted with was not only appreciated, not only valued but genuinely relished.

Oli is a brilliantly eloquent, entertaining, ambitious, loving and inspiring individual - but you don't have to take my word for it, simply read this extraordinary account of his life and make your own mind up.

My only advice: if he – or his brother – ever asks you to go for a drink with them, be very, very wary!!!

Ben Shephard
November 2012

INTRODUCTION

This book consists mainly of posts from my blog at SmileThroughIt.com, which was designed to highlight to as many people as possible the trials and tribulations of life on the transplant list.

It's not a pleasant or fun road to experience, nor one I would wish on the worst of my enemies. That's not to say you can't still have fun (as I hope this book shows), but it's not the kind of thing I'd recommend.

The text has been left almost entirely as-is from the blog posts themselves, save for fixing a few glaring spelling errors. I could have edited more heavily, re-written sections to seem more prescient or circumspect, or removed several of the more mundane episodes, but I chose not to because what I think you will gain, over the course of the next 12 months-worth of posts, is an insight into the true roller coaster lifestyle that anyone awaiting a transplant must endure.

You'll read about some of the most exciting times in my life – raising over £20,000 production managing a comedy gig for Live Life Then Give Life, being invited on to Radio 4 and speaking to national newspapers about organ donation and transplant.

You'll also read about the terrible toll all of these took on my body and my brain. You'll see how periods of activity are followed all-too-closely by enforced inactivity and the frustrations and anger that comes with them.

I hope more than anything that this book will serve to give people an illustration of just why it's so important to sign up to the Organ Donor Register – or whatever the service is called in your native country – in order that others may be saved the agonising wait I had to endure and that friends of mine are currently going through.

You'll also see just what a dim-witted, self-indulgent, melodramatic, pretentious muppet I can be.

Hopefully, you'll end up smiling through it with me.

PROLOGUE

It's dark outside and I wake with a start. The mask clamped to my face – supposedly to help me breathe – feels like it's not giving me enough air. I fight against it, grabbing at the straps to pull it off, but it's unfamiliar and not as easy to release as the one I'm used to.

Eventually, it comes away from my face and I scrabble to turn the machine off as it starts to alarm. As I turn in my bed I realize I can hardly move for wires trailing all over me, most of them permanently attached to me under my skin in various places all over my body.

I manage to take a breath and look around. I'm in hospital, that much is clear, but I don't recognize it; it's a larger room than I'd normally have and oddly decorated. Without my glasses I can't see much, but I do manage to grab the call-bell and hit it.

I hear the familiar drone of the buzzer out in the hallway and moments later a young nurse enters. She's young – not more than 20 – and I don't recognize her, either, but she smiles kindly and crosses over to me from the doorway, deftly leaning over to cancel the call as she does.

"Everything ok?" she asks.

"I don't know where I am," I respond.

"Where do you think you are?"

I pause and look around again: an unfamiliar hospital room with unfamiliar staff. A sea of colourful cards on the noticeboard opposite the foot of the bed. I'm wearing a hospital gown and see two very, very large tubes sticking out from underneath.

Something starts to dawn; a slow but certain realization that, at first, I don't want to give any credit to because to wake up from a dream like this would be the worst kind of self-inflicted torture.

The nurse stands patiently at my side and I understand that I'm not dreaming. The pain alone helps with that.

"I'm in Harefield," I tell her. "And I've had my transplant."

November 2006
(12 Months)

A Statement of Intent

Saturday 18 November

Blogs. There's millions of 'em. The world has blogs coming out of its ears. The world has blogs coming out of pretty much every orifice. So why am I adding to the over-crowded madness and what's this all about?

I'm here for me, mostly, but I'm also here in the vain hope that someone, somewhere, someday may find some useful knowledge or comfort in the words that will follow and the journey I'm embarking on.

18 months ago, in June 2005, I elected to go onto the active transplant list for a double-lung transplant. I have Cystic Fibrosis and over the course of a few years I had slowly declined to the point where my specialist team at the Churchill Hospital in Oxford arrived at the conclusion that I was now eligible for transplant.

I say "eligible" because transplant is a very odd thing: to be considered for the list you need to walk a very fine line between being ill enough to warrant a) taking the chance of a new life away from someone else on the waiting list and b) taking the risk that such a massive surgical procedure places on your already frail body, but at the same time being well enough that, complications aside, your body will have enough in reserve to withstand the rigours of surgery.

Since I went on the list in the middle of last year, my health has been stable and I've been *relatively* well. With CF, things are all relative.

In September this year, however, things took a turn for the worse and I'm now facing a countdown to the end of a race that is going to end on one of two sides of a coin.

Only 50% of people who go on the transplant list actually receive the organs they require to go on and live a full and happy life. The other 50% die while they wait.

Throughout my life coping with the ups and downs of CF – and believe you me they are myriad – I've learnt one thing above all others:

If you don't laugh, you cry.

Hence the title of this blog.

Whatever happens over the coming months and years, wherever my health takes me and whatever else life throws at me, this blog will be here not only to document the process, but also to remind me when the going gets to its very toughest, that the world is really a very funny place and you have to keep on smiling, because the other options are too dark to think of.

My intention in this blog is to chart my day-to-day progress, both physically and mentally, as I race the clock towards its ultimate conclusion – one way or the other.

I'm not (quite) vain enough to think that I'm going to change the world with a little diary-cum-biography-cum-progress report, but as with all things I do, both for the Cystic Fibrosis Trust and in my life in general, if it makes a difference to just one person and helps them get through a tough time, helps them realise they are not alone or just shows them that life's not always so bad after all, then it will be worth it.

Whatever you do in life, always have courage in your convictions – throw yourself into it with all your energy and strive every day to be the best that you can be. You truly never know what's around the corner and regrets in life are the hardest thing to deal with when you face a ticking clock.

Adaptation

Sunday 19 November

The hardest thing to come out of my recent downturn in form – as it were – is the adaptation I'm having to make to the way I do things and the things I do.

Yesterday, my big bro took me out in the afternoon to catch the new Bond movie (which is fab, incidentally, if somewhat dumbed-down Hollywood in parts) in the Xscape Cineworld in town. The trouble is it's about a 200-300 yard walk from car to screen, including going up a floor, which took me a long time to negotiate and a lot more energy than I was used to.

I've recently become accustomed to walking a lot slower than I used to, although I did go through a patch of setting off at marching pace for 10-15 yards before being pulled up by unhappy lungs protesting at the work rate. I've now learned to start out slowly and continue in the same vein, but this latest infection has left me with a real need for permanent oxygen supply – something my pride has not quite caught up with.

Last night, K had some old work colleagues over for a girlie night in, which I couldn't avoid and actually really enjoyed (she's really quite girlified me). But even though it was in our place, and spent entirely sat on the sofas in he lounge, I couldn't bring myself to wear my O2 in front of the group.

Silly, I know, but a good example of the adaptations I'm having to make to carry on as normal. I've got to get used to the idea that I'm going to have to have my nasal specs on when people are here and, more troubling for the moment, I'm going to have to get used to taking a portable cylinder out with me when I leave the flat.

It's hard to describe the battle of heart and mind that's going on at the moment – my head knowing that things are not only easier but also much better with the O2 on, my heart not wanting to be seen as a "sick person" by all and sundry who see me in the street.

One of the few blessings of CF is that to the untrained eye (and often to the trained, if you ask medical students patrolling the wards in hospital), the average person with CF doesn't look any different to the average person without CF. Slightly skinny, maybe, but skinniness is somewhat in vogue at the moment anyway (for the girls, at least) so it's not a big thing.

Going out with nasal specs and an O2 cylinder is another matter altogether. No one else does that. "Normal" people don't travel adorned with extra air. Which means admitting to the world that you're not the He-Man you wanted them to think you were. Or, at the very least, admitting that you're "different".

It's one of life's little ironies that I've spent such a lot of my life championing individuality to my friends, family and, more than anyone, the kids in my workshops, and now here I find myself aching to conform, to fit in, to *blend.*

But needs must, and I know I'll come around to it. I just need to be more forceful with myself and understand that if I'm wearing the O2, I'll be able to do more than I can at the moment, and hopefully "freedom" will be the spur that allows me to come to terms with it.

Failing that, anyone with any other ideas, please let me know!

A flare for the dramatic

Monday 20 November

23.01, Sunday 19 Nov

K brings me the phone, which she's just answered, "It's Nicky, from Harefield."

"How are you feeling, Oli?"

"Okay." Shitting myself.

"Any problems that you know of?"

"Nothing new." My heart's just stopped.

"We have a match for you on paper. It's early in the process at the moment and our retrieval team is on the way there now, but we'd like to get you in. It might be a wild goose chase."

"Okay." Okay.

Surprisingly calmly (this being my second call from Harefield since I was listed 18 months ago), I gather my things and K gets un-ready for bed. 20 minutes later, we're at Mum and Dad's and squeezing into Mum's Polo, my bro having borrowed my dad's nice spacious estate for the week to move his stuff out of his barracks in Canterbury.

It struck me as we sailed down the empty, wind-swept, rainy M1 towards London that this may prove to be the most short-lived chronicle of a run-up to transplant in the history of the blogosphere. Wouldn't that be upsetting?

We arrived at the hospital about half twelve and Nicky, the coordinator for the night, told me that the retrieval process was just starting and that there would be no news till after 3-3.30am.

The ever-efficient team then set about the myriad tests and odd jobs the docs and nurses have to do pre-op.

In no particular order (it's somewhat of a blur, to be honest) I had 14 vials of blood taken, a venflon inserted (small cannula in the arm for giving drugs through), height, weight, temperature, blood pressure and O2 sats checked, a chest X-ray, and ECG (heart-monitor thing) and a few pieces of paperwork about me to fill in.

The most wonderful part of the exercise was without doubt the full-body shave and alcohol shower. Wonderful little clippers provided by the NHS did for what little body hair I had above the waist, and there were certain other bits of delicate work to do, too.

Followed immediately by a shower using a full-body alcohol scrub like soap. And yes, if you've just sucked the air in through gritted teeth, that's exactly what I did, too. Nice.

Prepped and gowned by 2.30am, we set about waiting. And waiting. It all seems to have passed in a blur now, but it was interminable at the time. As the clock ticked past 4am, I began slowly to unravel from my tightly-wound coil of security and self-knowledge.

Bizarrely, what starting playing on my mind wasn't the fear of the op itself, nor the fact that I might not make it through. Instead, my mind fixated on what it would be like when I came around and I was enveloped in a fear of claustrophobia should I happen to come around while still attached to the ventilator afterwards.

The thing about anaesthetics and post-operative sedation is that it tends to meddle with your memory. So while you may be fully awake and alert and responsive, you may not actually remember it afterwards.

Not remembering means that, to all intense and purposes, to you it didn't happen. So I became somewhat obsessed with wanting to know at what point I would "wake up" – when my awareness post-operatively would kick in.

It wasn't until 4.30am that Nicky came back to us, by now huddling close together in the room with everyone trying to seep strength into me. The retrieval surgeons had been in and looked and while, on paper, the lungs looked good, on closer inspection the team weren't happy with what they saw and decided to abort the retrieval process.

It was a no-go.

It's hard to describe the deflation of news like that – the total release of tension and relief mixed with bitter disappointment mixed with adrenaline-fuelled exhaustion.

Venflon removed, gown cast off, re-dressed in street clothes, I shuffled my way into a chair for a ride down to the car and the journey home. Arriving back at the flat at 6am, I flopped onto the sofa and did my morning dose of IVs which were now due, then slipped into bed, slid onto my NIV mask and promptly fell asleep.

Looking back on the experience today, after a totally lost morning and an afternoon of bleary-eyed chilling-out, it has been a lot easier to cope with than my first false alarm.

All the way through the process I was a lot calmer than I was last time, largely helped by the fact that there were no surprises, I knew the drill and knew what to expect.

The deflation, while marked, isn't anywhere near comparable to last time and the roller coaster of emotions is much more sedate. Gulliver's Land compared to Alton Towers, tea cups to waltzers.

I was interested by my reaction and how my fear manifested itself. The post-operative period has never really bothered me before, but that's what my mind chose to focus on last night. With hindsight, it's clear that it was merely the way my brain dealt with the general fear of the unknown, latching on to one element and amplifying it to take control and form a focal-point.

I spoke to Dad this afternoon and he's already started a book on how many times from now we hear, "Third time lucky," from people. I'm confidently predicting double-figures.

The best thing to happen today, however, is nothing to do with CF, Transplant, false alarms or anything else. Suzanne, the practitioner and workshop-leader I work with at MK came over for a cuppa with her hubby this afternoon on their way home from Costco, the bulk-by warehouse and brought with them what can only be described as a *vat* of Flumps, the little marshmallow shapes. I haven't seen proper, official, perfect little flumps for YEARS and I've been searching high and low. And now, I've got a vat full of them!

It may have been a roller-coaster day, but my flumps will keep me smiling through it…!

Stranger at home

Tuesday 21 November

The dynamics of my home have changed.

I used to live in a small, 2-bedroom flat on the 1st floor of a block in a small court at the southern end of Bletchley in Milton Keynes, just up the road from the Bletchley Park of Enigma code-breaking machine fame. It was just the right size for me and my best friend, K, to co-habit peacefully yet maintain our own private spaces. It was cosy.

Geographically, I remain on the 1st floor in a court just up the road from Bletchley Park, of Enigma fame. There are, however, no longer 2 bedrooms. Since K and I got together some 5 months ago, we have discussed getting rid of the 2nd bedroom and giving me somewhere to write and us both somewhere to use the computer and to have a desk for all the usual household administration-type stuff that was taking over our table in our lounge/diner.

While I was in hospital over the last two weeks, K took it upon herself to enlist the help of some very good friends of ours to transform her old bedroom into our newly formed study/library. Out with the bed, the chest of drawers and the telly and in with the bookcase, a desk and chair and a lava-lamp (for good creative-juice flow) along with a filing cabinet and desk-drawer unit for storage. A perfect little work-hole for both of us.

But that's not the significant change.

What's changed is that far from being a small, cosy little flat, when I returned from hospital I discovered my home to be a vast expanse of space around which is had become necessary not to pop from room to room, but to hike breathlessly between oxygen stations.

I spoke previously of the adaptations I'm having to make following my recent challenges and down-turns in health and this is simply another one, but it's one I have to confess I didn't see coming. I love my flat – I love it all the more now I'm sharing it increasingly with K, who is slowly moving herself back across from her parents' house – and I just never thought that somewhere this compact and beautifully self-contained could present these sorts of challenges.

I now have oxygen piped into every room of the apartment, but it still necessitates switching from supply to supply between rooms, with O2 support-less journeys between piping points.

Whereas I used to merrily flitter away all over the flat, tootling back and forth between kitchen and lounge and bedroom as many times as my delightfully dim-witted brain would require before collecting all the bits I'd need for, say, doing a nebuliser, I now find that forgetting an element of the cocktail requires a 5 minute break before setting out to correct the mistake.

K is doing amazingly at running around after my forgetfulness, but it's infuriating to me that I can't do the simple things without gasping for air, that checking on dinner in the oven requires preparation, precision movement and a recuperation period.

I know it's something I'll get used to, just the same way as I'm slowly getting used to sleeping with my NIV, the way I'm getting used to wearing my O2. I've adapted in the past; even as recently as September I learnt how to budget my time so that I had the energy to do the things that matter most and not waste my daily or weekly quota on frivolous or unnecessary things.

And I know I'll adapt to my new home, too.

Already, I'm loving my study (our study) and my brain is starting to whirl with possibilities of new scripts and projects and ideas – seemingly freed by the knowledge that if I so desire, I can shut myself away from the rest of the world and tap at my keyboard 24/7 until my masterpiece emerges.

After all, they say if you give an infinite amount of monkeys an infinite number of typewriters, they'll eventually turn out the Complete Works of Shakespeare. I just need my new lungs to give me that little bit more time to bash at the keys and see if I can't luck into Hamlet.

Trains of thought

Wednesday 22 November

A good friend of mine has recently been seeing a psychologist to help them through a particularly tough time in their lives and we were chatting about it a little while ago. They told me something their Crazy Doc had told them about managing negativity that really stuck with me.

Negative thinking is like standing at a train station. When something happens to provoke "bad" thoughts, a train pulls into the station intent on taking you off on a journey through all your worst fears and insecurities, dragging up all the things which will drag you down and leading you on a sombre dance of distress.

But if you learn to recognise the triggers, you can provide a platform announcer in your head who can flag up the destination of the train pulling in and you can choose to stay on the platform. You can elect not to take the train to the dark place, but instead to board the daylight express to the end of the tunnel. You just have to be able to recognise the moments when you need the announcer.

It's all well and good noting wisdom and realising its benefits, it's quite another to put it into practice in everyday life.

Which is why I'm so happy about my day today and the way I've managed to avoid getting on the wrong train and instead enjoyed my time at home and looked forward to other things later in the week.

K took my mum out for a girlie shopping trip this afternoon, nominally looking for Christmas presents, but largely to look at pretty things and coo. I stayed at home in the flat, mostly to sleep.

In days gone by recently, this would have upset me. Not because I yearned for the chance to run around town pointing at prettiness (I'm not *that* girlified…), nor because I had a desire to nick a *melange* of treats from the sweetie barrow, but simply because they were doing something that I felt I couldn't do.

But I chose not to get on that train, to avoid the Sloppy Bollocks Express to Tear Town, and instead jump on the Chill Train to the City of Smiles.

Rather than see the afternoon as a missed opportunity to go out, it was instead a perfect opportunity to sit back, relax and pop on a DVD that I love but rarely get the chance to enjoy. (That's The West Wing, not anything best "enjoyed" alone, you dirty minded older-brother-types. Yes, I'm talking to the twins.)

I find myself at my computer this evening not sullenly relaying stories of my abandonment, but finding ways of communicating how far I feel I've come in the last 24 hours in breaking the back of my adaptation process.

Life's all about the ups and the downs – riding the waves and hoping not to fall off. But you always know that even if you do, all you have to do is paddle back out and you'll pick up another one soon enough.

I may not get back to the level I was at before this summer, I may have to make changes and adjustments, I may want to scream and shout and tear the place down, but I know that with the love and support of all those around me, I'll keep on going.

Kipling once wrote, "If you can meet with Triumph and Disaster / And treat those two impostors just the same," then, "Yours is the Earth and everything that's in it, / And – which is more – you'll be a Man, my son!".

My Triumph is waiting for me in the wings, and Disaster may be in the way, but you know what? I can take it. Hurl whatever you want at me, World, because sooner or later I'm going to have new lungs and I'm going to hurl it straight back!

One more day, one more ride

Friday 24 November

Last night was a toughie.

Having just about managed to get myself off to bed without succumbing to narcoleptic attacks in the hallway between bathroom and bedroom after staying awake until nearly 11pm for my IV's to finish, my NIV started playing up and cutting out on me while I was dozing off to sleep.

NIV essentially works by blowing air into your lungs and helping to suck it back out again, "assisting" your breathing muscles and respiratory system and ensuring a better flow of air – oxygen in and carbon dioxide out – through the night, thus avoiding CO2 build-up and the morning headaches I'd been suffering from for some weeks previously.

NIV is delivered through an almost air-tight mask strapped to your face, which ensures a seal around your nose and lips to make sure that the appropriate amounts of air are being supplied at the right time, with just a small exhaust port to make sure that you're not re-breathing your own expelled CO2.

When the machine starts cutting out, you find yourself strapped into an air-less chamber which is not only no longer helping you breath, it's now positively hindering you. Thus, when you're nodding off to sleep, the odd sensation of forced breathing is replaced by a sudden lack of air and O2, and ever alert to the change, your body wakes you up again.

After drifting off and waking up three times in the first hour of "sleep" last night, I finally threw in the towel and took the mask off. The question now was what to do for the rest of the night. It was now 1am and I had to be up at 7am to do my morning dose of drugs.

I knew if I slept without oxygen, I would hardly sleep at all as my body won't let me fall into a relaxed, shallow-breathing state of deep sleep since my oxygen levels then drop dangerously low. But with oxygen on, my CO2 retention skyrockets and by morning my body is slowly starting to poison itself and I wake with an almighty headache.

I think in polite circles they call it Hobson's choice.

I got up and out of bed and sat myself on the sofa, nasal specs on, trying to decide my best cause of action. By 2am, my eyes couldn't pretend to be awake any longer and I had to take myself back to bed, where I gave in and popped on my specs and tried to get comfy.

Having not tried "normal" (i.e. – unaided) sleep for weeks, I was surprised to find that my body didn't take kindly a lying down and insisted on a more propped position than I had been used to with the NIV working. Eventually, after much tossing, turning and gasping for air at occasional moments, I managed to drift off. Surprisingly, I slept fairly continuously until my alarm woke me.

As I'd suspected, my headache attacked. On the plus side, I wasn't as immobilised as I often can be by it, but it's still not a pleasant sensation to wake up to. I did my drugs and took myself back off to bed, where I reattached my NIV and tried, fairly successfully, to sleep again.

Finally waking at 11am, I was dismayed to find that far from blowing off the CO2 from my system, the NIV appeared to have simply maintained the same levels and left my headache in situ – not part of the plan. But having got up out of bed and taken some painkillers, things soon righted themselves.

Once the headache had passed, I was delighted to find that I actually felt pretty well-rested and not near as shattered as I'd expected to be after such a late night and rough sleep. I set about sorting through the mass of disorganised paperwork in our new study and catching up with all the bills and demands that had been made of me since before I went into the Churchill some 3 weeks ago.

In fact, after a bad start, today has been remarkably productive. Not only have I caught up on a lot of stuff, I've also proved to myself my capacity for work and concentration now I've somewhere to shut myself away when I need it. Prevarication is going to get harder and harder now I'm making more and more steps in the right direction and continually proving my abilities and boundaries to myself.

A mate of mine, S, who had been instrumental in helping K make-over the study – taking things apart, building things, moving things, juggling things, drinking tea – popped round after work today, which was cool as I hadn't seen him since I broke out. Even better, he came bearing a gift, which blew me away.

Everywhere my bro travels (and he travels a LOT) he always brings me back a piece of artwork, however large or small, so that I can at least taste a morsel of the culture he's explored. Over the years, I've collected up pieces from Australia, New Zealand, Tonga, Malawi, Egypt, Brazil, America, Italy and others. Last Christmas he bought me a panoramic photograph picture of Rio de Janeiro from his visit there. S has always been a big fan of the pic, but until now it sat rolled up on a shelf in my room, looking for a place to live.

Seeing a vast expanse of wall open up above the desk in the study as they assembled it, S took it upon himself to liberate the pic from my stuff and take it off to get it framed. He brought it back today looking nothing short of majestic and I can't wait to get it up on my wall over the desk. I must confess, though, I am slightly concerned about losing myself in it every time my eye wanders from my keyboard.

The day improved so greatly as it went on that I don't want to sully it with the Great Allied Respiratory Saga, but rest assured that this will not be the last you hear of it. The new home oxygen service has come in for a substantial amount of criticism in the past few months since its inception, and today I found out why.

For now, I'm going to quit while I'm ahead and remember that the qualities that make a day good or bad come merely from what you choose to highlight in your day.

Oh, I'm so wise...

Friday 24 November

I thought I had it all figured out. I thought I had it licked. I'd crested the hill of negative thought and was rolling hurriedly down the other side with a devil-may-care glint in my eye and a skip in my oxygen-enhanced step.

But as if to remind me that roller-coasters have downs as well as ups (are we all enjoying the mash-up of metaphors today?), life turns around and bites me on bee-hind like a snake interrupted in the middle of dinner. A really nasty snake that bites really badly and hurts a lot. Like a cobra. Not an adder.

Last night I toppled over into full-on insomniac territory. I managed a grand total of 90 minutes sleep, and for the pedants among you, it was from 5.30am-6.30am and from 6.45am-7.15am. I also managed a brief nap between 8.15am and 8.45am, which I don't count as sleep as technically I'd already got up in the morning to do my drugs. Even counting the nap, that's still a whopping 2 hours of sleep.

There are few things worse than lying in bed, waiting for sleep to envelope you, only to find that the Sandman appears to have left you off his rounds for the night, or made his house-call while you were in the bathroom brushing your teeth.

I would have been tossing and turning all night, had my NIV not insisted it was only going to work when I lay on my left side. That may have been a blessing, mind, because if I'd have been lying on my right hand side I'd have spent the night staring at K sleeping soundly all night next to me, which is bound to wind one up a little…

Today, then, has not really followed the pattern of yesterday, nor managed to continue the wave of optimistic advancement. It has passed, and is indeed still passing, in a fog, a mist, a veil of heavy-eyed melancholy as my mind has struggled to make sense of the simplest little thing going on in the world.

It took me so long to respond to K this morning that you'd have sworn her enquiry was more closely related to the implications of Chaos Theory when applied to Newton's First Law rather than the desirability of a high-temperature, caffeine-enhanced morning beverage. In fact, I'm not entirely certain I actually gave her an answer, but I got a cup of tea all the same.

I think it's fair to say that nothing productive has come from my day so far today. I managed to get to Oxford to have my levels checked for my IV's, and I managed (just about) to absorb the necessary information from my physio to operate my new NIV machine that they've given me, but beyond that, very little has actively passed through my brain and come out again in any semblance of comprehensible fashion.

I'm perfectly expecting to wake up tomorrow morning (oh to wake up – what a joy it would be, to be so far asleep as to be able to define oneself as actually waking up!) and read this back to myself and discover nothing more than a thrice-too-long stream of consciousness resembling more closely a collection of randomly-arranged letters than an essay understandable to students and natives of the English tongue.

If you've made it this far down today's entry, I commend you. Personally, I think I'd have given up after paragraph 2, but I suppose there is something of the car crash in the nature of it that may have been appealing enough to endure an extra few minutes' worth of reading to see if I may actually have lost the plot completely, or merely temporarily misplaced it.

Perhaps, after a night's rest and – dare I say it – sleep, I will be able to look back on today and pick out the moments of levity that helped me through, but right now, I'm nodding off to daydreams of a bed made of such softness that its entirely possible to lose an entire person into the mattress without the merest hint showing to the outside world.

So long, farewell, *auf wiedersehen*, goodnight.

All in a day's work

Monday 27 November

A week has passed since I ejected myself from Geoffrey Harris Ward in the Churchill in Oxford and my adaptation process has continued apace, not with 100% reliable or positive results.

I have to confess for all my jaunty little exploits that have made it up on to here, there have been a number of far less jaunty moments, and some which have had me fairly close to tears.

The interesting thing is the pattern into which life has settled over the past 7-10 days since I got back home again. Oddly, although every day has been different, they all seem to have followed the same arc from morning to night.

First thing in the morning, once sleepiness has subsided and the world is in focus, I feel positive and upbeat and keen for the day ahead. I wrap my head around the things I want to do for the day and assess what my energy levels are like and what I think I can realistically get through. Then, after 2 different nebs, a physio session, some breakfast and a shower, I set about whatever it is within the confines of the flat that I've set myself to do.

By the early afternoon, it's time for a recap on the benefits of sleep, and I get my head down for an hour or so, before stirring to do my IVs. For a patch of about and hour or two after I wake, I'm recovered enough to pursue things I want to do before the early evening, when tiredness bordering on exhaustion begins to settle in and things become a bit more of a battle.

My chest will start to moan and complain about the strain of, you know, breathing for an entire 12 hours without any supplementary support from Neve (as I've Christened my NIV machine, thanks to K's thinking and Em's bright idea of making things less scary through anthropomorphism).

Joining in the fun, my stomach will announce it's desire to be sated with a sacrifice like some built-in God of Food who will readily close up and not accept offerings should they not be timed appropriately according to it's very own desire.

As my body protests, so my mind – and my mood – takes a dive. The tiredness takes over my faculties for divining the logical and illogical in the world around me, the easy questions of everyday life become heart-wrenching, brain-busting trials of wit whereby turning over to Channel 4 can be the sum of a good 15 minutes worth of hard cogitation coupled with inner debate about the relative merits of watching Nothing Very Much on either this channel or that and wouldn't-it-be-good-if-we-had-Sky thinking.

The spiral continues into the night and I'm plagued mostly by the fact that I have to stay up until at least 10pm in order to administer my nightly third dose of IVs before I can retire to bed and the warm comforts of Neve.

(If anyone ever here's me suggest that an NIV machine is either a) warm or b) comfortable or c) in any way vaguely pleasurable, I suspect it has become time to skip the medication and proceed straight to a padded cell.)

The nights are the hardest, as my protesting lungs (even after a second, or third, physio session of the day) do everything they can to make getting undressed and ready for bed the biggest chore of the day. Breathlessness results from the most minor activity and washing my face and brushing my teeth become the greatest amount of exercise I've achieved all day.

And as I settle into bed, I have a tendency in my semi-conscious stupor to dwell on the things my life has lost in the last few weeks and months.

Even now, sitting writing this, I can see how the spiral starts and escalates, I can pinpoint the moments when everything starts to move in the wrong direction and I can see how my thinking patterns work against me almost constantly.

It may, to some, seem as if I'm outlining "a day in the life" for a sympathy vote, or in order to make people reading this understand what I "go through" every day. That is not my intention.

What I've found with everything else so far in this chronicle of mine is that by writing it down and reading it back, in a public domain where there is no where to hide, I can force myself into examining my thoughts, feelings and actions in a way I never would in my own head.

By illustrating my point as if to someone who knows me not at all, I simultaneously force myself to see things from a different perspective, to get out of my own well of self-pity and understand what's behind the changes in mood and strategic thinking.

Smile Through It, that's what it's all about – and if you know what it is that makes you stop smiling, you can keep your eye out for it and keep it at bay.

If it's not one thing…

Monday 27 November

Things have been steadily improving over my week out of hospital and after my insomniac murmurings last Friday, I was whisked to the Churchill for bloods to check the dosage of my current IV antibiotic regime. (The two things are, actually, unconnected, despite how I made them sound in that sentence…)

Just as I was leaving the flat, I got a call from my physio asking me to take mini-Neve in with me (mini-Neve being the smallest NIV I've been given, as compared to Neve and Fat Neve). It turns out that, as suspected, NHS employees have far too much time on their hands and often find themselves perusing the websites and weblogs of their patients. And, I trust, are now in the process of calling I.T. Support because they've just spat coffee all over their keyboard. Unless they're at home. (Don't worry, you can always blame Seb.)

But clearly, it's all part of the ever-expanded and improved NHS service and I'm certainly not going to mutter anything in the way of discontent, because no sooner had I been leeched by the vampires in pathology, than I was on the old ward (now the Treatment Centre) being shown the ropes on my New Neve.

New Neve (who will from now on simply go by Neve, because I'm a lazy git and typing New every time is far too annoying) is not as swish-looking or well-designed as the last one, and still stands with one foot somewhat in the analogue age, but appears to be much less inclined to a) stop breathing and b) stop breathing. Both of which I see as positive factors conducive to good breathing overnight.

And what a God-send she is, too, sorting out my insomnia with a breath of humidified air, perfectly in sync with my own breathing and without even a hint of giving up the ghost halfway through the evening's work.

Settled into my nice new overnight world with my nice, new

overnight partner, the weekend passed in a wonderful haze of relaxation and sleep.

Which is clearly not enough excitement for my body.

At 5.30am this morning, with Neve being somewhat cranky (well, it is Monday morning), I wake up lying on my side in bed with a pain in my chest.

"Nuts," I think to myself, "I must be sleeping on my port and making my shoulder ache." I readjust myself and rustle around a little. The pain stays. I realise I'm lying on my left side, the opposite to my port site, so the pain emanating from my right shoulder can't be port-pressure related.

I roll over. It gets worse. I breathe in deeply at the discomfort. It gets worse.

My by now increasingly awake brain sets into motion and starts ticking off symptoms on it's mental self-diagnosis list: stabbing pain in specific spot on chest: check; increases significantly on inspiration: check; spreads up into the neck and slightly down the arm on inspiration: check; lessens on exhalation/improves with shallow breathing: check. Previous symptoms-compatibility: pneumothorax, to the letter.

A pneumothorax, for those of you out of the loop on medical jargon, apart from being very hard to spell (and stumps most spell-checkers) is a partial collapse of the lung. I've had them before, four times as a matter of fact, although previously all on my left side, and they are usually identified by a "popping" sensation before the pain arrives, which I sadly appear to have slept through this time.

They can vary in severity, from minuscule to major, the very worse being only slightly less than an entire lung-collapse.

Luckily for me, mine have never (including today's) been bad enough to warrant any kind of emergency treatment. Frequently, the only course of action for pneumothoraxes (check the correct plural usage!) is to insert a chest drain, a process that I'm assured is as painful and uncomfortable – not to mention as inconvenient – as it sounds.

Sticking to my propensity for drama without the critical edge, my lung has behaved itself in not deflating any more. It has, rather mischievously, managed to detach itself ever so slightly from my chest wall right around the point where my port is located, which means it's pretty much impossible to spot on an X-ray, although I know for certain it's there.

So the recovery and adaptation process is thrown into turmoil once again. Having spoken to my wonderful Doc at Oxford, I have managed to avoid immediate admission, but I've had to retire to Mum and Dad's to recuperate as with the combination of pain and decreased tolerance to any kind of movement, I'm going to need more babying than K can afford me at the flat right now.

It's a massive blow, if I'm honest, as the last week or so has caused a rather marked sensation of losing my independence and to now be taking a further step back to living at home with the 'rents is a bit like having your face rubbed in it.

That's not to say anything against my parents, and indeed there's nowhere right now I'd rather be, because it's intensely relaxing and easy to cope with, knowing that I can get whatever I want just by asking and I don't have to worry about doing anything for myself. But in the grand scheme of things, it feels like another step backwards.

I'm aware of just how bizarrely those last two paragraphs read: at once mourning the loss of my independence and celebrating being back at Mum and Dad's and the security and reassurance it brings, but that's kind of the place I'm in mentally at the moment. Every situation has 2 sides to it and I seem to be constantly experiencing both of them at once.

Right now, the painkillers are working and I've had a rest and a sleep this afternoon, things are looking OK and I know I just need a few days of rest and I'll be good – or improving at least – but I also know that tonight, when I wake in the middle of the night with chest pains, and quite possibly with a headache since using Neve is out of the question with a pneumo (the pressure being too much risk of causing a much bigger collapse), I will struggle to see the positives here.

All I can hope is that if I fail to get back to sleep, I can come down here and log on to this blog and remind myself of the positives – that they are there and they will be tomorrow and that improvement is just a matter of small steps taken one at a time. Sometimes they go a little the wrong way, but I know if I wait long enough to recover between missteps I'll end up striding forward again.

When the media calls…

Thursday 30 November

It's certainly been an interesting last 12hours.

Following the announcement last night that Gordon Brown's 4-month old son, Fraser, has been diagnosed with Cystic Fibrosis, I've already done three breakfast radio show interviews – 2 on the phone for BBC 3 Counties Radio in Luton (Beds/Herts) and BBC Radio Berkshire, and one in the studio for BBC 3 Counties Radio in Bucks, which happens to be just up the road from my Mum and Dad's house where I'm holed up at the moment.

I first heard the news when Em phoned me last night and told me about it. It must be horribly upsetting for the family, especially having it "outed" as it appears to have been by a Sun scoop. But they seem to be dealing with it in the best possible way, staying upbeat and positive and looking towards the future with hope.

And there's no reason for them not to. With Fraser being diagnosed at birth and going straight onto a regime of necessary treatment, there's no reason to think that he should be capable of having a really good stab at a normal life. With the Gene Therapy trials just around the corner, babies being born with CF stand an infinitely better chance of leading a full and happy life than ever before.

Support for the Brown's from the CF community has been over-whelming, with the message boards on the CF Trust inundated with parents and PWCF leaving messages.

I was woken this morning at 6.45am by a call on my mobile, which is always on because of the possibility of a transplant call, and a researcher from the BBC asking if I'd do a phoner for them at 7am. Bizarrely, I agreed and while I was on the phone to the studio giving them my best "CF's rubbish but the Brown's needn't be all blue" I had a beeping in my ear from the other branch of 3 counties and a voice-mail left to call them.

No sooner had I come off air from my first interview (where I'd actually managed to leave the presenter speechless – go me!) than I was arranging an 8am studio visit for the MK branch of the breakfast show, whilst getting a call off a producer with Berkshire who is engaged to the first researcher I'd spoken to who had obviously relayed my performance just minutes earlier.

60 seconds later I was doing my second phoner of the morning and within 5 minutes was back off the phone, lying in bed and

drawing up my morning dose of IVs. Having administered them, I got myself up out of bed and dressed as quickly as my puffy little lungs would allow and jumped in the car with mum to trundle up the road to the Bucks 3 Counties Studio, where Martin Coote does his breakfast show that I've visited twice before.

This time I dragged Mum in with me and she gave a great account from a parent's perspective, before I filled Martin in on my current situation and even managed to get a plug for the Live Life Then Give Life campaign in, which was a bonus!

I was back home by 8.30am having pretty much not stopped since the first phone call this morning. I'm now starting to feel the early morning slightly, so it's off to the sofa for me and – maybe – a bit of extra shut eye.

A long last 36 hours (Updated)

Thursday 30 November

Quite before the media maelstrom that's been hurtling around today, I spent almost all of yesterday feeling absolutely awful. It's remarkable when I look back with all the things I've done today that I wouldn't have been able to even touch on today.

In all since 7am this morning, I've done 3 phone interviews, 1 studio interview, 1 photo shoot and written a 700-word article for the Guardian website. This time yesterday I was sat on a ward in Oxford hoping to goodness that the docs weren't going to put their foot down and keep me in.

Yesterday morning I woke up with the worst headache I've yet experienced, all thanks to the vetoing of my NIV due to the pneumo scare. Not only that, but the CO2 levels in my blood had obviously started to cause havoc elsewhere and I found myself lent over a toilet bowl 5 minutes after waking up depositing whatever was left in my stomach from last night.

I haven't been sick in a very long time, and I'd forgotten how unpleasant it was. Not only that, but without oxygen on, it left me gasping for air.

I managed to find my way back to bed and do my IVs, which took a lot more effort than usual, and got pain killers down me with a banana to try to settle my stomach and help them absorb better.

We had to leave the house by 9.30, so I forced myself up and out of bed, but my head was swimming. Of all the things I'd meant to do before heading out, I accomplished at most 2 of them, and then only half-heartedly.

At Oxford, I had a session with my physio, which saw me bringing up some of the nastiest stuff I've seen come out of me for a while. Not only that, but my headache was refusing to go away and my exhaustion was creeping up fast.

The docs came round after my physio session and we discussed the pneumo/chest pain. Considering I had a good night's sleep (barring the morning doldrums), and the pain seems to have gone away in my chest, it would appear that it wasn't a pneumo after all, just me jumping to not-entirely-illogical conclusions on feeling more acute than usual pleuritic pains in my shoulder.

We decided that the IVs clearly hadn't done the job they were meant to, and so I've been put on an additional drug to marry with my Colistin, Meropenem. Usually, Mero causes me severe joint pain, but we discovered last time I took it that combining it with steroids was usually effective in taking that element away.

The only drawback being once steroid levels go over 10mg (I'm now on 20mg) transplant becomes less likely, for various medical reasons too detailed to go into here. But it's only for two weeks and it'll hopefully improve my lung function and exercise tolerance, so it's got to be worth it.

Eventually, after a supervised first dose to make sure I wasn't going to have a massively adverse reaction to the Mero, I got away from Oxford (chauffeured by Dad) just after 2pm, getting back home around 3.30pm in time for some shut eye before heading out again to stock up on portable oxygen cylinders from my stash at the flat.

After a "who's got the keys" palaver of indeterminate length, we eventually got back in around 7 pm and I was shattered, completely exhausted and good only for sitting on the sofa and wiping out.

Although I did get a bit of a second wind in the evening, around the time Em phoned me to talk about the news and the reactions on the message boards, I was still in bed as early as I could be.

The most important part of my day, though, was in the change of stance on Neve, now that the pneumo had been discounted. Going to sleep with her on, I drifted off into the land of slumber and only woke on a couple of occasions before my early-morning radio address.

It was remarkable and wonderful to wake bright and alert and with no discernible leftovers from a proper night's sleep – no headache, no sickness, no nothing.

It's paved the way for a wonderfully busy day, all of which has taken place within the confines of the house, with the exception of a quick trip up the road. I'll be back on here later, with a bit of luck, to outline where else you can see my distinguished self discussing life with CF and other interesting topics of the day…

Updated 01/12/06:

After a breathless day-and-a-bit of media storms, between myself and fellow CF Trust Ambassador Emily we have notched up 4 print articles, over half a dozen radio interviews and she bagged all the Telly attention (but then, she is prettier and much more of a draw than me…), not to mention the rest of the CF community's coverage, which has included local news country-wide, This Morning, Newsround and forthcoming features in the Daily Mail other weekend magazines.

Articles featuring Em and/or I are available at the Guardian, Herald, Independent and Mirror and Emily also gets a mention on Nick Robinson's blog on the BBC website.

Articles have also appeared in the Scotsman and Evening Times for our Scottish Brethren, thanks to work from Anders, a North-of-the-boarder friendly-type.

December 2006
(11 Months)

Still adapting

Sunday 3 December

So, it turns out I'm not really very good at this adapting lark.

On an evolutionary scale, I'd be stuck somewhere around the fish-with-lungs kind of level – broaching the edges of a vast transformation but not quite grasping the basics of the new world laying itself out before me.

Everything is tiring. Not just averagely sleep-making, I mean tiring. Moving from one room to another if I have to slip off my O2 to change supply can lead to a required recovery period of several minutes if not longer and the merest hint of further activity leaves me body screaming for bed.

The biggest problem I have is learning to listen to what my body's telling me and then making the appropriate decision and acting upon it.

For instance: this evening I am beside myself with tiredness. I didn't sleep incredibly well, waking fairly often through the night in discomfort and from odd dreams. Today, my wonderful Godson came to visit and we had a great day playing games and watching movies and just generally hanging out. But it's left me completely shattered.

The most sensible course of action would seem to be to take myself off to bed and sleep, but he left at 6pm, which means that if I'd slept for an hour or more at that point, which I desperately wanted to, I know that come 11pm tonight when I've finished my evening IVs, I'd have been unable to get myself off to sleep.

So I tried just taking myself to bed and relaxing with a book, which worked for a while before tiredness crept in and made the book a blur, on top of which the urge to spend a little more time with my soon-departing bro crept in.

I came downstairs and settled in the kitchen (comfortable but not sleep-able) to read some of the Sunday paper and we had some left-over scraps from lunch for our supper with Mum and Dad before he left.

But I'm still no better off in the tiredness stakes, and I don't really know what to do about it. I know that, listening to my body, I should be in bed right now, but I have a dose of drugs to do in an hour's time, which will take an hour to go through, and if I fall asleep before then and have to wake up for them, that'll be my night totally ruined.

I suppose one could argue that if I have nothing to do during the days, perhaps it doesn't really matter what time I sleep, so long as I'm getting enough rest in during the day. I could, for example, live like a badger and stay up all night watching the Ashes and take myself to bed when the day dawns, but I'm not sure that's the answer.

For one thing, being up all night on my own I know I wouldn't feed myself properly then I'd miss all my day-time meals and so end up losing weight, which I really cannot afford to do.

Further to which, if I needed anything, had a nasty turn or my oxygen went funny or anything like that, it would mean rousing the house to come and help me, which I'd be mortified to do – it's bad enough having to get someone else to make me cups of tea when I want them, or shifting oxygen tanks around on my whims, let alone getting them out of bed when they're supposed to be resting.

What I really need to do, I think, is to find something which will keep me happily occupied in bed for a large chunk of the day – a computer game, or internet-linked lap-top or the like. The problem with all of those options being that I don't know how long I'm here for and they're ridiculously extravagant things to entertain me when there's a perfectly good TV downstairs.

I just can't get used to spending a day on a sofa, though. Daytime telly is bad enough (and I still can't force myself to watch it, no matter how ill I am), but I'm also just not comfy on the sofa all day. Odd, really, given I'd be quite happy in my bed 24/7 if I had summat to occupy myself with.

This is all one big crazy ramble now, largely caused by the constant fight to keep my withering eye-lids from gluing themselves together and calling it a night, but essentially it comes down to an "answers on a postcard" poser, really. Any cunning plans for occupying myself whilst enforcing a strict "not out of bed" rule?

I'm determined to get better at listening and – hopefully, one day – pre-empting my body's mood swings. I used to be pretty good at it, but I seem to have lost my touch of late. Here's hoping it's not too long before I get it back again…

I'm learning

Wednesday 6 December

It may be slow progress, but I'm definitely learning – I'm improving my understanding of my body day-by-day and feeling better and better as a result.

The last two days (Monday and Tuesday) I've done absolutely nothing – the closest I've come to expending energy has been throwing a sandwich together or making a cup of tea, and even that I've done very rarely.

I've been incredibly strict with myself about sitting doing nothing, or next to nothing – watching TV or reading, not even letting myself work up to a blog (sorry about that) – and I can honestly say I can feel the difference.

Granted, I'm on new antibiotics and a not-inconsequential dose of steroids to boot, which I have no doubt are pushing things along, but lack of energy expenditure is certainly playing a big part in my improvement over the last few days.

Today for the first time in 5 days I actually left the house, heading over to Oxford for a physio session and a quick once over. For the first time since I started IVs back in November, I actually had enough blow in my lungs to check my lung-function, which didn't come out great, but the fact that I could do it at all was a step in the right direction.

We've opted on another week of IVs in the hope that the improvement that's been shown over the last 7 days continues and when I eventually finish next Friday (the 15th), I should be fit enough to get through Christmas and New Year relatively hassle-free.

I've very much stopped planning ahead over the last couple of weeks and have avoided arranging things that I may have to cancel, simply because it drags me down so much mentally when I do.

Christmas is rather unavoidable though (and I wouldn't want to avoid it, either, however much of a Scrooge I may appear from time to time) and so my best plan of attack is to make sure I'm as well as I can possibly be and that I know my body well enough (at its newest settings) to stay on top of things on the day.

The last few days have really energised me, though, and I feel a lot more positive in myself.

At home we have an old joke stemming from my Mum when we were little, whereby every time we complained of any small ache, pain or minor ailment she would eventually come back with the line, "You're probably just tired."

It was infuriating to everyone at the time and hilarious to us all now, but I the last few weeks and months have driven home to a large extent exactly what she meant.

When you're tired, physically and mentally, everything becomes a stretch. Things that wouldn't faze you normally can become the biggest hurdles when lack of sleep or simple exhaustion gets in the way.

Having bowed my head and accepted that yes, maybe mother was right (occasionally) I find things much easier to deal with. It helps that I'm in a well-supported environment and I know that if I need to sleep, I just take myself off and sleep and I don't have to worry about anything else.

Hopefully this new-found self-knowledge, when combined with my old self-discipline at staying on top of what I can and can't do, will help me into a new period of positivity and enable me to move forward in getting some of the things I want to do done.

Even if I don't get them done, here's hoping that perhaps I can muster enough time, energy and inclination to actually attempt them.

Watch this space…

Forward, onward, upward

Friday 8 December

So, in the grand scheme of things, this week has been a Good Week.

Following last week's major dip in form, interrupted only by a day of media insanity which appeared to coincide happily with an inexplicably good chest day, I finally appear to be getting a grip on

a) the physical recovery process, with more energy, more internal resources and less time necessarily dedicated to sleep and b) the mental side of the game, which has seen me first acknowledge then work to accept my newly imposed limits.

In fact, my biggest challenge at this moment in time seems to be how to write a blog when covered in constantly interfering kitten. Pepe, one of Mum and Dad's two new additions (alongside sister Tio), isn't happy about my paying more attention to the funny glowing box with movey-cursor thing and there's something distinctly antagonistic in my fingers on the keys, it would appear.

It's hard to type with a kitten biting your thumb.

As I improve I am working hard not to get too carried away with recovery and am relying rather heavily on K and my 'rents to keep me grounded for the time being.

For the first time today I ventured out of the house under my own steam and wanted to do more but was talked down by K. Dad has a Christmas party at work tonight and needed a lift there, but Mum had been to a Christmas party at work and was one over the limit, so I obligingly offered to run him into Town, from where I was planning to go to the flat and pick up some bits and bobs.

But, considering I've now gone two days without an afternoon kip (through lack of tiredness, not stubborn-streak staying awake), it fell to Lady K to suggest that perhaps racing round to the flat, up the stairs and back no doubt laden with odds and sods wasn't the best way of testing how sustainable my energy levels actually are.

That said, it didn't stop her urging me to boldly step back into Real Life by stopping at the chippy on my way home…

The point is, though, that as much as I feel like I'm striding forward at the moment and as positive and happy as that makes me feel, it's important not to lose sight of what a tight-rope I'm walking just at the minute and to do what I can to minimise the risk of a relapse.

Which means that while it's important to know my boundaries, it's equally important to identify them through gentle probing rather than smashing through them at a sprint.

The challenge now is how to ignore my natural instinct to plough ahead full-steam and instead to slowly reintegrate myself to life, the universe and everything. And those of you who know me will be only too aware just how big a challenge that is.

Improvement continues, support unbelievable

Saturday 9 December

Another good day today, and another day of what economists term "positive growth" – although I have to say I wish that referred to my personal economics rather than the state of my chest.

Actually, I take that back – I'd take empty bank over knackered blowers any day of the week. Still, it's got to show how much things have improved over the last week or so that I can actually write half a paragraph complaining about lack of funds as opposed to anything health-related. What a relief. I think.

Having spent a week away from K, it's been absolutely lovely to finally spend some time together yesterday and today. She's been so amazingly supportive and has been there for me all the way through and has also dealt superbly well with not being there when I needed it, which I know from personal experience isn't an easy thing to do.

While I'm on the subject of support, though, I've been blown away by all the messages of support I've had from people reading this blog – it really is something else.

It's a remarkable feeling to know that you're loved and thought of by people all over the world (and it really has been from all over) and I want to say that every single one of your messages have made a huge difference in encouraging me and keeping me going when the times have got really tough recently.

As a side note, those of you who've been emailing me at my onetel account, I have to apologise for lack of responses, because I can't access my emails from Mum and Dad's. I went back to the flat for the first time in a couple of weeks today and was there long enough to check my mail and discover a whole raft of messages to which I want to reply but didn't have the time. So please excuse my rubbishness, but I will get back to you, I promise!

As far as today goes, I've had a lovely day of chilling out and relaxing. This morning, after sleeping in nicely till 11ish (caused mostly by poor sleep and drug-related tiredness), K and I were visited by S&S, no longer the newest double-team on the block, but happily still going strong.

It's been a while since I caught up with them, so it was good to have tea and chats and to humiliate myself with my awful knowledge of music while we channel-surfed through MTV, VH1, TMF, Q and other letters.

When they'd gone and we'd had a nice big bacon sarnie lunch with Mum and Dad, with super-fresh bakery bread, I did my drugs and caught a cat-nap before K and I ventured out in the car for a bit of a spin and stopped over at the flat, where I checked my mail and gathered a few bits and pieces to keep me occupied at home for tonight and the week ahead.

It was good to get out of the house properly for a bit and I was impressed at my discipline in again not pushing myself too far in trying to do too much.

Our friends at The Lodge, including the aforementioned S&S, D and PS are throwing a Dirty C Word Hawaiian Luau at their place tonight, which I really wanted to pop my head into, not least because it was at least partly motivated as an opportunity for K to get out to. But it would have been doing too much and I doubt I'd have managed to stay for just the quick "hi" and "bye" that I'd wanted to because I'd have had so much catching up and gossiping to do.

Mum's got all of her book group over for the night tonight, but I'm shutting myself away upstairs and being anti-social. Although I get on well with Mum's friends, I'm just not sure I'm up to maintaining conversation with big groups of people at the moment, so I thought it best to opt myself out of it and sequester myself in my room with Dad's laptop on Wi-Fi and today's papers to keep me occupied.

I'm sure I'll soon have my Social Strength back up to full-speed, but like everything I'm working with at the moment, I'm trying not to take too big steps too quickly. Slow and steady wins the race, as someone once said about something to someone.

Profound, that.

Busy mind, settled body

Monday 11 December

I'm clearly starting to reach sensible fitness levels as for the first time over the weekend, my mind has started to whir with possibilities of things I could be doing, or would like to do in the New Year.

Sadly, most of them are all things that will be beyond my reach before my Tx, but I suppose there's no problem having some kind of roughly sketched plan for the future, however far away it may be.

At times like these, I find the difficult thing is to focus my mind on to one thing in particular and get something done.

Right now, for example, would be a perfect time to knuckle down and get some really good writing done. Perhaps one of the new play ideas which have been circling my head – written up into draft form, or even just solidified in story terms. Or perhaps taking an opportunity to look back over one of my few first-draft projects and hone them slightly.

Inevitably, though, I find myself enjoying my imagined new-life projects far too much and taking myself off into my fantasy new world while achieving nothing and taking no steps forward in the real world.

It seems silly, really, to become too swept up in the details and nitty-gritty of the grand schemes I have laid out post-Tx when right now, planning whether or not I'm well enough to make a trip to Borders to finish the last of my Christmas shopping or treat myself to some new reading material.

What I need is some focus, and that's what I'm heroically lacking in. I say "heroically" as I'm blaming it on my brain as a way of coping with ignoring all the negative stuff that's inevitably swirling around at celebration times and the turn of a New Year.

Yes, it helps to bluff oneself with the concept that you're looking after yourself in the long run, and right now while you're recovering physically, any kind of mental exertion is good, whether its practical or dream-based. At least that's my story and I'm sticking to it.

There's also the question of the "holiday season" as some loathsome people are wont to call it, which is arriving like a speeding train and is just as likely to derail any well-laid plans anyway, so it's yet another excuse for butt-sitting and job avoidance.

Indeed, it seems fairly clear sitting here bashing away at the computer during the half-time break of the Sheffield Utd vs. Aston Villa game on the TV that the blog is just now as much a procrastination tool as anything else.

Or maybe - just maybe - forcing myself to sit and write my little progress notes of an evening is going to finally instil a little bit of discipline into my daily routine and lead me down the path of finally focused achievement.

Any takers?

Plagiarism: my new best friend

Tuesday 12 December

On my usual daily tour of my favourite websites today, I stopped in on my friend Em's blog to discover the following paragraph, which so neatly encapsulated the to-ings and fro-ings of my mind and body at the moment I thought it silly to try to reword it to enlighten my readership and decided instead just to lift it wholesale and try to pass it off as my own.

"*Sadly after 22 years I still don't quite seem to have got my head round the concept of "improving" as opposed to "magically cured and reinstated with working lungs" and so the minute I feel a turn around I start jumping around and doing lots and then am surprised when said behaviour doesn't go down well with my lungs which were (for want of a better phrase) breathing a sigh of relief that I was finally operating on a level they can maintain. I mentioned to my physio that you'd think I would have learned by now, she neatly sidestepped this remark by laughing politely and neglecting to comment.*"

Sadly, my sense of duty and honour (and the knowledge that we have enough mutual friends for it to be highly unlikely that I wouldn't get caught) meant I just couldn't bring myself to fully commit to the stealthy liberation of the text.

I'd like to say my conscience was pricked by the knowledge that Em managed to write it from her hospital bed and went to all the trouble of emailing it to a friend and getting it posted for her, but I know if I did that then she'd eventually read this and send me huge screaming emails and numerous phone calls berating me for jumping on the pity band-wagon which we all so deplore.

Plus it's also untrue, for that precise reason – pity is a trait all people should deplore. (Doesn't that sound like a high school philosophy essay question? *Pity is a trait all people should deplore: Discuss*)

At the end of the day, when someone says what you want to say better than the way you wanted to say it, it's best to hold your hands up and admit defeat than drive yourself barmy trying to best something that you can't.

If you needed any proof of that, just take a look at what a complete and total load of waffle I've written trying to justify lifting a paragraph of a friend's blog in order to help explain the challenges of getting back on your feet.

I think I should go and lie down. Maybe this plagiarism lark is too heavy for me, after all. Next time I'll stick to my own drivel.

Writing my wrongs

Wednesday 13 December

I've been making myself chuckle this afternoon as my procrastination levels increase. In fact, I've found a whole writers' self-help website devoted to aiding folks like me to get down to the nitty-gritty of actually churning something out.

The last couple of nights I've hardly slept at all. Monday night I was up until around 3am before finally dozing off, sleeping through till 11am save for an hour's break in the middle around 6am to do my IVs. Last night was worse – I didn't manage to sleep at all until after my morning dose.

Oddly, it doesn't appear to be your regular, run-of-the-mill, thinking-horrible-thoughts kind of insomnia. Rather, it's just that as I improve health-wise my brain is staying resolutely five strides ahead of my body. So while I can't do much physically during the day, my brain is aching to be put to use and if it's not (as it hasn't been) then it settles itself into manic thinking patterns when I hit the sack and keeps me wide awake, no matter how much my eyelids beg to differ.

So today I have been resolutely trying my best to a) stay awake all day and not take my usual afternoon nap and b) do things with my day that will make my mind feel like it's had if not a real work out, at least a little bit of a gentle jog.

It struck me when I was writing out my Christmas cards this afternoon that getting myself writing would be the most obvious method of productive mind-occupation, so I set that part of my brain that never stops whirring creatively to spin on ahead whilst I wrote, corrected and re-wrote the cards that kept being incorrectly filled in due to my non-multi-tasking man-brain.

Perhaps what I needed by way of a spur, I figured, was to tackle a branch of writing I've not tackled before – something different and fresh and intriguing to me. I've written plays and I've written screenplays – I've even finished some of them, too. So why not try something more narrative – a short story or similar?

In fact, it was the Stephen King interview I watched yesterday evening that provided my spark of inspiration – if I wanted to stir my creative brain and really test my mettle, why not try what writers used to do when they needed to churn something out (albeit usually for the cash than the creative momentum) and knock out a classic piece of pulp fiction?

Pulp fiction is that stuff that used to be known as Dime-Store Novels in the US and is more commonly known these days as Airport Fiction - that kind of crime-based, semi-plotted, under-characterised pap that you whistle through when you're lying on the beach in the summer months trying not to remember that it's only four more days till you're back at work.

What better, I thought, than to pin myself down to knocking something out which needn't have any literary merit at all, but merely serve as an exercise to show that a) I can still write and b) I can make myself focus on one thing for at least the space of time it takes me to write a chapter or two.

Of course, we all know that my mind doesn't work like that. Instead, I set off researching into pulp fiction and it's current place in the literary world: is it still written, published, sold around the world? Could I, conceivably, sell my mini-opus for publication when I'm done with it?

And research it I did. I even answered most of my questions. Which was annoying because it meant I had to come up with more questions so I didn't have to actually start writing.

Surfing through the myriad writers' websites dotted around the 'net, I came across various tips for getting into good writing habits and avoiding said procrastination. Eventually, I discovered an entire website devoted to a 30-day programme to help writers get organised and write.

That's right: a 30-DAY PROGRAMME. That's an entire month's worth of tips and exercises designed so that, at the end of the allotted period, you're set to go write your masterpiece. 30 (Thirty) Days. To get organised. To AVOID procrastination. It's so funny, I can't even do it justice with a smart-arsed quip.

Needless to say, I shall be sticking point-by-point the programme and ensuring that I don't achieve ANYTHING by way of productivity before the New Year. After all, if I don't pay attention to the site I found, all my hard research work from today will have been for nothing, won't it?

Addictive personalities

Thursday 14 December

In the last two days I've come to a shocking personal conclusion: I'm an addict. Twice over. I'm now – 100% officially – addicted to Sky+. And I'm now – 100% officially – addicted to Borders.

Nuts.

I don't watch much TV – hardly any at all when I'm not around K. She's a terrible influence on me because she'll watch any old rubbish and claim it's interesting, happily squidged on a sofa all day long. Ironically, I can't get her to share my passion for films because she doesn't have the attention span for them. Hmmm.... there may be something in this "MTV generation" theory after all... but that's beside the point.

Anyway, I don't watch much TV – maybe an hour a day, possibly two and it's usually specific programs that I want to watch. I've never been much of a sofa-surfing channel-hopper. Well, OK, I was once upon a time, until my brother began to tease me about my being able to win Telly Addicts on my own and I started having nightmares of Noel Edmonds in family-knitted garish Christmas jumpers.

So it used to really bug me when I'd look at the night's listings and discover that the only two things I really wanted to watch were on at the same time. Or, more particularly annoying, given it's infrequent occurrence, when I had something planned which clashed with something important.

Since moving back to Mum and Dad's, however, I've been blessed with the genius that is Sky+. The best thing in the world about Sky+ is it means I don't ever, EVER have to watch daytime TV. Even if I do have those days when I really can do nothing but sit on my butt on the sofa and veg out, I can record a whole evening's worth of vaguely-entertaining fare, without having to resort to the daytime schedules of not-even-close-to-entertaining pap. Or Neighbours (which is another category altogether).

Most of all, what I love about it is being able to watch things whenever I want to. For example, I've developed a new routine whereby I keep myself busy for most of the day, but permit myself a "lunch hour" in the middle of the day to grab lunch and sit and do nothing. Which means I can record things from the night before and catch up with them today.

All of which is a really long way of going about saying that I watched a really interesting programme today. But actually, I've been prattling on so long about the genius of Sky+ it seems pointless to go into my new-fangled theories on positive thinking and instead I'll save it for another day and come back to it fresher and less Sky+'d up.

Back to my addictions, though. Borders: the wonderful world of literature and other stuff that's descended from on high (read: opened a store in MK as opposed to the nearest one being in Oxford) and plonked itself slap-bang in the middle of my everyday life.

I've been there 4 times now, 3 times in the last week and for a combined total of around 4 hours and I still don't feel like I've managed to have a really good look around. I maintain, in fact, that I still won't until I've settled myself into a comfy Starbucks chair and flicked through an un-bought book for half an hour, finished my coffee, put the book back and come home.

The great thing about Borders, and what really stands out when you walk in, especially for someone like me who loves books, is that it's just so wonderfully full of books. I mean, they're everywhere. And not just in a regular bookshop kind of way.

I mean they're EVERYWHERE and "everywhere" goes on for absolutely AGES. It's the biggest biggest biggest book-holding space in the whole widest world of Milton Keynes and is so spectacularly amazing it makes me positively dribble with excitement. I can almost smell the print.

So now I can't keep myself away. I have to have my Borders fix. Twice in two nights I've been there for an hour between 8pm and 9pm, just to wander around when it's not full of silly people doing silly things like trying to shop for Christmas presents when I'm trying to be there and just enjoy the SPACE. Inconsiderate little so-and-so's.

It is mildly – only mildly – concerning what effect this could have on my bank balance. I've been fairly good so far – so far – at keeping my wallet in check and not splashing out, but it's only a matter of time.

I see Borders, and my addiction to it, as rather like one of these new Super Casinos that are due to be hitting our shores sometime in the near future (you know, the one that should be in Blackpool that the Government are making everyone think they might put somewhere else, just to spite Blackpool and take away it's "UK's Las Vegas" tag, as if that was something to be proud of in the first place). You think you've got it under control, and that you're winning. But sooner or later the situation's gonna change, everything will turn around on you and you'll find yourself completely wiped out.

Mind you, at least when I've cleaned myself out, maxed out my credit cards and had to lock myself in the flat and barricade the bailiffs out I'll have something good to read....

Inevitably...

Saturday 16 December

For all the forward motion I've been making recently, the pendulum was bound to swing back. I'm sure someone far more intelligent than me said something once about equals and opposites and all that kind of thing, but I have better hair than him, so I can't be bothered to quote him properly.

Still, after confidently striding forward and warning myself strictly against doing too much too soon, I spent this afternoon in bed after, well, doing too much too soon.

I hasten to my own defence to say that a) I spotted it early and nipped it in the bud and b) actually the hour-or-so I spent in bed on Neve (hmmm... maybe not such a clever idea to name the NIV after all – that could get a little confusing) and the extra session of physio have done me the world of good and this evening I feel top-notch.

Yesterday I went to Oxford to finish IVs – that's a grand total of 5 weeks all together, my record for recent times. My chest is a lot better and my lung function was hitting the 0.7/1.4, which is about as high as I go these days. For those of you who work in percentages, that's very roughly 20%/25% predicted. More encouragingly, my SATs were running at 93% on 2 litres O2, which is unheard of for my since around August.

I'm coping pretty well off-oxygen now. I'm still using it almost all day, but I can cope with wandering around shops (ok, Borders) without it for an hour or so, which is good.

I try to justify it by saying that it makes shopping a whole load easier not having to lug a cylinder around the shop with me, and I reassure myself that I'm good and have it in the car when I'm driving and wear it all the time at home, but if I'm truly honest with myself, it's still very much a vanity thing.

K and I decided we wanted to cook dinner tomorrow for Mum, Dad and my bro, who's home for Christmas, to thank them for putting up with me for the last few weeks (well, not my bro, 'cos he's not had to cope with me invading his life, but it seemed a bit mean to cook for everyone else and not him when it's his home…). So we had the cunning plan of hitting Tesco's late last night to avoid the crowds.

At 8pm we thought we'd got it right and BOY were we wrong. It was still heaving and in one despairing moment of realisation I stood at the threshold of the store in Kingston and realised that it was WAY too huge for me to wander round, especially at the end of a long day.

It's always a little dispiriting to have to acknowledge your limits – especially when things are looking up again. But I'm proud of the fact that I didn't just try to "soldier on" through the shop and completely wipe myself out, but instead called it a night with two bars of Toblerone and headed home.

I think, actually, our late-night jaunt is probably the crux of what lead to my energy shortage this afternoon and, again, I'm pleased I spotted it and took action (or rather, in-action) to combat it without trying to soldier through. I feel much better for it physically and it's given me a boost in my mental confidence to know that I'm learning to listen to my body again.

So tomorrow I've prescribed myself a day of rest, doing nothing all morning and afternoon and plenty of physio so that I've got energy enough to help K whip up a storm in the kitchen and give Mum and Dad a proper thank you. And my bro, I suppose…

Not entirely successful…

Monday 18 December

The meal was nice – and everyone enjoyed it (including me) – but it was WAY too much physical activity cooking it and I left myself feeling really quite rubbish.

K cooked the starter and the pudding, I did the main, and it was clearly not a cleverly thought out plan. What I should have done was chosen something that needed preparation and slow cooking in the oven so I wasn't standing over the stove for half-an-hour odd while it cooked, but could have sat and rested. More fool me.

It was a lovely dinner and it was great to sit around with the whole family and just eat and chat (pretty much what my family does best). By the end of the meal, though, I was shattered and my chest was really tight, so I took myself straight up to lie down on the bed. I thought it would just be for a little while and I'd be back down, but in the end I was settled there for the night.

Today's been another pretty rough day, paying the price for the over-exertion yesterday. I've been pretty low all day, just feeling a bit pissed off with the seemingly endless merry-go-round of exertion and recovery. I know it's what I should be used to by now, but it still grates that I can't do things two days in a row or if I over-stretch myself it takes me days to recover.

Still, I've been trying hard not to be too gloomy about it all and had fun this evening playing a game with my bro, Dad and K. I won, which is rare for me, but still managed to prove myself stupider(!) than the rest of the family by trying to play at being banker. I should really know that maths isn't my strong point and if I want to avoid getting annoyed with myself should give up the job at the start not try to bluff my way through it again and again.

I can see, reading what I'm writing just now, that the sunny-side of my disposition is struggling to get through; I'm taking everything to heart and being downcast about pretty much whatever's going on today. It's just a bad day, though, and everyone has those.

Doubtless I'll hit the sack tonight and get a good night's sleep (I feel exhausted) and things will look much brighter and sunnier in the morning. These feelings never last forever; it's just a matter of buckling down, acknowledging the rubbishness and ploughing through it tomorrow.

Told me so

Tuesday 19 December

MUCH better day today, as I was sure it would be. Well, semi-sure.

But my body's been decidedly responsive and I've managed to pass through an entire day with remarkably high energy levels and not very much in the way of breathless episodes and other nastiness.

I slept pretty well, which is always a good start, and didn't lie in bed too long this morning, which is something I'm increasingly persuaded is a bad thing in terms of momentum for the day.

This afternoon I ran K over to an appointment in Northampton and used the spare time to visit Suze, my partner in crime from MKT, from where I've sadly been completely AWOL for the entire term. It was good to hear that all the work they've been doing is going fabulously well and that plans for the show in April are really rolling along.

I'm desperate to get back there and get my creative juices flowing again. The workshops really energise me – working with kids and young people is so inspiring because of the way they see things and tackle problems.

One of the things I always fall back on when I tell people how great it is doing what I do is how much we can learn from children.

The most important thing in a 6 year-old's life is whatever they happen to be doing at that moment in time, and that's absolutely the way that we should all live out lives.

The trouble is as we get older, other stresses and worries crowd in and take over the freedom and innocence we enjoy as children and everything becomes more complicated. But working with the younger groups at MKT has really helped me keep in touch with the old adage of living every day – and moment – for what it is, not what it could, should or has been.

The older groups at MKT simply serve to drive me forward creatively. There's nothing so powerfully motivating than seeing a group of people you've worked with for a long time learning and growing and expanding their experiences and outlooks on life, and to be challenged in your beliefs and understanding of the things around you.

They push me to better understand myself and my ideas and to make sense of what I'm trying to communicate, to them or an audience or anyone else.

And working with Suzanne has given me the opportunity to be involved in a whole load of things in a whole load of capacities that I never would have had chance to do were it not for her faith and trust in me and what I can (or can't) do.

Needless to say, I miss it mightily and I'm yearning to go back. What's fantastic about today is that having spoken to Suze and caught up on life, the universe and everything (sorry about the house!) it's helped me to remember just how much I do want to still be part of what's happening and it's making me more determined than ever to get a grip on what my body's doing and learn to play it properly so I can get myself back into sessions, even if it's only for a couple of hours a week.

So today has also proved to myself that although bad days come along once in a while, but that they will always pass and be replaced by a good day. I'm lucky in that it's turned around quickly this time, but even in the blackest of nights it's important to remember that there's always a light at the end of the tunnel – and you know you're going to get there in the end.

Here's to April.

Flying brothers, complaining lungs

Thursday 21 December

Had a really good giggle last night when I ventured out with the fam and K to watch my bro enjoy his birthday pressie from earlier in the year with 10 minutes fly-time at Airkix indoor skydiving centre in MK.

It's unbelievably cool – a little Plexiglas bubble one story up above a pair of jet turbiney things (that's their trade name, obviously), which serves to suspend people mid-air as if falling at great speed from a plane.

My bro, the sickening sports fanatic that he is, got on amazingly well. He did 4 "jumps" of 2.5 minutes each and managed to learn 8 out of 10 techniques of flight. His instructor told us afterwards you're supposed to learn one per flight, so he'd doubled the expectation and mastered most of them within his 10 minutes. I really hate him sometimes.

Mind you, it was hilarious to watch him with his little cheeks wibbling away in the uprush of air. He even managed to dribble upwards. It feels a little odd when you watch people do it, because you're the other side of a Plexiglas window about 2 feet away from them, so if they lose control a little, they end up nearly head-butting you. Nervous laughter abounds amongst the spectators getting a little weirdly close to people they don't know in zoo-like conditions.

It's an amazing thing, though, the Airkix centre, and I have to recommend it to anyone as a gift, or even as a treat for yourself. It's not cheap, I know that much, but it looked like so much fun. I was extremely jealous, but I've got something else to add to my list of post-tx "must do's" now.

After we watched his diving antics, we all headed off for a nice Tex-Mex dinner, which went down wonderfully. By the end of it, though, I was exhausted. It wasn't until we were in the car on the way home that K pointed out that I'd woken up at 6.30am that morning (no reason, was just awake and couldn't nod off again) and without a sleep in the afternoon, it was no wonder I was a touch on the snoozy-side.

This morning I woke up even earlier, 5.30am, with roaring chest pains. After my last little pointless jaunt to casualty with over-exuberant pre-diagnosis, I decided it best just to grab some painkillers and immobilize myself for the day, so I duly took to the sofa in a true grumpy-lung'd sulk.

Watching the sky-diving and at the restaurant I'd gone without my O2 and I think this is my body's way of telling me that it was distinctly unimpressed with my choice to move around quite so much without additional support.

I've been a lot more comfortable this afternoon than I was when I woke up, but I know a chiding chest when I feel one, so I'm sworn to "good boy" status for the next few days to make sure I can make the most of Christmas.

It was also pointed out to me today by the lovely Lady K that my last update vaguely referred to things going on in April without any real expansion. Apologies for the vagueness, and I promise I'll post with full and inclusive April updates shortly, but for the record there will be a fundraiser for the CF Trust through the MKT Activ8 Youth Theatre by way of a main stage performance in the middle of April.

More to come, so watch this space....

Resting

Friday 22 December

Today's been a really good day for me and I'm really pleased with myself for it, too.

Yesterday, apart from slumming it on the sofa trying to urge my chest pains to go away, I spent the afternoon writing another article for the Guardian's Comment is Free site – this time about Transplantation.

Em and Em, the partners in crime behind Live Life Then Give Life (from whom you should all have bought a T-shirt, not to mention signed up to the Organ Donor Register), organised another big publicity push for Christmas, which I sadly missed out on because of all my recent email hiccups and account confusions.

So, in order to still be doing my part, I mentioned the campaign to the guy who'd contacted me about writing my previous article to see if he was interested. He said he was, so I spent the afternoon writing up a general summary of the status of transplant in the country and the various different systems around the world.

What I'm most pleased about it that he particularly wanted to stir up a bit of debate about the subject and if you go and check out the article online (here), you'll find a lively exchange in the comments section underneath, which is really good to see. Except maybe for the comment about my hair…

After being in the study working all afternoon, my chest was protesting a little again so I stayed on the sofa watching a movie in the evening and headed to bed at a sensible time.

Better than anything was the fact that I got myself comfortable (not always possible with chest pains) and slept solidly through until 11am this morning – 12 hours sleep being something I've not enjoyed for as long as I can remember. It was blissful to wake up and discover I'd been out like a light all night. And it's really recharging, too.

What I'm most pleased with today, though, is that I've stayed true to my promise to chill for the next few days before Christmas and have done very little again today. I've been massively helped by the fact that I've had friends round to see me most of the day, which is good for sitting on the sofa chatting and not having to move or do other things.

But I've also been really good at doing physio sessions and stopping myself from "popping out" or sitting in the study at the computer for too long, or at the table in the kitchen reading the paper – all of which have a tendency to put extra strain on my chest and induce pain here and there.

Fingers crossed, I'll be able to carry my discipline over to tomorrow, when I've got a little more planned, but am hoping that when I'm not out of the house, I'll either be in bed or on the sofa doing nothing at all. And K's back from her parents' tomorrow afternoon, so she'll be around to police me.

A Christmas in keeping

Wednesday 27 December

Since I started this blog in late November, I don't think I've gone three consecutive days without posting, but I figure I'm allowed a mini-holiday over the Christmas break, if for no other reason than nobody's likely to be reading it anyway, unless they got a new laptop for Christmas and are testing out their Wi-Fi.

This year's celebrations have been entirely in keeping with the whole of 2006 before it: a total roller coaster.

Christmas Eve was a wonderful day of chilling out and seeing friends. In fact, over the previous two days I'd caught up with a good number of friends, some of whom I've not seen for a while and some of whom I haven't seen as much as I should recently.

On Christmas Eve two of my oldest friends came round to see me, which was unbelievably cool. All three of us are really quite rubbish at staying in touch, but whenever we do manage to meet up we have the best giggle and always pick up right from where we left off – something which I think marks out a true friendship amongst the ranks of acquaintances we make as we go through life.

It was brilliant to catch up with them and find out what they've been up to, although I always find it hard to update people on how things have been going for me. Luckily, the more tech-savvy of the two of them has been reading the blog, so she was pretty clued up and had, I'm guessing, filled in our technophobe friend on the drive over. It's difficult to talk about how you're feeling when it changes so often and talking about how hard things have been can be a really downer on any conversation.

We had a great few hours chatting, laughing and generally messing around. They're both doing really well and always seem to energise me creatively when I see them. They're both actresses and talking to them always reminds me of the passion I have for writing, performance, theatre and film – they always inspire me.

Things started to go awry that evening, though, when K woke up at midnight and spent the next 12 hours hugging the toilet. A few of our friends and relatives have had a vomiting virus over the last week or so and our next-door neighbour had it on Christmas Eve. Her husband and son came over in the evening and that must have been where K picked it up from.

Once she had stabilized enough to not be sick for 30-40 minutes at a time, Mum ran her back home in order to keep her quarantined away from me. One thing I really can't afford right now is to go 24 hours without eating, and any kind of a bug is bad news, but it was horrible to have to separate ourselves after all the planning we'd done to get through Christmas together.

What that meant, of course, is that our Christmas plans were totally shot. I think K was more upset about it than anyone, but it was really hard to be without her on Christmas Day. That's now 2 Christmases in a row she's been laid up in bed, and we had wanted so badly to celebrate together. It also marked our first 6 months together.

We did what we could to make the most of the rest of the day and carried on as normal as possible, down to just the 4 of us in our family unit again. It was really nice, actually, but having been up all night with K, I was completely shattered. I slept for nearly three hours in the afternoon and then we went up the road to a friend's for Christmas dinner.

It was a really lovely meal and we all had a lot of laughs, but after a couple of hours I was past my stamina levels and had to get Mum to bring me home. They all stayed on and played games and drank copious amounts, while I chilled on the sofa with my Christmas DVDs.

Things picked up again yesterday, when K had managed to keep some food down and was really just struggling with energy levels from having had no food the day before. She managed to come over to join us with Dad's sister and her Gang in tow.

We always have a fab time when my Aunt comes down – our two families are so similar in sense of humour and shared piss-taking that there is almost endless laughter whenever we're together.

Three days of busy-ness were really taking their toll by the evening though and my chest was tight and protesting at over-working. We had a second-mini Christmas to share presents with K – we'd saved all the presents to her and from her to open when she was with us.

By 9pm I was beyond shattered and had to take myself up to bed, where I promptly fell asleep by 10pm and slept almost completely solidly through until 10am this morning – my body is getting much better at taking the required rest when it needs it.

This morning, my chest is still protesting a little, and I know a good few physio sessions are going to be called for, as well as a full-on sofa-day to let my body recover properly from the stresses of the last few days.

I'm really impressed with how I held up over Christmas actually.

It was a lot tougher than I expected it to be, but looking back it was bound to be difficult as I was fitting more into 3 days than I done over the previous 2 weeks, so to expect it all to be plain sailing was perhaps wishful thinking.

Now it's time to start planning energy saving for New Year so I can make it to midnight to welcome in 2007 – the year of the Transplant.

Progress – even with 02

Thursday 28 December

Festive recovery is progressing well – I've had two complete days of doing very little-to-nothing and looking after myself and I'm feeling all the better for it.

I've got a voucher-splashing trip to Borders planned for the morning, under the guise of taking my Dad over to show him how fab it is, and I'll be merrily spending my way through the delightful vouchers supplied by K's big bro and troupe. (Happy now?;-).

I'm still not entirely firing on all cylinders, but I'm finding it much easier to get around at the moment – albeit always tied to an oxygen cylinder or concentrator – and I'm not nearly as breathless as I was yesterday or the day before, which goes to prove two things. 1) doing plenty of physio and getting plenty of rest really works and 2) TOBI, the nebulised form of the Tobramycin antibiotic, really does do it's job spectacularly well, as I only restarted it on Boxing day (it works on a month-on, month-off basis).

Also had an interesting conversation with O2 yesterday. I've been thinking a lot about getting hold of a Blackberry phone/email device thingy, mostly because it's a fair assumption that this year I'll be spending a good deal more time in hospital and that being the case, it would be great to have access to my emails from my bed. The hospital as it is doesn't have workable or affordable Internet access, so a Blackberry seems ideal.

What it would mean is that while I'm laid up with nothing much to do, not only can I carry on communicating with my friends without running up an insanely huge text message bill, but I can also carry on with most of the work I do for the Trust, which is handled largely through email with contributors, designers and the "bosses" there.

Now, I've seen a few really attractive deals on O2 for

Blackberry Pearl phones and contracts to go with them, namely one which tell me that if you sign up to a £30+p/m voice contract and £10p/m Blackberry Tariff, you get the Pearl for free.

So I phoned and spoke to O2 customer services and told them that although I'm only 9 months into my current contract, I'd like to add the Blackberry Tariff and get the Pearl. Fine, they said, that'll be £220.

Now, bearing in mind that the phone alone is advertised in Carphone Warehouse at the moment for £199, this didn't seem like a fabulous offer. I told them so. They told me that since I'm not due an upgrade, there's nothing they can do.

I outlined my history with the company – loyal customer for over three years, no problems or complaints, no other issues – and suggested that perhaps, since I'm only 3 months away from the end of the contract, maybe they could budge a little on the price of the phone. I didn't say I wanted it free, just a little leeway on the £220. But no, they don't do it and no one there is authorised to.

So I thanked them politely and hung up, redialled and went through to the option on their phone menu saying "If you are less than happy". I outlined the situation again and got the same response – nothing they could do because I was outside the upgrade window.

At this point, having reiterated the fact that I'd been loyal for 4 years, never missed a payment, never raised a problem with them, never kicked up a fuss about anything, I let them know I was feeling like a mildly undervalued customer.

In fact, it had occurred to me whilst talking to them that it would be cheaper for me to go down to Carphone Warehouse, take out a new contract – on exactly the same terms as my current one – plus the Blackberry tariff, get the phone for free and pay out the remainder of my contract with them than it would be for me to get the Pearl through them. I told them.

At this point he put me on hold and came back 5 minutes later telling me that having spoken to 2 different departments, the 2nd one told him that if I called them back on the 4th January, they would do the upgrade for me. Just like that.

Interestingly, when I asked what department I needed to speak to when I called back, he told me it was the "Safe" department – the people you talk to when you say you want to cancel your contract. So being a "valued" customer isn't enough to get you benefits and deals as part of O2 – you really only matter when they think you're going to defect to Vodafone or Orange.

Still, who am I to grumble, as of January I'll be my own personal walking office – marvellous!

Border Attack

Saturday 30 December

I'm still pretty impressed at myself just now for not pushing too hard and doing too much. The nebs seem to be doing their jobs and keeping me fairly clear, and I'm sticking to the O2 all the time when I'm not using Neve.

Yesterday I had a FANTABULOUS couple of hour tour of Borders – Christmas voucherage always being a good reason to get out and about. The best thing about Borders, among all the other best things it has, is that even in the height of the new-season sales, when the car park is full to bursting, the store's so big it doesn't feel busy at all.

Apart from finally getting to enjoy some proper browsing time – and by "proper", I mean time enough to look around, then grab a book and sit and read the interesting bits that you want to read and put it back on the shelf when you've garnered all the useful info from it – it also served as the first time I've properly worn my oxygen out in the big wide world.

Those of you who were around early on in this blog may remember my difficulties coming to terms with the idea of venturing out and about with my O2 on and my reluctance to do so. I still don't think it's entirely gone away, but I reasoned with myself that if I was going to be spending a couple of hours in the shop, it would be really silly of me to think I could do it unaided. Especially when I'm doing everything else I can to make sure I look after myself and don't take huge steps backwards.

So I grabbed one of the lightweight cylinders and trotted off with Dad and K to explore the store and we all had a whale of a time. It was brilliant flitting between shelves, digesting bits of books, moving around and sticking my nose into all sorts of sections I wouldn't normally look at.

I think we all struggled with not spending heaps of cash, but I did managed to spend the vouchers K's bro and his family gave me, which was cool, netting myself Inside Little Britain (which I'm ripping through at pace) and a book about Max Clifford that I've wanted for a while.

The rest of the last two days have been spent very sensibly doing little-to-nothing in order to save my energy for the weekend ahead. Tomorrow night for New Year, I'm hoping to bee able to make it over to a house party S&S are holding at the Lodge.

The plan at the moment is to chill out for the day and catch a late-afternoon nap in order to get up and over there for around 10pm, which should give me a couple of hours party time, followed by midnight and a bit of wind-down before scooting home.

New Year's day I have my Godson coming over, which will be brilliant, but again very tiring, so I'm forcing myself to stay in bed for the morning and do plenty of physio while resting as much as possible so I can make the most of the afternoon with him.

This is going to be a major test of my stamina-planning ability and may have a massive impact on my decision as to whether or not I can try to phase a return to work in the near future. What I'm hoping is that if I prove to myself I can manage my fatigue, then I will be able to take myself to work for a couple of hours on a Wednesday night to work with the oldest group.

So I'm looking forward to the dawning of the New Year, with the feelings of energy and hope that it always brings, and I'm hoping that my planning and self-discipline holds out for the weekend and I come out of it tired but positive.

Here goes nothing....

January 2007
(10 Months)

By George he's got it!

Tuesday 2 January

I think I might have cracked it. Not in a bad, going-to-need-to-replace-it kind of way, in an it's-about-time-you-silly-arse kind of way.

First of all, big Happy New Year to one and all – hope you had a good night's celebrations and woke up later on the 1st without too much of a fuzzy head and swirly stomach. Being the paragon of virtue that I am, I was enjoyably tee-total (or is that tea-total?) all night and felt super when I woke up. So bleh to you! (I don't know how you spell the noise you make when you stick your tongue out at someone…)

But most excitingly, I've managed to get through all of the weekend's festivities and back into normal life with no kind of a chest-related hangover whatsoever – how brilliant is that?

Not only did I save up enough energy on the 31st to have a really good night with S&S and the big C at the Lodge, but I lasted the course of a day with my Godson and family yesterday too.

Sunday night was great fun – just the 5 of us chilling out, chatting, laughing and watching the Hootenanny on the telly. I love the Hootenanny, mostly just because it has a totally brilliant name. Hootenanny has to be one of the best words in the whole language. And it is totally fitting for some kind of party!

Come midnight we all hugged and danced (some more energetically than others) and decided we were knackered and ran away to bed.

Monday was another cracking day of fun and frolics with my Godson, his Mum and Dad and bro. We played Uno and I lost by a lot, we played Game of Life and I lost by a little less, then after our second meal of the day – don't you just love those days when you have a huge roast dinner and then come back later in the afternoon to finish off the leftovers and clear out the fridge with some lovely crusty bread and pickles and cheese and other wonderful delights? – we played Game of Life again and I won. I didn't mean to, I sort of did it by accident.

The whole thing was interspersed with an hour's break in the middle when the two Dad's took the young'uns off for a walk around the lake and I laid on the bed with Neve strapped on resting myself up for the 2nd half of the day. It worked brilliantly – just as I was beginning to flag, my mini-break, semi-nap set me up for the rest of the day perfectly.

The best part of the whole weekend, though, without a doubt (aside from all the great bits) was waking up this morning feel fresh, energised and ready to tackle the day. Not a single sentence of moany-ness from my chest and not a moment of complaint throughout the day.

I'm so happy it's really rather silly and I'm aware of how fragile it all can be, but I can't think of a better way to start the New Year than to realise that I've worked out the limits of my ever-changing body.

I know I tend to push myself too hard and usually too fast, but it's fantastic to know where I can push myself to and to be able to recognise when I need to stop, take a breath or three and stop myself being silly.

Those of you who've been with me from the start will know that this whole escapade began with me searching for an understanding of the boundaries that were newly rearranged around my ever-more-protesting blowers, and to finally find something of an answer, or at least a vague level of comprehension, feels wonderful.

So now it's time to turn my attention to more long-term and practical goals, and see what I can't achieve with my year before Harefield get on the phone to offer me my part-exchange.

Anyone got anything they need me to do that involves sitting at a desk and preferably being creative, you know where to find me.

For now, I'm off to get my 10 hours sleep to make sure

tomorrow goes just as well.

Happy New Year everyone, bring on the next challenge!

Writing and watching

Wednesday 3 January

It's been a bit of a quiet, stay-at-home kind of day today, spent largely on the sofa chilling out. I have, however, managed to do my first piece of real writing for *ages* and I'm really pleased with it.

It's an odd thing, writing. I love doing it and when I sit in front of a screen with a real purpose to my ideas, I seem to be able to rattle things off at speed. The 6-page scene I wrote today, which is something that will hopefully be part of the Youth Theatre show in April, took me a little under an hour to write, although I must confess I wrote the verse part of it over the course of an hour waiting for K yesterday.

It seems that when I have a deadline to write to is when I do my best writing and when my mind focuses most clearly on what it's trying to do and say. If I'm just sitting there of my own volition, tapping away at the keys and seeing where I end up, it doesn't come in the same way.

What this means, of course, is that once I start getting commissioned and paid for my work and I'm a top-flight, in-demand scriptwriter and playwright, I'll be knocking out classics left, right and centre (OK, OK, but stay with me), whilst right now I need to find that spur to keep me going when I don't have an identifiable goal to achieve in front of me.

People say the key to it is to make sure you write a little every day, no matter what it is. Specifically, I've heard it said that you should set yourself a page or word target that you must hit no matter what. The trouble with those plans is that I always just end up writing drivel to fill the quota and end up hating myself for being so uncreative and unimaginative. And when you think you've lost it, your enthusiasm for the project drops off the face of the planet.

All of which does nothing really to solve my dilemma, but it's nice to be writing again and reading my own words on a page. There's still something wonderful about reading back over scripts that have just emerged from your head through your fingers and ended up as a formatted file on a hard drive and ink-on-paper in front of you.

It never ceases to amaze me when I sit at a computer that in a matter of a few hours I can turn out something really quite readable to fill a blank page and possibly more.

My head tells me that I need to set myself some time aside everyday to try to achieve something in writing, even without self-imposed artificial quotas and the like, but at the same time I know that if I set myself a timetable and don't stick to it or am too tired to achieve it, I'll just get down about it.

But enough of that – it's all a bit unnecessary.

Today I watched FIELD OF DREAMS with K on the sofa and absolutely loved it. It was a Christmas gift from her because I had told her I'd not seen it and I'd heard lots of good things about it from lots of people, so I finally sat down to watch it today.

It's a lovely little film, filled with a beautiful kind of magic that you somehow just don't question. It's one of those films with such wonderful heart that you forgive it it's little foibles and unnecessaries and allow yourself to get swept up with the characters and their journey and the magic they're experiencing.

And who knew Kevin Costner used to be so watchable? And not in dodgy-accented, car-crash kind of terms? I mean, he was almost like a real actor. You'd have sworn he'd never do something as silly as make Waterworld.

I also wasted nearly an hour of my day on a programme about the Archers, which promised in it's Sky+ blurb that it would follow the production team as they put together the show's 15,000th episode – the kind of behind-the-scenes peek that I've always been addicted to. But instead, it spent the vast majority of its time covering the whole of the back-story to this momentous episode.

Which, when you're covering a radio drama on TV, is somewhat dull.

Still, at least I watched that before I watched Field of Dreams, so I could have my memory of it wiped.

Also watched a great Mark Lawson interview with Armando Iannucci, one of the writer/producers behind things like The Day Today and Alan Partridge or, more recently, The Thick of It. I love watching programmes about writers and programme makers and getting a glimpse into their various thought-processes and working practices. It helps focus the mind onto things I want to do and ways in which I could drive myself forward.

Of course, we all know all I really need to drive myself forward is a deadline to write to.

Focus your prayers

Thursday 4 January

I've just this minute had a text message from a friend (the other half of the Live Life Then Give Life team) to say that Em has gone down to theatre for her transplant at Harefield.

Words can truly not express what I'm feeling at the moment – I've been through a lot with Emily over the last 12-18 months and we've both come across new challenges around the same time as each other (although I have to say I've been the lucky one and had things an awful lot easier).

Almost precisely two years ago, Em was told she had a year left to live – she's been close to losing her battle on at least two occasions but has never given up fighting and believing that her Tx would come.

And now it has and I'm delirious for her – it's just unbelievable.

But it's not all plain sailing from here – she's going to have a lot more fighting to do over the coming few days and weeks to get through and out the other side to where she can finally enjoy the rush of fresh air into her new lungs.

So I'll ask all of you out there reading this, whether it's tonight, tomorrow morning or any time in the next few days to say a prayer or two for her and help her in her fight.

Em, you're a legend and I couldn't be happier!

UPDATE:

I've been told that Emily has come through surgery with apparent flying colours (Em does everything with flying colours. It's not worth doing if it's not colourful, mainly pink!).

She's now out and in intensive care – her family have seen her and she's doing well although obviously she's still critical at this stage. Please keep praying and keep her strong to fight through and come out the other side.

Weird reactions

Sunday 7 January

EMILY UPDATE:

As updated on Friday, Emily came through the surgery well and is currently in intensive care. They made an attempt to wean her off her ventilator today, but she didn't take to it too well and has been sedated again. This isn't a major issue, as it is quite common for the de-ventilation (as it were) to take a little while, what with the mixture of sedation, pain meds and new cocktails of anti-rejection drugs. She has become slightly more awake and alert at points and is showing good signs of her old bubbly personality in flashes, so things are looking cautiously optimistic at the moment.

As for me, well, the last two days have been pretty up and down.

One of the weirdest things at the moment is how other people seem to think that I'd be really adversely affected by Em's transplant – perhaps expecting me to be jealous or angry, the old "why not me?" chestnut.

But the truth is, I don't feel anything like that at all. I'm completely overwhelmed with joy for Em and her family and devoted boyfriend – I couldn't be happier for them all, and especially seeing such a close friend going through what we've both been hoping for for the last two years. It feels odd, because there's a part of me that thinks I should be feeling some pangs of jealousy or upset, but it just isn't there.

It has made me think a lot more about my own transplant, but actually in a much more positive light. I have to confess that I have had moments, particularly over the last few weeks leading up to Christmas, where I have been doubting my conviction that this will come for me, and I still don't like to hear people talk about it with such certainty in their voices.

But I know that Em has been through patches like me as well – particularly in the summer when she had an exceptionally bad spell and was touch-and-go for a while, and we spoke about it afterwards. And I know that although she had her doubts, she never lost faith and never stopped fighting, right up to her call. She's set a kind of positive-thinking example to me and perked up not only my enthusiasm, but also my previously rigid belief that this will come for me too.

Secretly, I also have to admit I'm quite pleased she got in there first, because she'll now be on hand to help talk me through all the relevant stages of post-op recuperation as I come across them!

The last few days have been a bit rubbish for me, though, since I've started to feel really sick after my evening meal for the last three nights in a row now and the pattern is becoming a little disturbing.

The first night, on Friday, I had a horrible moment of thinking I was coming down with the same virus that hit K on Christmas day and that has slowly been working its way through her family. But so far I've not actually been sick.

Another theory that struck me yesterday was that, having spent two afternoons back at the flat trying to get it ship-shape before we aim to move back in over the next couple of weeks, all the dust and stuff we'd been kicking up has upset my chest and made me more productive, which in turn I've been coughing up and swallowing a lot – causing not-too-goodness in my stomach.

Although that seemed a plausible explanation yesterday, it seems less so today, when I've done nothing but chill out at my 'rents. And it also doesn't explain why it's only in the evenings, either.

It's not too bad, just annoying that I can't seem to eat in the evenings without feeling like I'm going to hurl for a couple of hours afterwards. It goes off slowly over the course of the evening, but it's not very pleasant to have to put up with.

Still, things could be worse and my chest is still doing very well a week into the New Year. I'm waking up every morning with lots of energy and get-up-and-go and I'm hopeful of a successful move back to the flat in the coming week or so, which will be lovely not just for K and me, but doubtless for Mum and Dad, too.

So next week is a chance to start focusing back on work, with the start of a new term at MKT and a show to build towards, as well as time to start turning my attention to the next issue of CF Talk. And then, of course, there's all my writing projects, too....

Back on track

Monday 8 January

I've had a brilliant day today, taken up mostly with a mammoth 4-hour meeting with Suze and Rheya about the MKT show this April.

The show, which is going to be in aid of the Cystic Fibrosis Trust, will be something of a gala performance for the Activ8 Youth Theatre, with whom Suze and I have worked (on-and-off on my part) for the last 5-6 years. We've never had the opportunity to start with such *carte blanche* as we've been given here, and it's fantastic – if a little daunting.

The Youth Theatre have been lucky in the past if they secured a single performance date in a 12-month period, so to have this show coming so quickly off the back of the summer show is exciting in and of itself, but to have such free reign to make the most of our stage time is a fantastic opportunity for all the children and young people involved.

So far, we're looking at doing devised pieces for the youngest three groups, and then a combination of devised, scripted and new-writing pieces with the oldest group – who have mostly been with us for a long time and will no doubt be raring to display the many facets of stage-craft they've had the chance to develop working with a practitioner as accomplished and, let's face it, off-the-wall as Suze.

Today's meeting was spent hammering out exactly what each group would be doing – allowing for the fact that the rehearsal process is sure to kick up a few new challenges and options on the way – and also going over a few storylines for some of the devised pieces which needed solidifying before we past them back to the groups to continue working.

The groups have already been working on some of the stuff that will be incorporated into the performance in the last term, but the ideas they've developed will all be picked up and run with over the course of the next 10 weeks leading up to the show. The idea is that we'll be using familiar material but probe deeper into it to make sure we're challenging them to come up with something that will push them and make the most of the showcase they've been offered.

I'm most excited about the fact that I'm due to return to rehearsals on Wednesday and Suze has offered me the opportunity to write part of the show and to direct a separate section with some of the older group involved. It's been so long since I've directed anything from scratch that I'm REALLY looking forward to it and can't wait to get going.

The section I'm working on is an amalgam of scenes from Hamlet and Tom Stoppard's Rosencrantz and Guildenstern are dead – a show I've always wanted to direct in its entirety.

I have to confess I've been a little on the tired side after our enormous brain-storming/planning session, but I feel so jazzed at the thought of being part of this show. It's wonderfully exciting to be working with the groups towards something that will really show their families and, hopefully, the wider community, what they are capable of doing.

In other news: my new BlackBerry arrived today, too!! After all my to-ing and fro-ing with O2 (the phone company, not the oxygen people), I managed not only to secure a free upgrade to the BlackBerry, but also to upgrade my call plan to double the minutes (400) and ten times the texts (1,000) per month for the same money. And I only wanted the phone....

Unfortunately, since it arrived I've been castigated by K after spending all morning and half the afternoon in a meeting for then getting so wrapped up in my new toy that I've hardly paid any attention to her all day.

I'd like to make a witty-yet-cutting riposte to show her that she's completely in the wrong and I'm smugly in the right as usual, but I really can't defend myself on this one, so I'm going to slope off and use my apologetic face.

EMILY UPDATE: For those of you still keeping tabs on Em (of which I know there are tons) she's still doing well. She's still on the vent for the moment, but her family say things are looking good for now. Thanks to you all for your love, prayers and support – I know they're greatly appreciated.

Preparation is the key

Wednesday 10 January

Who'd have thought I'd be back to studying, eh?

Not 24 hours after my mammoth meeting on the new show, I realised that if I was going into rehearsals on Wednesday, I'd sure as heck better have done some work on the script I'm tackling.

It wasn't till I sat down to piece together the sections of text from Hamlet and Tom Stoppard's Rosencrantz and Guildenstern Are Dead that I realised it was going to be impossible to work from copies of the script I had, so I'd have to type it all out fresh for the cast to use.

Laborious as it was, I'm actually grateful for the need to take the long way round, because it took me through both texts line-by-line, which got me much closer to them than I would have been if I'd just have given them a cursory glance through.

The basic idea of what I'm trying to do is use two of Shakespeare's scenes with Hamlet, Rosencrantz and Guildenstern (or Ros and Guil, as their mates – well, my type-worn fingers – call them) to book-end my favourite section of R&GAD involving a rapid-fire word game which is not only fun to watch, but also to perform and direct. The contrast between the language and the style of performance in the two different parts (ancient and modern) is a great opportunity for the actors to really explore and play with the text and their characters.

What I didn't count on, wading through the text as I typed it out, was just how much extra work I'd created for myself by going back to Shakespeare's original. Foolishly, having studied it for A-Level, I was hugely confident of my grasp of the material. But looking at it again I realised that although I still had a good hold of the sense of it, there were a hundred questions that leapt out at me from the verse which, as an actor, I would immediately have thrown at the director.

Being the director, that means I have to know the answer. Of course, it's not as simple as just throwing out an answer – I prefer, in rehearsals, to let the actors reach their own decisions and conclusions about what they're doing - but in order to keep them on the right track and not flailing off in random directions which take us round in circles, I needed to swat up on my ancient English and get to grips with Will's words.

Remarkably, I slipped back into my studying patterns without so much as a hiccup. In fact, I think I may have been better at it now than I was when I was studying it to be tested on. Whether that's a reflection on my abilities, or motivation, as a student, or on the problems with teaching Shakespeare in an English class I'm not quite sure.

Whatever the result and however well it goes in rehearsals, there is no doubt that getting back into creative endeavours – and practical ones at that – has refreshed my mind and my imagination and pushed my motivation to stay fit, healthy and able to work even harder than it was before.

More than anything else right now, I want to be able to see this through to the end. Ok, if I get my transplant call, I might just see fit to relinquish my role (provided, of course, I get comps to the show…), but beyond that, I don't want anything else to get in the way of me being able to do the thing that's been so missing from my life.

So it's double-physio, extra drinks (of the build-up kind, not the alcoholic kind) and plenty of rest throughout the day so that I can make the very most of the opportunity afforded me.

Emily and Watchdog

Wednesday 10 January

Anyone watching last night's edition of Watchdog would have seen the BBC taking Allied Respiratory to task for their abject failures in the oxygen delivery system – which you may have read me blogging about in the past.

You would also have seen that doyen of small-screen campaigning, my good friend Emily, performing admirably in berating the oxygen companies whilst simultaneously looking gorgeous and intelligent at the same time.

Frankly, there was very little of substance to the programme by way of solutions, but it was invaluable to help highlight the problems that oxygen users are facing and the poor job that Allied have been doing. It was telling that they didn't send anyone along to the programme, simply supplying an apology statement.

To this end – although not related to the Watchdog programme itself – I'll be going along to a meeting at the end of the month with the Chief Exec of the CF Trust at the Department of Health along with representatives of Allied. Although PWCF are not the only ones who depend on oxygen delivery, it plays a significant part in many of their lives and any benefits or progress we can make on our behalf will only serve to benefit others as well.

Of course, it should really be Em's realm to follow up her campaigning for better oxygen provision, but as we are all so wonderfully aware, she is otherwise detained at the moment!

Speaking of which, by way of an update – Emily was taken off her ventilator yesterday and is now breathing on her own with her bright, shiny, clean new lungs!! Hooray for her and here's to many more years of happy deep breathing!

Back and back

Friday 12 January

So the New Year has started proper now, hasn't it? First day back at work notched up and I'm relishing the challenges ahead.

It was awesome to be back at the Theatre and to see the group again. The majority of the girls are still the same people I've been working with for a while now and it was like slipping back into a comfortable pair of shoes, or a freshly made bed, or something similarly warm, comfortable and welcoming.

The guys I did know seemed so happy to see me that it really lifted my spirits and the ones who I didn't didn't seem to think of me as too much of a freak, which was good.

I have to confess, I was feeling pretty nervous ahead of time – it's been over 6 months since I last properly set foot inside the Theatre and whilst it's full of familiar and friendly faces, I couldn't escape the fact that for me, a lot has changed since I was last there.

Striding in with my oxygen cylinder (OK, strolling), I tried to embody the kind of confidence with which I normally arrived at the building, but I found it a lot harder to muster my usual sense of artistic bravado. Somehow the oxygen makes me feel weaker, and more self-conscious, and at the same time I know that it's only my attitude which is creating that impression.

As much as people tell me that no one notices the O2, I know that it's not true. It may not be as big a deal to other people as it is to me, but it's also nonsense to pretend it's invisible. My hang-up about looking "ill" came back with a vengeance and seems to be staying firmly put for the time being, although I'm trying hard to learn to ignore it.

I didn't wear my O2 all the way through the session – apart from any vanity-related reasons, it's hard to fully engage with a group when you're tied to a cylinder and I sure as heck wasn't going to have the energy to lug it all around the rehearsal room with me.

On reflection, I should have been more strict with myself and re-attached when I was sitting down discussing ideas or talking to the group and only coming off when we were doing something that demanded me being on my feet.

That's a big part of the learning curve that I'm going to be on for the next few weeks, though, and I know I'm going to have to push my boundaries to a large degree and see what I can and can't cope with. I appreciate that I don't have much room for error, but if I don't try things I'm never going to know how much impact I can have on things.

The rehearsal itself went really well. The group are all really keen and worked really well, incorporating the new people quickly and in a much more friendly and welcoming way than has often happened in the past.

They were also all really pleased with the ideas for the show that Suze had drawn up and happy with the casting for the sections we've decided on. There's going to be a few tough calls on casting for some of the pieces and I think the Hamlet section could prove a tough one to fill – whoever we choose is going to have to work hard. The great thing with this group, though, is that you know they all will work hard and give it their best.

The 4-hours I was out of the house was, I think, about my limit for the time being – although the strain was doubtless enhanced by my being off the O2 – and on Thursday I really felt it.

I woke up feeling pretty good, although tired, and I knew I had to take it really easy all day. Things seemed to go pretty well in recovery terms until about mid-afternoon when everything took a bit of a nose-dive and I completely ran out of energy.

About 5pm my reserves seemed to have deserted me and I was left absolutely shattered and dying for my bed. I eventually made it until about 9pm, but not before I'd managed to cause a mini-argument with K over the phone by trying to organise things when I was tired.

I really knew I was exhausted when I found myself in bed reading Ben Fogle and James Cracknell's story of their Atlantic rowing race and getting emotional with the ups and downs they were experiencing in their moods. When they talked of missing their wives and getting tearful and I started welling up too, I knew I'd let myself get WAY too tired.

Still, today has been a clear and bright day (mentally, if not meteorologically) and I've been to Oxford, where my lung function was only ever so slightly down (which I still put down to it being taken before not after physio) at 0.7/1.3 and my weight had risen to 50.8kg. I also spoke to the dietician about the sickness I've been feeling and she prescribed me... something I can't remember for a couple of weeks to see if it takes it away.

Tonight, with my Gramps here and my bro heading off into the sunset on another punishing course (who'd be in the army, eh?), we sat and ate dinner together before he high-tailed it away to colder, wetter climbs. Rather him than me.

Now all that's left is for me to get my beauty sleep before Phase 1 of the Move Home tomorrow. If all goes to plan, I'll be back living in my little apartment paradise by this time Sunday!

Home sweet home

Sunday 14 January

After nearly 6 weeks away from my little Oli-world in far, far

Bletchley (that's kind of like a Galaxy far, far away, only with less hospitable bars) I'm back and wonderfully happy to be in my own space again.

Mum and Dad have been fantastic over the last two months and have really gone out of their way to make it look like they've not been going out of their way to accommodate me, when I know it must have been a pain in the butt. I appreciate the fact that most parents would do whatever they could to make life easier for their offspring, but that doesn't make it any less wonderful when they do.

I suppose it helped that my bro was home for a good chunk of the time too, because at least I could pretend that maybe a little of the disruption was thanks to him, but I know that it's mostly me!

Still, I'm out of their hair now, although I dare say I'll be just as, if not more, reliant on them back here than I was at home. I know that when the going gets tough here, it's going to get really tough, even with K around to help out, but we're all prepared for it and we'll tackle whatever hiccups come our way head on and with true Lewington smiles plastered all over our faces.

It's just a really wonderful feeling to be back here, living with K and enjoying being just the two of us for the first time since November. More than anything, it's been lovely tonight just to curl up on the sofa and watch TV and chill out.

I'm possibly slightly sadly over-excited at the thought of getting down to work tomorrow in my newly re-mastered study – the story of which is an epic tale of human calculation and lateral thinking that only my Dad and I could get lost in. Even my mild-mannered mother started losing her rag with us yesterday. Suffice it to say that it's not too easy to work out how to fit 2 bookcases, a desk, a filing cabinet, a drawer chest and a soon-to come coat stand into one former bedroom.

All of the excitement of the move and the on-going tidying, sorting and clearing has drained my batteries for the day, though, so I'm off to bed for a good rest up in my own bed, with my own pillows, my own sheets and my lovely K beside me. Oh, and Neve, too.

Productivity

Monday 15 January

A new era has been ushered in in the House of Oli (like the

House of Usher, but hopefully not falling) – an era of cool, calm productivity which, I predict, will reign for years to come.

Sceptics would say that it will reign until a week next Wednesday, but I've never listened to the naysayers in my life, so I shall continue to thumb my nose at them and live in blissful ignorance for the foreseeable future.

Today, I have mostly been working diligently in my study – beavering away at my newly-imported (read: bought in John Lewis) keyboard which has made my entire office set-up both more ergonomic and more fun – the clacking of keys on a proper keyboard is so much more preferable to the tapping of lap-top keys, don't you find?

Of course, it may only be little ol' me who has a strange obsession with the noises made by keys on a keyboard, but when you're working life consists almost solely of one particular noise, it's good to find one that agrees with you. Not that laptop key noises are disagreeable, as such, they're just not as good as.... oh stop now.

Anyway, in addition to going a good way to clearing the backlog of emails waiting for my immediate attention in my three inboxes (don't ask, it's too complicated), I managed to commission two articles for CF Talk, take further steps towards establishing a dedicated DVD section on the Close-Up Film website, of which I am nominally DVD Editor but have yet to really start work proper, and also got involved in a really exciting charity project happening in March, which I will expand on when I'm able.

Not only did I achieve all that just from sitting at my desk, but I also cleared a huge backlog of clearing and tidying of the stuff we brought back to the flat from my Mum and Dad's, AND had time for a 2-hour brain-storming planning session for the video sections of the Youth Theatre show in April.

Now, those of you who followed the progress of the last show on my MySpace blog will know that the multi-media elements served to provide the toughest test of my unflappable Production Managership (it's a word, I said so!!) and my "never rip the head off a moron" motto.

Luckily this time we will be undertaking the filming work purely on our lonesome, Suze having handed over the reigns to myself and Rheya, my counterpart in the production management of the show and soon to be co-producer, co-director of the filmed sections of the show. We have no obligation whatsoever to involve Milton Keynes College or any of their students – Happy Day!

At the flat today we spent a wonderful couple of hours batting ideas to and fro and narrowing them down to a workable length and story line to open the show with. Obviously, it's all mega-top-secret and if I told you I'd have to kill you, so for both our sakes (don't forget I'm lazy) I'm going to keep my cards close to my chest. My eyesight's not good anyway, so it's easier to read them the closer they are.

Tomorrow, I'm aiming for more of the same, and I'm also going to try not to eat strange little badly-cooked frozen mini-pizzas for lunch. But that's another hurdle all together…

Barrels of Laughs

Wednesday 17 January

Today has been just as productive as yesterday, but also HUGELY more exciting because I officially climbed aboard a project being run by the Live Life Then Give Life campaign putting on a comedy night at the Mermaid Theatre in London in March.

The history to the night is quite long and convoluted, but mainly involves Emily getting a phone call a while back from Bill Bailey, who'd been told through the grapevine from a reader of her blog that she was a fan and had been having a hard time.

Now, there's a very funny story here about serial-schmoozer Emily getting hideously tongue-tied and not being able to form sentences, but I wouldn't like to embarrass her, so I'll leave that bit out. Oh wait….

Anyway, after chatting to her for a while, Bill apparently succumbed to what many people have come to know as the "Emily Effect" – that is, having spoken to a remarkable friendly, eloquent, funny, determined and energetic (in speech, at least) young woman about all the issues on which she campaigns, he offered to do whatever he could to help.

Some months later, Emily has decided that now is a good time to go get some new lungs (I'm told they're 2007's must-haves) and left her LLTGL partner-in-crime Emma high-and-dry staring down the barrel of a show in 6 weeks time with a whole range of "To Do's" still "To Be Done".

So, shining my armour and mounting my steed (yes, my steed!),

I fired off an email to Emma gallantly offering my services as Production Manager extraordinaire to fill any gaps she may have.

Now, there must have been some sort of miscommunication here, because Emma and her wonderful, throw-your-hand-in, get-stuck-in, jump-in-the-deep-end husband Brad seem to have developed the mistaken impression that I was actually offering to help them out and do some work.

Clearly, they don't know me well enough to know that when I offer to help it's nothing but an empty gesture and what I really mean is I'll be happy to sit on my rump in bed at home and watch Bill Bailey DVDs and tell people how funny he is.

Still, being the awfully polite person I am, I suddenly felt like it would be terribly improper of me to point out their error, so it looks like I'm on board…

I really don't know how I get myself into these fixes, but now I'm here, I supposed I'll just make a fist of it and see what I can't do to make things run a little smoothly.

Right now there's all sorts of bits and pieces remaining to be organised, including nailing down who exactly is going to be on the bill. Through Bill Bailey's management we've acquired a strong line-up of fresh comedians willing to entertain the masses, and we're still hopeful of getting a few last gasp names to pop along too.

I've got my list of To Do's passed down and am liaising with the venue and management about technical requirements and other such things, as well as sticking my oar in wherever I see opportunity.

It's looking like it's going to be a really good evening and, more importantly, is going to go a good way to helping support the LLTGL campaign's current objectives – of which more at a later date.

Not as knackered

Thursday 18 January

I'm sitting here tonight feeling very tired, but not shattered and still with some energy left in the batteries, which is a big step forward on last week, when come mid-way through Thursday afternoon (following the Youth Theatre sessions on Wednesday night) I was completely exhausted.

The sessions were great yesterday – we finished casting all the pieces, which is a job that remains just as difficult no matter how many times you've done it before, how well you know the people you're working with, or how much preparation you've done. As per usual, Suze and I spent a huge chunk of time in the session with people coming in and out to read for us.

What made it particularly difficult this time around was the strength of the group and the strength of the material. We want more than anything to make sure that everyone who is coming along this term, whether a new member or an old hand, gets a chance to really stretch themselves and do something which is going to challenge them. With this final round of casting, I think we've achieved that and I'm looking forward to the rehearsal process immensely.

This week was also particularly good because I got to hear my chorus piece in the mouths of the group and see whether it worked or not. I'm pretty chuffed to say it did – and I'm always amazed at the qualities that a cast bring to my writing over and above what I've written. It's exciting to see something you've written coming off the page and being performed – doubly so when it "works" and, for comedy, when it makes you and other people laugh.

I managed my energy levels a lot better this week than I did last week. I used my O2 a lot more in the session, making sure I was on it whenever I was sat down – either at the side of the room during an exercise or for the script readings and other parts of the session, too. I also took along snack food and drink to keep my energy levels up and ate well before I left, too, to make sure I made the most of my time there without exhausting myself.

It's an annoying process to have to calculate your energy expenditure before doing anything and working out what is an isn't possible, but it's also a part of my life now that's not going to change until my transplant, so there's no point griping about it. I'm a lot happier knowing that I'm getting to grips with it and can see potential trouble-spots far enough ahead to compensate for them.

Thursdays are now my designated "off" days, to allow for the fact that if I do over do things at work, I can spend the whole day in bed if I need to. My diary is always clear on a Thursday now, and it will remain that way all the time I'm still working at the sessions to ensure I can give them my all without having to worry about the impact it will have on "tomorrow" and having to cancel or rearrange plans.

Because of that, I've actually done very little today, but it's been nice to chill out a bit, since I've spent most of the week so far busying myself with my myriad different tasks in the study. I'm really enjoying being so busy and having so much on – particularly things that I can do from home without having to worry about expending energy going out and doing things.

More on my current projects as they develop, but lots of cool things happening, so keep 'em peeled. Offers of help always appreciated (Rob) and likely to be taken up – anyone know any well-known stand-ups we can call?

Just plain happy

Saturday 20 January

Believe me, I know how strange this sounds coming from someone who's spent the last two months writing about the various different ups and downs in his life, but just now I'm finding it unbelievably hard to find the right words to describe just how happy I'm feeling.

This is one of those periods of life that just make you sit back and smile – to count your blessings and realise that the world is not really a big, evil place that intent on wearing you down, but rather that if you put yourself in the right position to be the master of your own destiny and you look at the world from the right perspective, things will sooner or later start to swing your way.

I can also appreciate how bizarre it might sound for someone who is currently waiting for someone else to die so that he can have a chance of a fresh, new tilt at life to even begin to describe himself as the master of his own destiny.

But success or failure, good or bad, up or down is all a matter of perception.

Paul McKenna, in numerous published writings (not least Change Your Life in 7 Days, which I would recommend to anyone, even the most sceptical of self-help depreciators) cites the words of Thomas Edison when questioned as to how he felt after failing for the 700th time in his attempt to invent the electric light:

"I have not failed 700 times. I have not failed once. I have succeeded in proving that those 700 ways will not work. When I have eliminated all the ways that will not work, I will find the way that will work."

Right now, in as much as these things matter to me, everything is going my way:

I'm back living at home in my lovely little flat with my girlfriend whom I'm very much in love with and I'm honoured to say is very much in love with me.

I'm working on 3 projects which not only motivate and excite me, but also give me aims, objectives and reasons to keep well.

My chest is behaving exactly as I expect it to. It's not ever going to fire on all cylinders again, but that's why I'm on the transplant list. All I can ask it to do now is support me as best it can until such time as God sees fit to call time on these knackered old blowers and give me a fresh set.

I'm surrounded by people I love and who love me back – my friends are fantastic and don't ever make me feel bad for not being able to join in things, nor complain when I pull out of things at the last minute; my family all go out of their way to do whatever I need of them, no matter how little or unreasonable; people I work with make huge allowances for what I can and can't do and never bat an eyelid or make me feel like I'm stretching their patience (even when I know I must – I stretch my OWN patience with some of the last-minute turnarounds, it can't be easy for others to deal with).

Every once in a while all the pieces in your life seem to align just so – like the planets and the sun, or the cogs of a machine – and for a moment life seems just right. And it's so, so, so important to seize that moment, to recognise it for what it is: fleeting perfection of it's own kind which will last but a flicker, but if you see it and grasp it, it will last forever in the memory.

I'm under no illusions that this will continue unabated; I know there will be trouble ahead – harder times, darker times, more challenging and less fun times, but damned if I'm not going to enjoy the good stuff while it's here.

Like the song says: while there's moonlight and music and love and romance, I'll be the one on the dance floor.

Super Tuesday

Wednesday 24 January

Tuesdays are traditionally one of those nothing days, aren't they? They're not Monday, so there's no real reason to hate them, but neither are they Friday, with the joy of an impending weekend, nor Sunday, with it's laid back, pipe-and-slippers feel.

So it was a wonderful turn up for the books yesterday when we seemed to have a belated Christmas of good tidings all tumble into our laps over the course of a happy, exciting, smile-making morning, afternoon and evening.

First thing in the morning, we kicked off with a wonderful double-whammy for K where in the space of 30 minutes she discovered not only that she had she been accepted on her college course – a 12-month access to healthcare which will set her up to head to uni to study Speech Therapy next year – but also that she's been granted an interview for a job which would fit both her and our needs perfectly.

Coming directly on top of that, I had a HUGELY productive morning working on the Laughter for Life show, getting to grips with a number of pressing issues. Most unbelievably generous and fantastic for us was the agreement of Steve at Tin Racer, who do all the design work for CF Talk, to design the programmes for the night for free. Not only that, but he also offered to talk to his contacts to see if we can get it printed for free, too!

After beavering away on all things funny for the morning, we then popped out to Mazda to test drive the Mazda 6 – a proper, grown-up car which I have to confess I've rather fallen in love with. I've been looking to change my current car on the Motablilty scheme since November, when I realised that in order to stay mobile when I'm less well, it may be better for me to have an automatic gearbox, to take away some of the physical exertion of driving. It now looks like we've found the right car – and may well be off to order it tomorrow!

On top of all of that, K then started her college course in the evening (cutting it fine on the admissions front, MK College…) and came through the evening unscathed and looking forward to what the next 12 months hold academically.

I spent the time she was in college hanging out with a friend who I haven't spent a lot of time with for ages and we caught up. Adding to the Super Tuesday feel, he was filling me in on his new relationship (early stages, but hey, it's still a relationship) and I couldn't have been happier for him. I know he's feeling a bit conflicted about it all at the moment (loooooong story…) but I think it's fab and he should enjoy it!

Every now and again one of those days come along where everything just seems to go your way. So often in life we can only remember those days when everything seems to go against you, so I'm determined to hold on to the memory of my Super Tuesday and use it in future to blast away the cobwebs when I'm starting to doubt my productivity or the wisdom of things.

Everyone should have a Super Tuesday at some point, and when you do, make sure you lodge it in your memory and share the good news with all around you. Nothing like a ray of sunshine through the snow to make people smile.

Doesn't take much

Friday 26 January

Ah, well, you can't have it all going your own way, can you?

After the best part of a week spent luxuriating in the delights of life – happiness, exciting prospects, wonderful surroundings, beautiful people and all the rest of it – I knew that sooner or later things would come crashing back down with a bump. And bump they did.

Yesterday, as I hoped, we went down to Mazda to order our new car and things seemed to pass off without a hitch. But low and behold, I get back home this afternoon to find a voicemail message from the dealer telling me that Motability won't insure an under-25 on a category 9 car – so I'm 4 months too early to get the Mazda 6. How ridiculous is that?

Having phoned Motability, they've said I can appeal it in writing and they can take it to their insurers and see if they'll make an exception, but it seems crazy to have to go through all of that palaver for the sake of 4 months!

But actually, although the whole car thing is a bummer, I have to confess that that's not really what brought me down this week. What really dragged me off my happy perch was a visit to Milton Keynes College on Thursday afternoon.

K is doing an access course to get her set for uni entry in 2008 and had to enrol officially before her class on Thursday night, which meant we had to go down in the afternoon and do the enrolment necessaries.

I suppose I should have thought about it ahead of time and prepared myself for it, but I didn't. The surprise element may have been a factor in my difficulties, but I can't blame that entirely.

The problem, largely, is being around groups of teenagers and young adults, hanging out in corridors as they do and being themselves at their supremely judgemental young ages. I know that this is a MASSIVE generalisation and that not ALL teenagers are hugely judgemental, but I remember being a teenager, at school, and what I would think of people walking past me in the corridor and how much we used to jump on anyone or anything that was "different".

And, for the first time since my health dipped and O2 became a big part of my life, my worst fears came true – I felt like a total freak. It didn't help that we were forced to walk almost the entire length of the campus between two departments we needed to see, which had me not only navigating through huge throngs of students, but doing it even more breathlessly than normal while lugging one of my really heavy black O2 cylinders with me.

I also know that most of the negative vibe I felt I was creating almost entirely within my own mind, but that didn't make any difference to how I felt, or how I feel about the experience.

It was supremely negative – something I'm not very used to in my life. Almost any situation I can look at, take a spin on and come up with a positive side, or a brighter perspective. Even this blog is titled after my attitude to whatever life chooses to throw at me. But for the first time in a very long time on Thursday, I felt small, insecure and very, very different.

What made it all the harder is that I've spent so long now building myself up and repairing the somewhat fractured self-image I had in my final years at school that I don't have the coping mechanisms to help me through feelings like these. I seemed to go into a sort of semi-shock, no use to man nor beast for an hour or so.

I was only lucky in that I had to go straight on to another meeting, this time on friendly turf at the Theatre with Rheya to go over our video shoot, which managed to occupy my brain long enough to push the negative thoughts from my head and start me off on a clean bill when I got back to my own space.

I suppose what I have to take away from the situation is a knowledge of how bad it can get. Although this may sound mightily pessimistic on the surface, it's important to me and actually something I find quite positive.

Life is all about the ups and downs and I've now got a whole new barometer for the downs – college on Thursday was tough, and way beyond anything I've experienced like that for quite a while. But that also means that I'm unlikely to find another experience like it for a while, either.

And when I think I have, I can just remind myself how bad this was, and almost immediately make myself feel better that it's not that bad.

I was saying all through the ups last week that I was enjoying them because you never know when the downs are going to come in the roller-coaster of life, and having them to cling to when the week's got rough has made a big difference. Where once I would have been bummed out for days by an hour's worth of bad experience, instead I can focus on all the good things that have happened and are still happening and turn my face away from the rubbish that I don't need on my mind.

Enjoy the good times and remember the bad – just don't let them rule your thoughts.

Whoops, dropped the ball

Wednesday 31 January

After my somewhat self-pitiful mini-rant last week I seem to have slightly dropped the blogging ball and not had a proper update – the longest I've gone without an update since I started this blog I think.

I blame many things – anything really that absolves me from accusations of being too damn lazy/forgetful to write something interesting on here – and deny all such mutterings from the kids in the back.

Still, things have picked up mightily since last Thursday – I knew it would only be a blip, and it was, albeit a two-dayer, but a blip none the less. I struggled for a couple of days to shake of the negative thoughts and not-so-nice images in my head, but I've got a pretty good daemon fighter in my head after all these years, so I get back on top of things pretty quickly.

This weekend was a weird one, because I had lots to do but couldn't escape the fact that during the week I'd actually been far too busy and needed to take a bit of time to myself to make sure that I stopped myself from sliding down hill.

I headed to Oxford on Friday to see my physio and we made plans with my CF nurse to start a course of IV's at the end of this week. They wanted me to come in, onto the ward, for the first week of the course, but I managed to negotiate a stay of execution until the week after to ensure that I didn't have to miss another week of work. (I'll now be in hospital for half-term week, so not nearly as bad as going in next week).

It also means that I can still attend the meeting I've been invited to at the Department of Health next Tuesday, the subject of which is sadly under wraps at the moment, but I'm sure I'll fill you in on at a later date.

Today, however, I was coincidentally down at the DoH as well, meeting with the team who deal with oxygen provision to discuss the problems that I and other PWCF have been having with the home oxygen service, mostly with relation to Allied Respiratory.

It had originally been scheduled as a meeting between all three sides, but in the end the decision was taken by the DoH to have a separate meeting with Allied, which the CF Trust will also do, to air the concerns directly.

The purpose of today's meeting was to express as clearly as we could the importance of so-called ambulatory oxygen to PWCF and their needs for portable O2.

It was actually a really positive meeting, with the two representatives of the DoH really keen to take everything on board and correct things. It's fair to say that things are a good deal better with Allied than they were even 3 months ago when I first started using them, but it's important for the issues that did come up to be properly looked at to ensure nothing like that happens again.

I'm confident following the meeting that good things will come from it, including a commitment to looking at lighter, more portable forms of oxygen to make getting out and about easier for people like me who find the cylinders a weight.

I also hope that the feedback with regards to customer service is picked up on and driven home to the company, because their staff training is simply appalling.

The meeting did exhaust me, though, so it's an early night and restful day tomorrow on the cards.

Worse than expected

Wednesday 31 January

Today has been a really hard day. Despite being exhausted by the day's activities yesterday – heading down to London and back, with an hour and a half's meeting in the middle – I slept terribly, hardly managing longer than an hour asleep at a time, and waking up this morning feeling totally drained.

I knew that the meeting was likely to take a chunk out of me, and need me with a need to recuperate, but I wasn't expecting to be bed-bound for three-quarters of the day.

Even now, sitting in the study writing this I know I'm not right – my brain isn't really turned on and my chest is protesting. I need to do some physio, which may help the chest, but I don't know what I'm going to do about my brain. I'm just waiting for my neb to work before getting some physio done.

I'm supposed to be going in to work tonight and I desperately don't want to miss another week, not with the show starting to loom and only 2 weeks till half term. I'm having all sorts of horrible thoughts of missing out on the whole term again and not being able to do anything for the show, not to mention landing Suze in the proverbial by missing sessions at such short notice that she doesn't have time to get cover or re-plan.

It's just not fun – my body is rebelling and my mind wants to go with it and I'm fighting tooth and nail not to let either of them win. And yet, I'm stuck on that see-saw between doing what I want to do and making my chest worse – there's no telling whether it will or not.

The smart part of my brain is telling me not to go into work tonight and to stay home, stay in bed and get some rest, but the fragile part of my brain is telling me that I need to get up and out of the house to avoid getting chronically cross with myself and my chest for not supporting me in the things I want to do.

I don't want to be here now – I don't like being back in this place where everything I do has to involve a sacrifice somewhere else. I want to be able to book myself to do something on two consecutive days and not feel like a slave to the whims of my lungs.

I know I have to accept that that's exactly what I am now, and that I have to learn to work with them as much as I can for the time being until I get a shiny new set which will let me do what I want when I want. There's really no point in me sitting here harping on about how poor old me can't do what I want to do and isn't life unfair, because it's not like I didn't know that already.

Pull yourself together, get a grip on the realities of your situation and stop letting little things rock your boat. Focus on the good things, do what you can manage to do and forget about the rest of it – there's no point pining for something you *can't* do, you might as well make the best of what you *can* do.

February 2007
(9 Months)

Laughter for Life is ON SALE!

Thursday 1 February

Nothing like a break through in planning and organisation of a big project to stimulate the happiness and reenergise you (see – it's not just the steroids…). As of this moment, tickets for Laughter for Life, hosted by Bill Bailey and featuring Dara O'Briain, are ON SALE.

This is undoubtedly the coolest thing to happen this week, and will totally keep me charged full of positive energy until at least six o'clock. And then I'll come back here, read my excitement and get excited again.

But you must *hurry*, because this is a fabulous evening of hilarious comedy from fantastic comedians (and other such hyperbole) and it's going to sell out fast with a capital FAST (not hyperbole, actually true).

So if you're really my friend, buy some tickets, otherwise I won't like you any more. And if you want to be my friend, buy tickets and I promise I'll like you.

So there.

Did I mention it would be funny…?

Radio 4 no less…

Monday 5 February

Back at the start of the year, I was sent an email by the press officer at the CF Trust asking if I'd be willing to talk to Radio 4 about my diet and having to take on an inordinate number of calories everyday. Being the self-confessed media tart (MT) that I am, I nearly bit her hand off.

Having spoken to one of the team on Radio 4's Saturday Live show, I was told the following day that they'd decided not to go with that story, but that they'd keep my details on file for the future.

I didn't realise that meant a matter of weeks – just last Thursday, JP from the show called me back to see if I was free to come to the studio in London to do a segment on the same subject with presenter Fi Glover and stick around for the whole show.

Excited doesn't quite cover it from my side of things – I love the media: TV and radio have always intrigued and excited me and to think that I was stepping up for 2 minute 2-ways on local BBC 3 Counties to a show that people had actually heard of was unbelievable.

So I roused myself at 5.30am on Saturday morning and stumbled around to do my morning dose of IV's before I left for the studio in my Dad-powered taxi at 6.45am.

I did manage to doze on the way down a little bit, but arrived at Broadcasting House – yes, THE Broadcasting House!!! – at 8.15am feeling every-so-slightly-very nervous. I've got so used to doing local radio and press that it didn't occur to me how nervous I was going to get going on a big national radio station.

As it was, the whole thing was fab. I was on the show with Fi, the presenter, the regular poet they have on every week, who was a really good giggle and an Asian music producer who was fascinating to talk to and is doing some really interesting work in fusing musical sounds and styles from all over the world.

My section of the show – which I think ran about 10 minutes, although I totally lost track of time – went really well, although I was annoyed with myself for tripping over my tongue at the beginning. I covered all the bases they wanted covered for the piece and even managed to get in a plug for Live Life Then Give Life and organ donation in general.

Further to the on-air discussions, though, I also got chatting to Fi after the show about Laughter for Life and she has promised to help out with publicity if she can – passing our details to a 5Live producer and to the London Radio listings people, which should carry a bit more weight than just randomly attacking them with a press release.

As exciting as it was, it has also made the start of IV's even tougher going, since my body disagrees mightily with Meropenem anyway (the drug I'm on) and adding into it early mornings and irregular sleep patterns doesn't help.

I know I'm going to have to take a few days to recover, but annoyingly, it's hard to tell how much of this is IV-related and how much is down to over-work/exhaustion. If I knew that, I'd be able to look after myself a bit better and space my workload, but as it is I have to assume the worst and take it as easy as I can for the time being till things pick up again.

Still, I was on Radio 4!

The big IV slowdown

Tuesday 6 February

IV's are great because a) they keep you alive longer than you otherwise would manage and b) ...... well, I think (a)'s pretty convincing so I guess it'll have to do.

On the other hand, the list of why IV's suck is much, much longer.

This time, top of my "Why I loathe IV's" list is the unfortunate and highly rubbish side effects that my Meropenem (drug) is having on me.

Now, I have a bit of a history with Mero (as with many of the drugs I take), mostly that it gives me hugely painful joints and muscles, but we have discovered that a short course of steroids to coincide with the Mero seems to do the trick in alleviating the pains.

Not so much this time, though. Although I am doing better than I have been, it's still giving me the weirdest and most annoying pain in my right hand. It's not even that it's particularly excruciating, it's just almost permanently there and refuses to go away. But since it's only in my right hand, it seems a bit silly to moan about it.

I did check in with my friendly family on-call doc (my all-knowing Aunt) who looked it up on the web and assured me that it wasn't doing me any harm, but probably lots of good and to persevere with it, which I have.

The hand aside, I'm also suffering the simple and commonly

acknowledged IV slowdown – the high doses of super-powerful antibiotics being a good stimulant of sleep and restfulness. The only issue being my body seems to have set itself on the weirdest clock at the moment, not letting me sleep till the early hours of the morning, then letting me be deceived into thinking I'm wide awake in the middle of the day until it hijacks me and cuts off all brain and motor-function mid-afternoon and forces more sleep on me.

It's weird this IV lark, and you'd have thought I'd have got used to it by now after regular courses 5-6 times a year for the past goodness knows how long – but I still seem to be taken by surprise when it knocks me for six the next time I'm on them.

Still, I'm booked in for a week of rest and extra-physio (although I'm not sure the two necessarily go together…) in the Churchill next week, so hopefully I'll have a storming second week and come out of it in tip-top fighting form for the big Laughter for Life publicity push and the run up to the show.

Not to mention getting the new issue of CF Talk off to the designers and shooting 2 days of video for the Activ8 Youth Theatre show.

IV's may suck, but in the long run they let you do the things you want.

Something always comes good

Wednesday 7 February

Today has been, frankly, a pretty rubbish day.

Yet again last night my drugs and brain conspired to keep me awake almost the whole way through the night, letting me finally drift off for more than an hour just before my 6am alarm call for my morning IV's, followed by my usually solid sleep-time of 7-11am being interrupted by phone calls, deliveries and other distractions.

So a bad start to a long day as it was, which put me in a less than fabulous mood for the rest of it, which in turn annoyed me because my cousin Katie was down from Brum to catch a show at the Theatre and we were planning on having a bit of a day of it.

As it was, I could hardly muster the energy to entertain, although we did have a good chat and a cracking Game of Life with K (which I won, natch…). But I still had to collapse into bed mid-afternoon to catch up on sleeps.

My body was simply not keen to play ball today though and

stubbornly refused to wake itself up from my nap, which dragged me further into struggles for general awake/happiness.

The thought of getting through an hour and a half's work session was, I have to admit, less than appealing, so it came as some relief when Rheya phoned to pass a message from Suze to say that since most of my group weren't in for tonight, it made more sense for me to stay at home, so I delivered Katie to the Theatre and sorted her tickets before heading straight back home.

No sooner was I back than my chest started playing silly buggers again and giving me all sorts of grief – mostly muscle-related pain, I think, from where I've been sleeping and holding myself a little strangely due to the IV access in my shoulder.

Being both exhausted and in pain is never a great mood-enhancing combo, so I was getting spectacularly downbeat and po-faced when I discovered perhaps the funniest thing I've seen on TV in a long time.

Curled up in bed with K, we flicked onto Never Mind The Buzzcocks and I laughed so hard I'm sure the pain from my chest has migrated to my stomach.

I've really no idea who Donny Tourettes is – or even if I've got his name right – but he made for some of the most unintentionally hilarious TV viewing since You've Been Framed made people laugh.

Watching Bill Bailey and Simon Amstell (both newly minted personal heroes of mine) ripping into Donny's bizarre attempts at either rebellion or humour, coupled with his own self-image of sex-god punk rock star out to diss the world had me doubled over in laughter and nearly falling off the bed.

It goes to prove that no matter how lousy things get, I was right all along when I said that the only way to deal with the tough times is to smile through it.

God bless you, Buzzcocks.

Bloody rollercoasters

Friday 9 February

Have I mentioned in the last week or so how much IV's annoy me? Methinks once or twice…

Yesterday was a really good day – I didn't sleep very well, but I re-organised my drug schedule to get me out of bed at 8am instead of 6am, which meant I could get up and start my day immediately, rather than going back to bed after an hour when my drugs were done and sleeping till noon.

It also worked well because it let me take my catch-up sleep (that's just me trying to avoid the word "nap" really) straight after lunch, before my afternoon dose, rather than having to wait till after it and then sleeping too late into the afternoon, which in turn appeared to be disrupting my night-time sleep pattern.

Not only did it seem to work pretty well, the new schedule, but it also seemed to give me a lot more energy and get-up-and-go and as a result I had an enormously productive day, leathering through work on the new CF Talk, Laughter for Life and the Activ8 Show, all of which had been somewhat neglected over the previous week.

Having gone to bed tired and ready to sleep after my late dose last night, I was eagerly anticipating a good night's sleep (which I got – YAY!) and another energy-filled, super-productive day. I was even starting to plan my to-do list for the day as I drifted off.

But high doses of whopping-strength drugs will go and do odd things to your system. After a great night's rest, I woke up not full of the bouncing, work-attacking energy with which I'd gone through Thursday, but with the apparent wakefulness of your average 3-toed Sloth, which saw me lumped on the sofa most of the morning working out how much of the to-do's could be un-done for the day.

After lunch, I slept, again anticipating a post-snooze pick-up to revamp my day, but again seemed only to wake more tired than I had been when I went to sleep. Worse than that, though, was the fact that my brain saw fit to simply shut down and not operate for the rest of the day until about 9pm this evening.

I've thus spent almost all of the day/afternoon in a semi-comatose state on the sofa wondering where on earth all the energy and pizazz I discovered yesterday had gone.

It would appear that I'm back in the old give-and-take world of IV's and energy which had me so frustrated in the run up to Christmas. As much as I want to be pushing myself forward and keeping ploughing on, I keep having to give in to my body and accept defeat on a day's work.

If there were just some kind of indicator as to whether tomorrow was going to be better or worse, I think I could cope with it easier – it's the apparent lottery of energy levels that's really riling me at the moment.

I suppose I just have to look at it from the point of view that it makes each day more interesting and exciting because I never know what's going to get thrown at me: perhaps there'll be something new to spur me on tomorrow, or maybe I'll be finding new depths of reserves to drag myself through the day. Who knows? Isn't it fun?!

Saturday Night Live

Sunday 11 February

I did it!! I actually managed to go out on a Saturday night without a) running out of steam after half-an-hour, b) not being able to get out of bed the next morning and c) feeling too self-conscious about wearing my O2 while I was out.

It's a big step for me, really, and I'm really happy this morning. It was K's Dad's 60th this week and the whole family (the 4 off-spring and relevant +1's) headed out to Sam and Maxie's, a new place in the "Hub" where the new business/hotel-type district of MK is going up.

If I'm honest, I've been fretting about it on and off all week, what with my somewhat unpredictable blowers and anti-biotic reactions at the moment, because I really wanted to be there and share the night with the rest of the family. K and I have known each other for a long time, and I've known her family for most of our friendship, but it was also the first time I was joining up with a full family gathering as "one of them" and I really didn't want to have to bail out because my chest was being belligerent.

It's probably going to sound funny to people who know me, but last night really did feel like a bit of a watershed moment for me – like I was being welcomed into the family. There was no fanfare or special treatment or anything like that, but just that feeling of comfort you get when you stop worrying about whether or not everyone is *really* happy that you're there and accept that it really does appear that they can tolerate your company.

Of course, it was helped hugely by being able to bribe the twins round to my side my being a taxi, but you never get anywhere in life without the odd backhander, eh?

But I think most importantly for me last night, helped by feeling welcome and comfortable, was that I managed to get through the whole thing without worrying about how I was feeling. I seemed to have the perfect energy levels for the night. I didn't arrive home exhausted, nor did I feel that I had to not do something because I wasn't up to it.

I was about to say that I suppose that sitting in a restaurant having dinner isn't too taxing, so I shouldn't really make a fuss, but actually, on reflection, it shows how far I've come in my recovery since before Christmas that my mind is working like that. Back in November/December, the idea of spending 3 hours sat in a restaurant, oxygen or no oxygen would have been enough to send me to bed to sleep for a week – so it really is a big deal for me to have got through it.

It's funny how these little victories often nearly go unnoticed and it's one of the things I love about doing this blog. In the same way I said when I started out that I hoped writing it all down would encourage me to see the wood for the trees and not get bogged down in hard times, but remember to keep smiling, I think it helps me not to overlook the upsides which might otherwise get glossed over.

Whatever way you look at it, I've come a long way since the turn of the year – like any period in life it's had it's ups and downs, but it's worth reminding myself that I've done some amazing things and I'm doing better than I perhaps would have hoped in terms of moving forward both physically and mentally.

A week in hospital for respite pre-show this week should also do me a lot of good and although I know I'm not going to like it much when I'm there, it's been reassuring to have the knowledge of an impending stay to let me prepare for it, rather than the usual course of getting it hoisted on me when I'm at my lowest.

The next week can't really go quick enough, but at least I'm on a high going into it, which should stand me in good stead for keeping my spirits up through it.

Note to self

Monday 12 February

I was convinced that this time round I was being a sensible, grown up, clever boy in deciding to come into hospital for a stay on the ward for my second week of IVs – its good for me, I know I need it and, well, its good for me.

What I'd also convinced myself was that it was going to be much, much easier to deal with coming into hospital having had it all pre-planned.

It's always rubbish and ever so slightly depressing coming in for a stay, usually made worse by the fact that you're not feeling great in the first place and it normally comes as a bit of a shock when you think you've just popped in for a clinic visit and they strap you to a bed.

So logic dictates that if you're feeling ok to start with, as I am, and the stay is pre-planned, as it was, then you shouldn't struggle as much with admission.

But, as we all know by now, my logic is frequently fatally flawed – especially when it comes to dictating what tricks my mind is going to play on me from moment to moment.

So I spent last night and this morning in mopey-child mode, being generally glum and po-faced at the prospect of losing my liberty.

It wasn't helped by the fact that the ward phoned early to tell me not to come because they didn't have a bed for me yet, but to wait for a call to say it was ok to come in.

It threw my carefully planned day off and led to a distinct raising of hopes that they might in fact not find a bed for me at all and I'd get another night at home. Or even better, if I stayed out Monday night I might be able to convince them I didn't really need to come in anyway and could avoid the stay altogether.

I tried incredibly hard to ignore the persistent niggling hope that I'd get away with it, but I was still decidedly deflated when I spoke to the ward just before 4pm and they told me to come in. If only I'd not phoned to jog their memory, who knows?

Luckily I'd been persuaded by K to listen to my more pessimistic (realistic) instincts and had done most of my packing, but it was still a distinct struggle to gather myself up and drive over to Oxford.

As it is, now I'm here, it's really not as bad as I built it up to be in my head. I know most of the staff so well now that they're like friends and I've already had one HCA tell me she heard me on the radio!

It's much nicer on the ward here now since the move to their new building, with *en suite* rooms that are actually nicer than some Travelodges I've been to.

I also spoke to my bro, who's decided that his motivation for getting through this week of his commando course for the marines is going to be that no matter how hard, cold and horrible things get for him this week, it could be worse: he could be in hospital.

Which is funny because the thought struck me earlier that the way I'd get through the week would be to remember that not matter how dull, lonely and unhappy this week gets in hospital, it could be worse: I could be on Dartmoor in the cold and the wind and the rain on the commando course.

I think my bro and I maybe the perfect yin-yang.

So, note to self for the future: just because you plan it doesn't always make it easier to deal with. But just because you dread it doesn't always make it as bad as you expect.

Nothing happens

Friday 16 February

Avid readers (do I actually have any…?) will no doubt remember my excitement at the turn of the year to receive my – free – upgrade of my mobile phone to the office-in-a-phone BlackBerry Pearl.

Now, apart from having it banned in the house, things have all been pretty rosy and happy with my new toy and I've enjoyed having it very much. You will also remember that the main reason for getting myself the 'Berry was so that I could stay in touch with the outside world while I was in hospital – I could continue work on CF Talk, I could stay in touch with my mates via email, this saving enormous text-message bills, and I could keep abreast of all the other various random emails which come my way from time to time through various different sources.

In particular, I was keen that I would be able to use it to email updates through to my blog when I was incarcerated at Dr Majesty's pleasure – so that people would know what's been going on and how I'm doing.

The problem I discovered with my theory throughout this week was simple: nothing happens.

In hospital, unless you're on the critical care list and you're hanging by a thread (and thank heavens I'm not there yet!), then time spent in hospital is mind-numbingly boring and NOTHING happens to you during the day.

I realised the idiocy of writing a blog on the goings-on in hospital when I sat down to consider it on Wednesday night and realised that the single most interesting, comment-worthy thing that had happened to me all day was that my dinner was delivered 45 minutes late. I mean, people, it was AFTER 6pm! Can you believe it?

Now, I've surfed some pretty spectacularly dull blogs in my time and I'll confess that this isn't always a riot of colour, but even that is beyond me.

Mum and Dad are decorating the house at the moment and I was more inclined to YouTube a video of their paint drying than to blog about my days in hospital.

Hence, you'll gather, the lack of updates this week.

Happily, I'm now back residing in my own house with real, important things to blog about.

For instance, today I've had three cups of tea and I've had my glasses re-glazed with a new prescription so I can see when I'm driving. I've also delivered a letter to the council regarding my benefits.

See – you're life's better for knowing all of that now, isn't it? Doesn't it just fill you with that rush of enthusiastic, finger-on-the-pulse sense of truly politically-hot, fresh news without which you'd be not only more ill-informed, but also a few minutes younger?

OK, so maybe my day's still aren't riotously crazily excitingly busy, but give me a break, I've only been back 24 hours.

Tomorrow is Shoot Day 1 of the Youth Theatre film shoot, which will go at the head of the show and is shaping up to be a draining but rewarding day, followed by a hectic week of organisation for Laughter For Life, which is now only 2 weeks away and COMPLETELY sold out!

Hospitals are rubbish, but they do one thing really well: make you better. So now I'm better – in fact, flying high on top form, better than I've been for an exceedingly long time – and I'm breaking out into the world of doing things, achieving things and really getting a kick out of life.

Nothing happens in hospital, but it's all go when you're out!

Frowning through it

Sunday 18 February

I'm in a bad mood: a grump, a fog, a depression, a dip, a lull, a negatively-buoyant, anti-happy smudge of a grey-day melancholy. And I don't really know why.

It could be the over-exertion of spending a day on my feet shooting the Youth Theatre video yesterday, where I was less than proficient at keeping my energy levels boosted and trying to stay seated as much as possible so as to conserve as much energy as possible.

It could be because this afternoon I went out to the cinema to see Hot Fuzz (which is great) when I should have been lying in bed forcing my body to recover from yesterday's runabouts rather than forcing more activity on it.

It could be because I missed my dose of steroids at lunchtime and didn't catch up with them until nearly 6pm this evening, so my system is significantly down on its currently beefed-up power supply.

It could be that after going to the cinema, which I shouldn't have done, following a day of shooting which I didn't manage well, forgetting my steroids and driving over to Mum and Dad's and back again just for a bite of dinner and not taking oxygen along for the car journey, I'm just a little bit pooped.

It could be that I'm just tired.

Whatever it is, I'm in a really bad mood.

This is supposed to cheer me up – my blog and blogging on it. It's supposed to remind me that when the going gets tough, the tough get going – or at least in my case the tough laugh in the face of the other toughness and tell it to be on it's merry way because tough isn't welcome in this part of town and if it doesn't go away swiftly-and-I-mean-right-now then I'm going to do something really drastic like laughing even harder.

It's not.

I'm still just feeling pretty grumpy.

So I'm clearly beyond help. Far beyond the outer reaches of the depths of the far side of the distant part of somewhere that's really not very close to the vicinity of the place where I am and help's ability to reach me.

So there's only one thing for it: I've just got to go to bed. And sleep.

Like all big problems in life that at times seem insurmountable, I'm confident that this will see me through.

Actually, thinking about it, there's not many insurmountable problems that are cured by sleeping. Insomnia, maybe. But not cancer. Or AIDS. Or even HIV, for that matter. War is rarely solved by sleeping, although I suppose if all the people on both sides were sleeping then they couldn't be shooting each other, so it's a kind of solution, but not really practical or workable as peace-plans go.

Murders aren't solved by sleeping, and dogs aren't walked by sleeping. Sleeping does nothing to stop the spread of malicious rumours regarding the alleged illegal exploits of footballers or politicians, nor does it make any headway into the resolution of global warming.

It does, however, stop mindless, idle drivel like this, because when I'm asleep I can't type.

There are many things on this earth and in this life for which we should all be thanking the Good Lord who watches over us. And me being asleep and not writing any more of this is one of them.

Good night all.

A strange yo-yo

Tuesday 20 February

I'm thoroughly confused.

I should be used to being confused by my body by now, I really should – nothing should really throw me about its day-to-day fits and wobbles and ups and downs. But somehow I just haven't got used to the unpredictability of it all.

Take yesterday, for instance: after a really rather awful, moody, tired Sunday, I slept averagely well and woke up at 8.30am full of energy and enthusiasm and raring to go. I actually wanted to eat breakfast, which is something almost wholly alien to me, since my appetite doesn't usually kick in until mid-morning at the earliest, so the extra energy boost was great, too.

I spent all morning ploughing through mountains of work and knocking things off my To Do List left, right and centre. I amazed myself at the speed with which I rattled through all the things I wanted to get done and I'd almost achieved everything by midday.

I felt entirely un-guilty about taking some time out in the afternoon to pop over to K's brother's to play with the little ones – one of whom has just discovered how amazing it is to be able to propel yourself towards whatever it is you want. I wouldn't so much call it crawling, just yet, it's more like commando-crawling as he doesn't appear to have worked out that using your legs can help, but he's on the cusp of a major revelation, that's for sure.

Back home after an hour of fun and games (OK, an hour of sitting on the floor playing with Fifi and her Flowertots – don't ask me who they are, we were just sticking them to the magnetic board....), I settled in to polish off the rest of the pressing bits and bobs which needed dealing with before close of play, then settled on the sofa to watch some TV and hit the sack.

Now, today, after an identical night's sleep, with perhaps an extra hour in bed, I have managed to achieve almost nothing. Since getting up this morning I have felt entirely drained of energy, lacking in any kind of resource to keep my eyes open and my brain switched on.

Compared to yesterday, I've got next-to-nothing done, although all the important stuff has actually been dealt with, but I had to go back to bed at lunch time and it's really only since taking K to college this evening and sitting back at my desk around 6pm that I've been able to engage myself to do anything at all.

It's immensely frustrating because I just don't know where this energy-drain has come from. I seem to be yo-yoing up and down from day to day with little or no reason behind the ups and downs.

I remember saying here previously that I'd be OK with it all if it made sense and was plannable, but it's impossible to know what each day is going to be like at the moment and I can't work out whether it's OK to plan things or if I should just wipe my diary and play each day by ear.

I don't suppose I can really start doing anything differently, other than, I guess, be strict with myself at stopping when I don't feel I've got the energy and making sure I rest myself when my body says no. But when you're trying to plan for a major event just 10 days away (how exciting!), it's frustrating not knowing how much you're going to be able to do all day.

Still, all moaning aside, I can't really complain about today because I did get to further explore my media-tart side of my personality with a live phone interview with Peter Allen on Five Live Drive for the BBC this evening.

The wonderful Fi Glover, who's Radio 4 show Saturday Live I did a few weeks back, passed on my details to the editor of Drive and, sure enough, I got a call at 11am this morning to talk about things and asked if I'd come on the show live this evening at 5.25 – pretty much prime time.

It was a bit of a tough interview because, obviously, I was mostly interested in plugging Laughter for Life and transplantation, but it seemed that they were more interested in the CF angle of things. Which was nice but, you know, not really "news".

Still, I managed to get through all the CF awareness stuff, plus a plug for the gig, plus a load of awareness-raising for organ donation AND a mention of the Live Life Then Give Live campaign. Not too bad for 3 minutes air time, I thought. Even if it did involve a little bit of talking over Peter Allen as he tried to interrupt...

So the publicity machine ploughs on and the date of the show gets ever closer. Things get more exciting by the day and I'll be sure to post updates on here as soon as I get them. Hopefully, I'll have more warning of the other interviews and things I'll be part of, which will mean I can put heads-up posts on here ahead of time.

Trying hard

Wednesday 21 February

It's funny to read people's observations on my posts on here, both in the comments on the site and emails I receive. A lot of people seem to have had the same thought: that I do too much on my Good days, which in turn leads to the Bad days.

I have to admit that this is something I have thought of before, but I just don't seem to have taken heed of my own warnings. I think my family probably think the same thing, but then how often does one really listen to one's own family when they're telling us something unpalatable that, to an extent, we already know?

I certainly think that the thought must have occurred to my Mum and Dad but they've refrained from bringing it up with me because they know it's a lesson I need to learn for myself and won't accept being told from outside. It's the way my family has always worked, and it's made me all the stronger for it. It's a strong parent who can take a step back and let their kids make "avoidable" mistakes in order to help them learn and grow – and it's something I'll always be grateful for.

But having had comments on here now confirming my worst – and most hidden – suspicions about my general approach to getting on with things, it really seems to have sunk in. Well, I say that now, but we'll have to wait and see where it goes from here.

I feel almost like I'm turning over a new leaf – making a pledge to myself to try to regulate the amount of things that I do so that I can either maintain a constant energy level throughout the week, or else build in sufficient rest periods for the times immediately following major (or minor) exertions.

Yet again, I'm reminded of the value of this blog as so much more than merely a record of what I'm doing with myself from day-to-day. It's helped me to learn and grow and stay in touch with the essential elements of making sure I live my life to it's fullest for however long I'm given.

I have to accept that things aren't going to be a breeze and I'm not going to be able to do all the things I want to do. But I can also promise myself that I will do whatever is necessary to get the most out of the experiences and activities that mean the most to me.

So thanks to everyone who's emailed, commented and talked me through my highs and lows – you make a big difference to the way things go around here.

Keep smiling, because I am.

Rubbish

Thursday 22 February

Today's been rubbish.

I woke up fine but by midday I was totally out of energy. I've no idea where it all went, because I'm sure I wasn't using that much – i was only sitting at my desk trying to work.

All afternoon my brain has been mush. It's not listening to what I want it to do and as for focusing on anything vaguely work-like for more than 10 minutes at a time, you can forget it.

My chest feels OK – bit full of rubbish but nothing majorly out of the ordinary. I'm sleeping OK. I don't think I've been doing too much.

But something is clearly not right. I just don't know what it is.

Man, this is frustrating.

Better day

Friday 23 February

Today has been much better – certainly a little more stable and less energy-crazy.

I have taken what struck me as a very sensible and mature decision at the time to not accompany my parents and K to the Theatre tonight in light of the fact that we're shooting for the Youth Theatre film all day tomorrow.

With my energy levels being as unpredictable as they are, it's clearly a good idea for me to rest up today (tonight especially) and make sure I'm on top form for the shoot. It's a bit of a drag and I know K would have much preferred that I was there, too, but if I'm going to get out of my vicious circle of lustre-lacking, then I'm going to have to make unhappy choices now and again.

It feels like we're accelerating incredibly quickly towards Laughter for Life now – it's just 8 days away, which seems insane. There still seems to be a remarkable amount to do but while I would normally be ever so slightly panicked by now (well, a little) I actually feel confident that this is all going to come together and pass off marvellously.

It's promising to be such a fun event, with such great support and we can only hope that not only will everyone have a great time on the night, but also that we manage to really push people's awareness of Organ Donation, whether through people's attendance at the show, or through the press and publicity the event gets.

It feels a bit odd going into the week before the show being really aware of all the avenues of publicity we're still pursuing – both locally and nationally – but with nothing yet confirmed. My diary for next week is pretty empty at the moment, but it may well start to fill up rather quickly from early on Monday, when press releases and things go out and we really hit the campaign trail.

Of course, it could be that none of it comes off at all and we end up with next to no coverage, but let's hope that's not the case. Even if we don't get as wide coverage as we'd hope for, the main thing is the event itself and the money it's raising to help transplantation in the UK.

It's going to be a hard week this week, balancing the work that needs to be done with the rest that needs to be had to make sure I'm in top form for the weekend and the night itself. It's going to be a long one, and likely a hard-working one, too. But it's also going to be one I won't forget for many, many years to come.

Steady as she goes

Monday 26 February

I'm always loath to jump up and down and rave about having a good few days without any enforced bouts of bed rest. Well, let's face it, I'm always loathe to jump up and down full stop any more. All right, I've ALWAYS been loath to jump up and down. Even when I could.

Still, it seems that the last few days have been particularly encouraging for me – a full day's shooting all day Saturday, a nice, restful Sunday which still managed to include a trip to K's parent's for a lovely Sunday/birthday lunch for her Mum and a middlingly-active day today getting K sorted for her new job and fixed up with sexy new specs.

I seem – *seem* – to have found a nice equilibrium with my energy levels for the moment – succeeding in balancing a need for restful periods with achieving the most important goals of the day without running myself completely into the ground.

I'm hesitant to be fully excited until I get a couple of days further into the week with no repercussions, but so far, so good.

The day's shooting on Saturday was really good fun. Although we had quite a bit of time pressure to ensure we were out of the public areas of the Theatre by the time the matinee audience came in, we actually got all of the stuff we wanted relatively quickly and with very few hiccups.

We did, unfortunately, realise later that we'd miss-shot one scene and made a fatal error known in the trade as "crossing the line". This is far too hideously boring to explain in full to anyone not familiar with the term, as it's a bit of a pedantic, anally retentive technical thingy to look out for, but unfortunately it's one thing that can completely ruin a film when it's all cut together. Most of an audience would never be able to point it out, but would undoubtedly know there's something wrong with what their watching.

Luckily for us, the scene in question with the minorly-major technical hiccup (or f**k up, depending on your view) is one which we still have to shoot a couple of additional shots for, so shouldn't be too much of a problem to go back and rectify. Fingers crossed.

Today I spent another morning in front of a camera, this time giving an interview for a student film for Bournemouth University's journalism programme about transplant and life on the list, as well as what can be done to increase donor rates.

It's nothing major, but I was put in touch with the filmmaker through UK Transplant and as I said at the time I agreed to it, any publicity is good publicity. I think it's particularly good because there's a chance it'll be seen by a good number of students at the uni and that the message it sends out will get through to one of the most campaign-aware sectors of the population.

There's huge amounts of resources sitting around university

campuses in way of students who can be incredibly vocal about any subject close to their heart. Make just a few of them aware of the importance of having people signed up to the organ donor register and there could be a whole new wave of Live Life Then Give Life supporters coming through the system and shouting louder than we have before.

Arrangements continue apace for Laughter for Life and I've spent a large chunk of the day on the phone to various people and rapidly swapping emails to finalise press strategy for the week, with local MK releases going out tomorrow. Our national campaign should begin in earnest this week, too, although we're a little disappointed that Bill's not able to help us with shouting from the rooftops due to his already manic schedule.

That said, we've got an entire 3-hour gig lined up for Sunday night with some of the country's top comedians donating their time for nothing and for which we've already sold out a 600-seat Theatre, so it's pretty hard to be unhappy about anything!

Here's hoping the rest of the week stays as smooth as today. We've got a few auction lots to finalise and gather, as well as the press and media work to cover. I've got some technical gubbins to double check and artists to liaise with. We've got an auction to plan and sales to figure out, and I don't even know what I'm wearing yet!

Gosh, it's all go!

Pace gathering

Tuesday 27 February

We're 5 days out from Laughter for Life and things are gathering pace with alarming speed. It feels constantly like there's a thousand things to do for us to be ready on time, but actually, when I sit and analyse where we stand, there's really very little to be done.

It's reassuring (in a sense) to think that the night could actually go ahead and probably run perfectly smoothly if we all completely stopped working now and did nothing until Sunday. Of course, that's not going to happen – we're all far too committed to making this night the best it can possibly be – but I think it may serve well to remind ourselves as we fret over the final details that actually the leg-work is behind us and we're now adding the icing/gravy/hair gel/analogy-of-choice to an already fab night.

Today was press release day and with the help of our awesome PR-guru Paula, who's done a whole heap of work for Live Life Then Give Life in the past, we've mailed out press releases to local and national media. I think the national ones are due out tomorrow morning, but all my local ones have gone today, so I'm hoping that tomorrow and Thursday should be full of phone calls and sparked media interest. We'll have to wait and see.

Also today, we've made great strides in gathering some great lots for our auction which is taking place in the VIP party afterwards, which include some signed Might Boosh stuff, a raft of Theatre tickets with accompanying bonus features which are still being pulled together through various wheeler-dealings around the place and some great pamper packs and treatment sessions and some awesome original artwork.

Emma is really struggling with a new course of IV's, which is incredibly rubbish timing for her, but goes to prove that CF pays no heed to any other masters and will wantonly and brazenly do whatever it can to intrude on life. But, she is showing the classic resilience of all PWCF and not letting the little bugger get in the way. "Chest infection? Pah! I laugh in your face! You shan't stop me!"

Patrick, from Bill Bailey's management agency is being a total legend in helping us get things squared away and sorting last minute bits and pieces with us and Steve from Tin Racer, who do all the artwork and design for CF Talk is ploughing through preparing the programme for the evening for us.

It's amazing how helpful and kind people have been in coming together to make this event happen. People have given us things, offered extras, consistently gone the extra mile and done whatever they can to help us along, with goods, services, money or support.

It's amazing to see just how much goodwill there is in the world and a sobering thought when you consider the cynical times we live in. People seem to expect so little of other people and often assume the worst. What I've found throughout the last six weeks or so that I've been fully involved with this as a project is that people are far more ready to support and help people than I would ever have expected.

I've always prided myself on thinking the best of people and often wondered if I'm being just a little naive in my belief in the goodness of the human race. But this project has taught me to stick to my guns even when the world around me is presenting a universally cynical view of itself through the press and TV – people are fantastic and if you give them a chance, they will bend over backwards to help you out.

There is no way this night would have been possible without the MASSIVE assistance of a huge number of people and each and every one has made contributions that could have stopped the whole show in its tracks.

This is more than just a gig: it's a chance to tell a whole new crowd of people about the importance of organ donation. But more than that, it's reaffirmed my belief in people and it's also given me the confidence to believe that if I want to do something, I really can do it.

Five sleeps and counting until the night of the year so far!

What a day!

Wednesday 28 February

Blimey, life moves at a hundred miles an hour sometimes, doesn't it?

A friend asked me the other day how I think of things to put in this blog everyday – and I have to admit sometimes it does seem a little pointless to be writing when nothing much has happened.

And then you get days like today, where it's ALL happened!

It all kicked off at 10am this morning when the phone woke us up. Until today, I've been up and about by 8.30am every day for over 2 weeks – completely naturally, waking of my own accord. But the first day I sleep in, it all kicks off.

Steve from Tin Racer Design was on the phone, asking if I'd got his proof of the programme through yet, which I had to confess I'd not seen because I wasn't out of bed. Hastily rolling out of bed, I plonked myself in front of the computer and checked my mails to discover not just the proof, but also an email from the printers we thought were handling the printing for us saying they could no longer do it.

To say I panicked would be overstating it slightly – I'm not really a panicky person - but let's say my calm took a bit of a dent. Rolling K out of bed, I thrust the phone, a yellow pages and an outline of what we needed into her hands and got her dialling while I jumped on the job of proofreading the awesome-looking programme.

In the middle of the chaos, other emails kept firing in from various sources, all seemingly demanding instant attention. I can go days without getting any emails (well, ok, not at the moment) and usually you can sort them into various piles of urgency, but almost every one that came through today seemed to need an immediate response.

Understandably, with all my activity and the prospect of an exhausting rehearsal session at the Theatre tonight still to come, K was getting anxious that I pace myself and make sure I was keeping enough in my tank.

I pride myself on working well under pressure and although I had a couple of moments of dread at points today, I managed not only to address everything I needed to, but also to make sure I had enough time to have a proper lunch and take time to lie down in the afternoon to recharge before work.

As well as signing off on the programme, today has seen me: get hold of a follow-spot for the show, finalise two auction lots, get a sponsor for the programme (the legendary Dunham's Solicitors in MK), confirm all the technical details with the venue and recruit a stage manager to handle the back-stage organisation for the show (well, nearly recruit, anyway, as it's dependent on getting hold of someone else first – but we're nearly there).

Not only that, but I've had a three-hour rehearsal at MKT for the Youth Theatre show, including an hour-and-a-half working solely with my three wonderful Hamlet cast members who have taken to the whole thing so much better than I could possibly have hoped.

Shakespeare is not an easy thing to grasp and there's a lot of nuance and little touches to the text which can take an age to go over and discover in the rehearsal process. I was so happy tonight to find that the cast have already got a good grasp of the text, but also that they are keen to share ideas and work with me and with each other to find a balance between their characters.

It's been a long time since I've worked specifically as a director in a rehearsal setting and it felt great to be putting something together again – I realised tonight just how much I miss that area of the Theatre and how much more I want to do down that avenue.

On top of which, I also delivered the final part of the piece I've written to open the first and second acts of the show and it went down really well with the cast, which is always a good place to start.

I was concerned it might need a bit of redrafting, which would have been a headache considering how limited the rehearsal time now is, but it's actually looking like it's going to be OK as-is.

And now I find myself back home in front of my inbox again (with another 12 emails come through since I left the house at 5.30 tonight) and discovering a whole new load of greatness to polish off my day.

We've got some really good media interest, which will hopefully convert into coverage, and a few more pieces of the auction have fallen into place – including securing a workshop for people to see behind the scenes on Avenue Q, which I'm so insanely excited about it's funny.

I'm now tired enough to go to sleep almost immediately, but I'm also pleased that I don't feel totally exhausted. I suppose the true measure is going to be how I feel when I roll out of bed and drag myself over to Oxford for clinic in the morning, but I think I've got the Big Guy on my side this week and he's making sure I've got the fuel inside to see me through the weekend.

That said, I'm not taking anything for granted: I know I have to look after myself and pace myself or I'm not going to be able to make the most of what's going to be one of the best night's of my life.

Four days and counting!

March 2007
(8 Months)

The ball keeps rolling

Thursday 1 March

Three days and counting and the pace is non-stop. The great thing about the whole thing now, though, is that we really are just dotting I's and crossing T's on the event itself, plus chasing what media coverage we can over the next few days.

I found myself staring out of the pages of MK News yesterday, in a beautifully placed story on page 5 – sadly, it was with an awful old photo of me from one of the stories they'd run previously when they sent their photographer round. They also managed to make the simplest and yet most glaring of sub-editing errors by spelling my name wrong in the headline. I don't know how on earth you spell it correctly all the way through the piece itself and still manage to get it wrong in the headline, but there you go.

I've yet to see a copy of today's MK Citizen, but I'm hoping I got my ugly mug in there, too. I had a call from BBC 3 Counties Radio this afternoon to ask me onto their breakfast show with Martyn Coote tomorrow morning, which is great. I've been in there three times before, so they know me and it's a nice, friendly place to stick my head into.

Technically, the show is coming together nicely – we've got our follow spot, and our follow spot op. We've got our Stage Manager for the night, as well as a stand-by team of MK techies to help out if need be. They're actually paying customers coming to see the show, but I've warned them I may need to collar them for a hand during our SUPER-quick get-in on the night.

We've sent info packs out to all the acts about the night, with the running order, information on the campaign and general goodies (a pin-badge, no less!).

Most excitingly – and this is the bit that had me doing the closest thing I can to jumping up and down – we've secured a 2 tickets to see Avenue Q, the puppet musical in the West End, along with an exclusive, private 30-minute workshop with a cast member to see the puppets up close and learn how they go about bringing them to life on stage. It's an unbelievable lot (in my humble opinion!) and I'm so excited about it.

That said, we've actually managed to come up with a generally awesome collection of things to auction off at the VIP party – we should not only raise some really good money with the things we've got, but also offer people some really exclusive stuff for the cash they're parting with.

Among other things, we've got an original artwork by an artist whose life has been transformed by a double lung transplant, a facial at a top London beauty salon, tickets to no less than 4 West End shows, including super-special extras to go with them, and the ultimate war-fighting day with a company which promises to supersede paintball in both value and realism.

It's amazing how things are coming together and I'm getting more and more excited by the minute.

It's going to be an amazing weekend and I can't wait for it to be here. Three sleeps 'til Laughter for Life!

On me

Thursday 1 March

Amid all the hullabaloo (gotta love that word – never thought I'd use it here!) surrounding L4L, I have actually been looking after myself, too, you'll be pleased to hear.

In fact, I was booked for a check-up at clinic today. I popped along, with K in tow for waiting-room entertainment, and saw all the necessaries, who all seemed to be buzzing about my appearance on Radio 4 and/or the upcoming gig. It was almost like a taste of celebrity…

But most importantly, things went really well. Off to a cracking start when I weighted in at 52.6kg – the heaviest I think I've ever been at clinic. According to my notes I've put on a kilo and a half in a month – pretty good going! Especially considering a week of that was spent in hospital, where eating enough calories in a day is more like a carefully managed game of skill than a diet-plan.

While I was up there, since I was due to start back on my TOBI neb (a nebulised form of the antibiotic Tobramycin), I asked them to do a check on my lung-function before and after, as the last couple of months I've had of TOBI (it's taken on a month-on, month-off basis) I've noticed my chest getting tight after a dose and I wanted to check it out.

Sure enough, my before and after L-F showed a drop from 0.7/1.4 to 0.6/1.3, which doesn't appear overly significant, until you work out that actually what shows up as a 0.1litre change on paper calculates to a 14% drop in the "real world". And I challenge anyone to lose nearly a 7th of their lung capacity and not notice.

So after a quick conflab, the powers that be (that's my CF nurse and Doc B) sent an order to pop me on a Ventolin neb to see if it would relax my airways back from the TOBI.

I haven't taken Ventolin in years, and even then it was only as an inhaler, not nebulised, so I don't have a great deal of experience with it and didn't know what to expect.

What I didn't expect – at all – was to find that after a single 2.5mg dose, my L-F jumped to an eye-watering 0.9/1.6 – a scale I've not reached in over a year!

To say I was happy is to do understatement a disservice – it's unbelievable that a quick 2-minute neb can make such a difference to my breathing. But more than just the numbers on the page, I really noticed it in my freedom and ability to breathe and walk and just generally not feel breathless.

In fact, there's a good story that will show you how good it was. When I got up to leave the ward after the trial, I switched from the hospital-plugged oxygen supply back to my walkabout tank and wandered up the corridor to Pharmacy, from where I then walked back to the car with K, had a 5 minute telephone conversation, walked back to pharmacy, returned to the car and then popped quickly back inside for a pit-stop before we left.

When I finally got back to the car and switched to my "driving cylinder" (long story), I discovered that I'd forgotten to turn my walkabout cylinder on when I left the ward. So I'd spent the best part of 45 minutes walking up and down and all over without once noticing a shortness of breathe and questioning my oxygen supply. What's more, I actually remember noting to myself how I seemed to be walking faster than I normally would without noticing any adverse effects.

You don't get much better than that. Consider me not only well chuffed with my day's activities, but on a personal high both physically and mentally. Things have a way of turning themselves on their head – it only takes a bit of positivity and something to add a bit of meaning and purpose to your life.

Oh what a night

Monday 5 March

Well… wow.

Over the course of the last 7 or 8 weeks since I first officially came on board the Laughter for Life project, I've sat down or laid in bed at night and thought about how it was going to go and run all kinds of best-case/worst-case scenarios through my brain. But none of them came even close to last night.

It was, without doubt, one of the best nights of my life and one of my greatest achievements. I felt both proud and privileged to be part of such a spectacular and successful event and I can't even begin to express my gratitude to all of those who were involved, helped out, donated or just encouraged us to do it.

Shattered now, yes, but boy was it worth it.

We didn't have access to the space until 6 o'clock, so we turned up *en masse* at the venue around 5.30 to put our stuff down in our function room and lay out our battle plan. Emma, myself, Paula and Rose all took on various jobs without much discussion and everyone just seemed to fit in around what we were doing.

I don't want this to be a stupidly prolonged thank you session, but I think it's safe to say that without the assistance of the "significant others" – Brad, K and Julian – things would have been a lot more bumpy.

I left everyone to handle the front-of-house goings on and found my way to the auditorium and found Suze all ready and raring to go as our Stage Manager for the evening. I had no idea that she was going to be as busy as she was – having assured her it was just going to be a case of jogging each act with a 5 minute call before they were due on stage.

As it happened, she was completely invaluable, doing all the legwork that I couldn't have done. I think our partnership for the night was rather like the proverbial swan, with me sitting serenely above the water looking calm and controlled and marshalling people here and there, whilst Suze paddled away furiously under the surface making sure everything I was marshalling was where it should be to be marshalled.

The acts all turned up in plenty of time (more of an achievement than you'd have thought, let me assure you) and were absolutely brilliant to a man. Kind, generous and fun to chat to, I managed to have a good giggle before we even got to the show itself.

I had Rob, my documentary cameraman, following me around getting all the madness on tape, so it's going to be interesting to look back on it in a few month's time and see just how calm I was (or wasn't!) looking.

We had just over an hour to get everything set up, including rigging a follow spot, getting the band set up and sound-checked and giving the acts a chance to familiarise themselves with the space and the set-up.

They all wandered on stage from the green room just before we opened the house (let the audience in) and chatted with the band to arrange their walk-on music, which was great for them to be able to choose.

The house band – Big Buzzard – were brilliant and added such a sheen of professionalism to the whole event.

They were something of a last-minute addition, having offered up their services at relatively short notice, but I'm so glad we took them up on their offer – they really added that extra dimension to the show.

The show itself was simply stunning. The entire bill was nothing short of hilarious and several times throughout the even I thought I was in danger of embarrassing myself with loss of bladder control. If I'd not be tied to an oxygen cylinder, I'd have been rolling in the aisles.

Bill Bailey strung the whole thing together perfectly – giving everyone perfectly distilled little pieces of his humour whilst linking between the acts. Geoff Whiting, Glenn Wool and Rob Rouse tore through the first half and had me coughing with laughter the whole way. After the break, I had managed to compose myself enough to be less of a distraction through Ian Stone and Dara O'Briain's sets.

During the interval, I popped backstage to the Green Room to grab a fresh O2 cylinder – it being the nearest secure place to leave them through the show – and was planning on heading out front to catch up with all the various friends who'd made the effort to come along.

As it was, I ended up in a really long chat with Rob, Glenn, Dara and Ian about my O2 and then segued into CF and its various effects/characteristics. They were all genuinely interested and keen to learn, and being the Ambassador I am, I'm never going to pass up an opportunity to educate people on CF!

After the show, I was keen to make sure everything got sorted backstage, but was hurriedly ushered off to make my presence at the after-show drinks reception felt. Although I think what I actually ended up doing was making sure that Richard Madeley understood all of my gobbledygook on his crib sheet for the auction.

Emma stood up and started things off with a run of thank yous and talked for a bit about where the money we raised was going and what we were all here for. I then followed up with a brief heartstring-plucker to get everyone in the mood to dig deep in their pockets for the auction itself.

I have to say I'd not done any prep for it apart from thinking about my opening line, and I was pretty impressed with what I came up with. I knew I'd have to talk about some difficult stuff, but I think I'm so used to it now, it just rattles off without me having to think about it too much.

It seemed to set the tone well though, ("Thanks a f**king lot" was Richard's response when he took the mic from me) and the auction went really well. Considering all the lots we had were donated for nothing, everything we cleared was money straight in our coffers and we did a great run for 11 lots – over £1,800.

That figure will be swelled over the coming few days with cash from programme sales and the collecting buckets (somewhere in the region of £1,200), and individual donations (which is currently over £1,000 and expected to rise) – all of which is to be added to our ticket sales, which is somewhere around £15,000. All told, we're looking pretty good to hit £20,000 for the whole night – an astounding and truly humbling amount of money.

I think one of the biggest compliments of the night for me, though, was to hear today that there were people in the audience who had no idea they were at a charity gig at all – they had bought their tickets purely on the strength of the bill we presented (no pun intended) and when they realised it was for charity and learned about the cause, couldn't wait to dig into their pockets and drop cash in our collecting buckets.

I said last week that this whole experience had taught me how wonderful people can be and to believe in the spirit of human nature and it's only been reinforced over the last couple of days.

This whole event has been one of the greatest – and most rewarding – experiences of my life and I have to thank Emma and Emily not only for letting me be a part of the project they started, but for allowing me to feel so much a part of the team and the cause.

If you're not already signed up to the organ donor register, you have time to do it now. If you've just read through the whole of this blog entry, you clearly don't have enough to do today, so you've got enough time to take out 2 minutes of your day to go to www.uktransplant.org.uk and sign up right now – it's fast, it's electronic and it could make a difference to up to 9 other people's lives.

Don't let your death be in vain, and don't let the 400 people who died last year while waiting for a transplant have passed for nothing. If there's any message that should come from this weekend, it's Live Life Then Give Life.

Recovery Road

Thursday 8 March

It's been a bit of a weird week this week – I appear to have been either out of the house working or running errands, or asleep. It's a bit all-or-nothing.

After travelling home on Monday I was shattered, but ok with a bit of an afternoon nap, then I had Tuesday morning to laze around before being on Taxi duty for K (through choice not compulsion, I must add).

Then yesterday, K started her new job (yay!), which meant I was up at 8am to get her there (boo), and then found myself coming home and passing out on the bed again till the afternoon – not intentionally, but when your body's bossing you around after a weekend like mine, you listen.

Then last night it was back to normality with my session at MKT with the Youth Theatre.

I say "normality", but it's not every week that I get to spend 20 minutes shooting part of a short film with Samantha Janus just after she's come off stage in Guys and Dolls. Even by my celeb-bumping-into standards, this was a bit on the surreal side, my friend Helen (who's the dep wardrobe mistress on the show) having spoken to her and got her to agree to do us a favour and pop up in cameo in our opening film for the YT show.

She was lovely, and very accommodating, especially since we literally accosted her straight off stage, at a time when I would imagine most performers just want to be left alone to veg out – especially with another show starting in just over 2 hour's time. But she happily stood around and delivered her line of dialogue for us enough times for us to cover it and we left her to it.

The rehearsal itself was very good again. I spent the first part working with the Chorus on the piece I'd written, which was good fun, although slightly odd to be blocking something I've had in my head. It's what I love about working with performers, though, because it really gives you a chance to work through things and see how they work -and if it's your own script, you can chop it and change it as much as you like.

The second half of the session was back with my Hamlet trio, who again worked diligently and have formed a great little grouping. They were struggling slightly to get to the meaning behind some of the Shakespearean waffle, but we worked through it and managed to get through to what lies underneath the flowery poetry and make it make a bit more sense.

Although the show's not too far away now (and if they're reading this, they really need to be learning their lines!!), I think this piece has the potential to really show how talented some of our young people are. Combined with the piece that Suze is directing – called After Juliet, a modern take on the aftermath of the Romeo and Juliet story – it's a chance for our older members to really show some flair for the dramatic, and we both know that they've got the range and the power to do it.

That's not to say it's not going to take a considerable amount of work on their part, and support for them on ours, but if the work goes into it, they could make it something really special. Of course, if they don't, there's the worrying prospect of it coming out as a group of youngsters lost in a mire of misunderstood poetry. But that's the challenge.

I'm hoping that this weekend is going to provide a nice window of relaxation for me – a chance to stay in bed, or veg on the sofa and do as little as possible, whilst shoe-horning as many calories as possible down my throat to keep energy levels high and infections at bay.

It may have left me struggling for energy, but I'm determined that the weekend isn't going to take me down!

Wallowing

Saturday 10 March

Sometimes people really make life hard for themselves – and they don't seem to realise how much they're contributing to it themselves.

It struck me watching the BBC's new Fame Academy thing for Comic Relief first off. Every night they all step up into the "circle of fear" to perform slightly out-of-tune, glorified karaoke versions of well-known songs to varying degrees of success (and even I'll admit that Ray Stubbs had me smiling tonight with his version of "Lola"). But what kind of a mind-set does it get you in to call your performance space the "circle of fear"?

If you want to ward off your nerves and give of your best, you need to be feeling positive and confident when you step up to the mic. Telling yourself you're stepping into the worst 12 feet of space in a building is hardly gearing yourself up for success, is it?

But that's not the thing that's led me to this. What's bothered me tonight is reading another blog of a lady who says she's "not coping" with all the things in her life.

She lists all the many things going wrong with her – some unavoidable, some unbelievably sad and some which, to me, are a matter of pure perspective.

Some people – and this isn't aimed merely in one direction – don't seem to know how to let things go. They like to wallow in their failures, their mistakes, their foibles and to make sure everyone else knows how much they are suffering.

You know what? We all are. We all have our own demons, our own battles to fight, our own mountains to climb. Bad things happen – that's a part of life.

But the measure of a man – or a woman, or a child – is whether he can take the knocks on the chin and get right back up, look life in the eye and say, "Is that all you've got for me?" It's not easy, but neither is it meant to be – nor should it be. Where is the joy in victory if you've not had to fight to get it?

Sometimes you fight and sometimes you lose, but there's no good to come from dwelling on your losses. That's not to say you can't learn from them, but you've got to take your lesson and move right along. A rolling stone gathers no moss, it's said, and why open yourself up to being over-taken by weeds when you can keep on moving and break free?

Blame is the hardest thing in the world to accept, yet some people choose to heap it on themselves. Why go through life carrying a burden that you've given yourself? Come on, life gives us enough to carry on our own, there's no point adding to it. Blaming yourself for things you can't change is a sure-fire way to get yourself into a vicious circle of personal degradation.

I don't mean to sound like I'm belittling people's problems, nor do I intend to suggest that I'm forever rosy and never have my dark days – anyone reading this blog over time will know how much I've struggled. I merely mean to suggest that sometimes, you need to offer yourself a fresh perspective on your situation – to look at it from a different angle and see if the insurmountable is actually just really f***ing hard.

"Fate doesn't hang on a wrong or right choice,
Fortune depends on the tone of your voice."

Where did all the steam go?

Sunday 11 March

You know how sometimes you just keep rolling along, a certain sense of momentum propelling you forward regardless of how you're actually doing? And you know how eventually, you find time to stop, sit down, take a rest and chill out – and then you discover just how exhausted and run-down your body really is?

Well, that's me.

I seem to have somehow bluffed and blundered my way through the last 6 days and now I've reached the weekend, I've taken two days out to rest and supposedly recuperate, and I find myself more exhausted now than I did when I went to bed on Friday night.

It's good to know that my chest can be relied upon to perform to it's best at the right times, although a bit of warning of a delayed-reaction strop would have been nice, if I'm honest.

I feel somewhat aggrieved that I've spent my weekend doing nothing to recover and my body feels like it's been forced to do an

Iron Man and a marathon back-to-back – but I suppose that running the backstage side of a comedy night and partying 'til 2 in the morning, coupled with a "normal" working week including early mornings and evenings out is pretty much my body's equivalent to the Iron Man-Marathon combo.

The important thing is to stay on top of the treatments, make sure I'm getting my physio and nebs done and keeping the flow of calories as high as possible to make sure that exhaustion doesn't lead to any other nastiness. If I can't do much but the vital things this week, it's not the end of the world – I need to make sure I'm not trying to carry on as normal and running myself into the ground – always a danger with me, I'm aware.

So it's early nights, lots of rest, little to do during the day and plenty of food – when I can get my appetite to play ball. The rest of the week will have to stay on stand-by until I know that my body's ready to come back out of its shell.

A new ball rolling

Tuesday 13 March

I'm nothing if not reliable – I'm quite liking this new era of being able to work out what my body's telling me, it's certainly better than the confusion leading up to Christmas this year (see Nov/Dec's posts for more) – as yesterday and today I find myself back on the wagon and with enough energy to get through the day again.

Not only that, but I've also found the time (and inclination) to start a new ball rolling. Yesterday, for the first time in nearly 3 years, I think, I actually sat down and started writing a new play. It's only small, and not very grand, but with 8 pages down on the first day, I can really see where it's going, which is something of a rarity for me when I first start projects.

It's actually based on a couple of ideas I've had for quite a while, but have only recently strung together to make a sensible whole. The whole thing kicks off with an image/scene I've had in my head for ages, but not been able to find the right context to put it into.

One of my biggest problems when I start out writing is knowing where things are going to go and knowing that there is some conflict there which will drive the story/plot. Many of my abandoned attempts at plays in the past have fallen by the wayside because nothing happened in them. As good an ear for dialogue as

I think I have, all talk and no substance doesn't make for a very interesting play.

So I've kicked off the new one with a cracking first 8 pages at the first sitting and I'm hoping to keep up with around 5 pages a day in the hope of getting a first draft done by the time I go into hospital for my next planned course of IV's at the start of April. From there, if I like it, I'm thinking of submitting it to the Verity Bargate Award which Soho Theatre runs every year.

It's about time I actually started to put my scripts out there and stopped sitting around at home calling myself a writer with nothing but a couple of 10-page Youth Theatre pieces to show for it. I also plan to redraft an old script of mine which I workshopped when I was out in Texas – I've got reams of notes on it, but never seem to have managed to get into the groove of turning it around.

I don't know if it's the spring sunshine, the move away from the cold, dreary winter nights, or the knowledge after Laughter for Life that I really can achieve something if I set my mind to it, but I seem to have found not just inspiration, but motivation thrown in.

I'm all too aware of the ease with which my motivation can drop, so I'm keen to harness it while I can. And once I've built up some momentum, hopefully it'll just keep coming.

And now I've blogged about it, of course, I'll have plenty of people popping their heads in to ask how it's going, which is only going to make me work harder, since the only other option is learning how to lie convincingly about what I've managed so far – and that's just not me.

Dot com

Tuesday 13 March

All those of you who visit and read me avidly (or just slightly bored-ly) and long to pass on my blog address to others to entertain, or bore stupid, but have trouble remembering the site address – REJOICE!!

For the benevolent Family Matlack from Texas, with whom I managed to HUGELY over-stay my welcome in early 2004 (which is an epic tale far too long for this post) have once again come up trumps, totally out of the blue.

Clearly worried that far too many people were missing out on my myriad ramblings and mighty rants against the world/my chest/other people's blogs/life in general, Adam – the techno-savvy gadget-freak I always wanted to be – has not only registered smilethroughit.com for me, but also done all those little bits of re-directing and stuff that I would never have known how to do.

So now you can email all your friends, update your MySpace, add to your favourites and generally pass on to the world that the greatest blog in Knaresborough Court is now officially SmileThroughIt.com

Woo-hoo!! And YAY for our American cousins (when they're not duping Tony B into war....)!!

AND I bet I still can't beat him on the X-box...

Other things

Tuesday 13 March

On top of the new play, there are more things bubbling along in the Oli-melting pot at the moment, all grabbing my attention here, there and everywhere – that's how I love it, though.

First off, and most importantly, there's the Activ8 Youth Theatre show at Milton Keynes Theatre, which is coming up on April 22nd and is coming together really nicely in rehearsals at the moment.

We're currently chatting about marketing strategies and getting all the info on the show out to a wider audience than would normally support a Youth Theatre show, mostly because a) the kids and young people taking part really deserve a full house to show what they've achieved and b) it's all in aid of the CF Trust.

Beyond April, the LLTGL team have a couple of projects we're starting to look at, including looking ahead to a repeat of Laughter for Life next March, following the immense success of this year's show.

We're also looking at the possibility of organising some kind of a rally – maybe in super-cheap cars – which would take place in early autumn and involve a jaunt around the British Isles in some form or other. And, naturally, would end in a nice big party when you reach the finish.

There's lots of good ideas bouncing about and I think it's something we're going to pursue soon, but it's just a case of nailing down the format and looking at logistics and things like that.

Keep your eyes peeled for more info as and when.

On top of all of that, I've got the new issue of CF Talk to turn around and get off to the designers so we can get it out at least vaguely in the right timescale. OK, so it's still going to be as late as ever, but I promise it's going to be good.

So just a few bits and bobs going on for the moment – nothing too drastic.

Oh, and I also received an email from Bill Bryson yesterday, letting me know how hugely successfully the organ donor campaign has been going at Durham University, where he is currently chancellor. Not only that, but that he was taking the campaign idea to chancellors of all the other uni's today to see if we can't take it nationwide.

I met Bill around this time last year at the CF Trust's Breathing Life Awards and immediately hi-jacked him for an interview with CF Talk at some point later in the year. Sure enough, he obliged only too happily and our brief 15-20 minute phone chat turned into nearly an hour.

In the middle of the call, while I was supposed to be interviewing him, I mentioned the fact that I was waiting for a transplant (it was actually in the context of a question about holiday destinations) and he turned the interview around and positively grilled me (in the nicest possible way) about transplants, the organ donor register and the problems that we have with donation in this country.

From then on, things seemed to take a life of their own and it only seemed that a light jogging was needed from Bill to his students for them to shoot off and go crazy with the idea – running off T-shirts and organising the campaign with amazing professionalism, it would seem.

Apparently, although I've yet to see the "merchandise", it all centres around the hook, "My friend Oli…". Being the naturally shy, introverted type that I am, I obviously feel very uncomfortable about all of this, and the prospect of yet more attention being focused not only on transplant, but on me personally. However, sometimes in life you have to make personal sacrifices for a greater cause, and I feel that this is one of those times.

I mean, come on, a campaign named after me!?! Pretty soon it won't be lack of portable oxygen keeping me in the house, it'll be a head too big to go through the door….

Stupid viruses

Thursday 15 March

There was me thinking I'd got thing under control after my weekend dip and I manage to get myself laid low with a virus. Not a regular, all-singing, all-dancing kinda virus, mind, but a really pathetic, weedy one which is just enough to prevent me doing what I want to do without making me feel REALLY ill.

The last few days I've been struggling with a bit of low energy and this morning I woke up feeling very lethargic, but also with all sorts of aches and pains all over my body. My lower back was hurting, and I felt like I'd pulled the muscles in my groin (which I think is pretty much impossible when you're asleep).

Added to that, when I got up I had aches through my knee joints and around my shoulders and pains in my hands and fingers. Chest-wise, I feel fine – no better or worse than usual, but I just can't seem to do anything that involves moving without either wincing or nearly losing my balance.

After talking to a few people from the CF Trust message boards, it seems that it's just a virus that's going around, which should wear off in a few days with some decent rest, but it's no less annoying for it. The best news, really, is that it doesn't seem to have done any harm to anyone's chest, or caused infections or anything, which is a definite plus.

So it's a few days in bed/on the sofa for me, which I'm going to find exceedingly annoying because – as you'll have seen from my last post – I've got a whole load of things that I really want to be getting on with.

Ah well, the sensible, mature me will have to take charge and remind myself that having projects is all well and good but if I don't keep myself well enough to enjoy them, what's the point?

Send me get-well vibes!

Stillness and Bookcases

Saturday 17 March

I still can't move, but on the plus side, we have nice new bookcases in our study, which means the floor no longer resembles a preparation area for Fahrenheit 451.

Ever since we created our new study out of K's old bedroom in the flat, we've had a desk and filing cabinet, but nowhere near enough shelf space to collect together the frankly bonkers number of books we both own.

But now, thanks to a mercy visit by both sets of parents, we have two gloriously beaming new bookcases which not only hold all of our current collection, but also have enough room for us to "grow into" – for the next six months or so, at least…

I was entirely useless at helping put them up, though, as I'm still pretty much immobile with whatever this virus is I've picked up. For variety, the pain today has focused itself mainly in my neck, making me unable to glance sideways at people in that wonderfully comical manor which I so enjoy.

Not only that, but it's meant that every time someone sitting next to me asks me a question, I answer them with a half-hearted wince as I momentarily forget my aches and turn quickly to answer them, only to be reminded instantly that turning my head 90 degrees is exactly the one movement that I'm incapable of today.

Still, at least I've not lost my sense of humour. (At this point I'll gladly thank my parents, K and her parents for not correcting me in a comment below).

Generally, today (and yesterday) have been pretty rubbish. Not only have I been in near constant pain – or at least major discomfort – but I've also had to miss out on a really good friend's birthday celebrations and also to sit idly by and not be able to help put together things to go in my own flat. Not a highlight of my year so far, I have to say.

I'm trying incredibly hard, however, not to let it drag me down, although to be honest it's starting to. I'm not ill, so I can't complain really, but I don't feel well enough to really "do" anything, which is unbelievably frustrating.

It's so hard to define what's going on with my body, or my head, at the moment and it's really rubbing me up the wrong way. All I can hope is that another day or two of rest will be enough to drag me out of it and that as my physicality improves, so will my mood.

If not, heaven help poor K as she's had to put up with enough of a monosyllabic, sour-faced, misery-guts of a boyfriend for the best part of half a week now. Please God I get better soon, for her sake if no one else's.

Swinging

Monday 19 March

No, not like that, you dirty-minded little ratbag. Hehe – I said ratbag.

No, swinging as in mood-swings, as in ups and downs and roundabouts – a very Milton Keynes kind of blues.

Today's been full of it. Every particular kind of "it" you can imagine. Except that one. I've been up, down, and all around, trying to work out what on earth my head, body, mind, brain, chest, feet and hands are up to.

I've decided the answer is that I don't know.

Having spent the weekend doing nothing, following two days of doing nothing, I'm feeling somewhat bored of nothing-ness. Today was supposed to be a better day because a) I've spent 4 days doing nothing, so I must have improved, even just a little and b) I actually had something to focus on – a telephone interview with David Seaman (ex of England and Arsenal) for CF Talk.

It started slowly (the day, that is, not the interview), taking me a while to wake up, but I did get up with a good deal less pain than I've had for the last few days. This morning's discomfort was more in the line of "aches" than pains, which I attribute largely to muscular discomfort after over-compensating for the positions that caused me pain over the weekend.

After dropping K off at work, I prepared for the interview, but when I phoned, David was out (how inconsiderate).

I then sat around for the rest of the morning and I have honestly no idea what I did in the 3 hours between phoning DS and speaking to him when he phoned me back this afternoon.

I'd rather given up on the idea of speaking to him today, actually, and was hugely tired before he did call. I toyed with the idea for a while of leaving an out-going voicemail message saying, "Hello David Seaman, thanks for calling back, I'm just having a bit of a nap at the moment, but let me know when you're free and I'll call you back when I wake up."

Thought it might seem a bit odd. Especially if the BT man rang.

Still, I managed to prise my eyes open long enough to hang on for his call. I managed to stay awake all through the interview, too, which I took to be a good thing because I can't help feeling it's a little rude to nod off when talking to a celebrity over the phone.

As it happened, I'm not sure he would have minded, since he seemed like a really lovely bloke. I managed to glean lots of interesting bits and bobs from our half-hour chat today, including the fact that he is a huge INXS fan, which I promised not to hold against him, in the same way I tried not to hold it against him that he captained the Arsenal side which beat Southampton in the 2003 FA Cup final I was in Cardiff for.

I also learnt he owns a Geri Halliwell album. He claims it's his wife's.

After that, though, things seem to have gone downhill. (In my day, not the interview).

I picked K up from work and took myself off to bed, where I dozed for an hour or so, then propped myself up in bed with a cuppa to read for a while, but found myself feeling distinctly unpleasant after not too long. This rampant seesawing of wellness has started to drag in the most incessant way.

I'm finding it harder and harder to stay on an even keel mentally when my body sees fit to flip-flop all over the place physically. It's not that I seem to be changing from day-to-day, it's that I can change from hour-to-hour, one minute up and full of energy, ideas and get-up-and-go and the next minute with less energy than a battery-run bunny after a 10-hour run-off against the Duracell dude.

If only there was a pattern or a rhyme or reason to what was happening or when it happened, I would at least be able to square it in my head so that I was prepared for the sudden on-rush of bleakness. But the constant swinging from state to state creates such an enormous flux through the day that I find it impossible to anticipate and I find myself being dragged down mentally as soon as I flag physically.

I am hoping against hope that the next few days bring a renewed strength and chance to focus myself on to some of the things I really want to do, because much more of this flip-flopping, see-sawing, up-downing and I think I really might go mad.

Either that or I'll find myself watching daytime TV, which is the same thing, really.

Back on the Inside

Sunday 25 March

As steps go, it's difficult to know whether this is backwards or in the right direction. As I sit here on the ward in Oxford looking at the plain white walls and interestingly green doors, I realise it's a bit of half-full/half-empty kind of moment.

My instinct is telling me that after convincing myself I'd dealt with the virus and kept it off my chest for the last 5 days, it's a bit of a massive step back to find myself not only incarcerated, but also missing more work and rehearsals for the activ8 show.

But my sensible, well-perspective'd head tells me that no matter what I'd managed to convince myself, my chest wasn't what it should be and if I want to be in any state to enjoy the show itself or to carry on with any of the projects I so enthusiastically outlined not so long ago, then I need a stay at the doc's pleasure to set me back on the right track.

Still, it doesn't take away from the fact that this weekend I'll be missing not only the second mate's birthday celebration in the space of 8 days, but also the Christening of a really good friend's first child. You can be as upbeat as you like about missing things for the betterment of your health and ignore birthdays as repetitive annual events, but missing a once in a lifetime ceremony to welcome a child into the Kingdom of God just plain sucks.

There's nothing I can do about it, though, so I suppose getting stressed or moping about it is fairly pointless. After all, I would much rather be around to see several more significant birthdays in her life than make it to a Christening and not see her 1st. It's all a matte of perspective, which at times like these can be hard to come by.

Much as you search for the better angle, it's frequently masked by the obstacles in the way or the apparent unfairness of life. I'm determined not to be dragged into a mire of negative thought. I know that the next few days are going to be tough and the weekend especially so, but I know I've got the resources to see me through both within me and around me in my wonderful family and fantastic friends.

Just knowing that there are people out there thinking of you, rooting for you and praying for you makes such a massive difference. So don't stop now - I need you to shout your loudest!

Who am I?

Monday 26 March

Ups and downs are par for the course in life, and we all learn to live with our own particular roller coasters and merry-go-rounds.

Right now, I'm in a pretty substantial dip, enclosed as I am in my hospital room with what appears to be very little day-to-day improvement or sign of change.

I've been in just under a week now and, while I do feel better than I did when I was admitted, I don't feel like I'm somewhere the docs might describe as "better".

What's become worse over the last few days is my intense focus on my transplant and when it's going to come.

For the last 20-odd months, I've lived with the ever-present likelihood of that crucial phone call at any time of the day or night, but it's always been something which I've lived with in the background and not paid much heed to.

Now things are looking less rosy, and with landmark moments being missed and life being put on hold, the urgency has been brought to the fore and the once-in-a-while thoughts have turned to a daily dwelling.

What upsets me most about things at the moment, though, is how much this borderline obsession is changing me as a person.

Not only do I feel more negative than I have for a while – finding myself struggling to see the fun side of life or consider anything that might be conceived as residing in the "future" – but I've also developed what can only be described as a jealousy towards others.

One of my closest "net-friends", with whom I've shared many of the bizarre, amusing, surreal and downright scary moments of the transplant process, has been granted the gift of life which had so long eluded her.

But rather than finding myself eagerly awaiting news of the new joys she's discovering every day, I can't bring myself to catch up on things because I am constantly hit by a wave of "what about me" feelings.

I don't recognise this as a trait in myself – it's just not me. I'm not a jealous person and I've always delighted in the triumphs of my friends, family and all those around me.

So why the change now? What is it about my life at the moment that has brought out parts of myself that I never knew I had?

They say you learn a lot about yourself in adversity and "they" are often right. But how much of my current mood and outlook is a deep-rooted personality defect that's been dormant for years and how much is it merely distorted through the prism of life-threatening illness and the hope of salvation?

I honestly don't believe I've changed as a person, nor do I think that my current health-hurdles are insurmountable. Similarly, I don't expect my run of negative thinking to go on forever, but see it merely as a darker period brought on by hospitalisation – an effect I'm all too aware of from past admissions (both recent and historic).

The trouble with lung damage and infection is that it's incredibly hard to know when you can reasonably expect to regain your lost lung function after a bout of infection and when you have to accept that you've waved goodbye to the portion of lung for good.

Clearly, the lower the function in the first place, the less there is room for movement either way. So when lung function drops, it's hard to keep the fatalistic wolf from the door – both physically and mentally.

I'm not giving up yet, though. I've been through tough times before and although I've never considered myself quite as close to kicking it as I have this time, I'm confident that I can get past it.

This is largely thanks to my ever honest and sensitive team at Oxford who know what goes through my head and aren't afraid to tackle the issues – and fears – as they come up.

I may not be able to bring myself to stay fully abreast of a good friend's post-transplant progress, but I can still remind myself how often things looked bleak before the big day arrived.

Everything comes to he who waits, and while my new lungs may be the longest-settling pint of Guinness in history, I'm sure I'll soon be frustrating someone in my position with my tales of new wonder in my life.

What a difference…

Thursday 29 March

…a discharge makes.

It took a while, but I finally managed to get myself kicked off the ward yesterday afternoon. Probably more significantly, it was at the prompting of the docs and not through me harrying them as much as possible to get them to let me go. In fact, in contrast to my usual practice of starting my "let me out now" lobbying campaign from the moment I arrive on the ward, I actually didn't mention it to the docs until they raised it with me.

The thing about hospitals is that they provoke mood swings more severe and frequent than turns of a steering wheel in a rally car. It's possible to go from happy-go-lucky, ain't-the-world-gorgeous, by-jove-what-a-wonderful-place to weight-of-the-world, deepest, darkest blackness in a matter of seconds, and it can take a similar amount of time to recover back to normality.

None of which helps much when you're trying to make sense of the random and rapid variety of things going on in your head throughout the course of the day.

If I said that's the main reason I'm happy to be out and to be comfortably ensconced back at home in my study in my PJ's and dressing gown, I have to admit I'd be lying. Above all, it's just nice to be back in control of my own day – not having to rely on the timings of physios, doctors, nurses and ward staff to decide when I can and can't sleep, how long I'm allowed to rest for and the quality of my rest periods.

Back home, everything is part of my own control. Except, ironically, my chest. But I suppose you can't have it all.

I still don't feel 100% – in fact I'm still wavering around 70% at the moment, but it's a whole lot easier to be positive about outcomes when you're not staring at the same 4 walls for 18 hours a day, or being woken up to eat a plate of mush which used to be vegetables.

It's alarming when you spend as much time looking on the bright side as I do to find yourself in a situation where you can't see a chink of light, let alone a whole side of brightness. I'm sure that the very fact of feeling down about the world enhances itself because I get annoyed with myself for letting it get on top of me – a self-perpetuating circle, I suppose.

Now I'm home I just have to concentrate on doing what's best for me and not over-working myself in my bid to get back to normality. The last time I came out of a lengthy stay in hospital, I went back to Mum and Dad's to recuperate, but this time I'm trying to skip that step and stay at the flat with K.

The next few days will tell us whether that's a good or bad decision – largely depending on whether or not I can discipline myself to remain inactive as long as I need to be. The danger of being at home as opposed to Mum and Dad's is that there is far too much temptation to "just do" this and that, and all the this's and that's soon add up to being way too much and I find myself over-exerted again.

The main thing is that being back home I feel much more myself – more easy about things and less penned-in to someone else's routine. Now I'm back I feel like my mind's my own again and while it's naturally going to take me a while to wash away all the negative thoughts, they're certainly going to seep away much quicker in this environment that they were ever likely to on a ward.

I want to say a huge thank you to all of you who've left me messages and sent me emails – it makes such a difference to know that there are people out there rooting for me and willing me on. It's hard to explain the feeling of knowing that someone's getting something valuable from a blog like this – it's part of the reason I set it up but also one of the things I least expected to actually happen with it.

If nothing else, I hope the last few weeks (and hopefully the next few) will help to show that no matter what lows you sink to in health – be it mental or physical – there's always a way back. I'm under no illusions that sooner or later the physical is going to become insurmountable, but with a positive mental attitude (oooh, the PMA cliché!) and the support of my family and friends, I aim to make sure that I make it "later" – and preferably long enough to get a fresh set of blowers.

Take care, all of you, and look after yourselves. Every single one of you is important to someone, and chances are you're more important to some people than you will ever know. Never forget that you're amazing.

All right, love-in over.

But I just want to have fun!

Friday 30 March

I'm sure this is a sign that I'm improving and getting better and more active, but I've been frustrated again today by my body's inability to handle more than a couple of hours of activity.

I seem to recall, as I sit here moaning, having exactly the same problem last November when this blog first started, and was forever moaning that I didn't have enough energy to tide me over through more than a few rumbles of busy-ness.

So I already know that the answer is simply down to discipline and time, and that my recovery will be greatly aided the more I have of the former and the more I allow of the latter.

But being me, I don't like it.

Yesterday, K and I nipped round to Mazda to collect our new toy – the brand, spanking new Mazda 6 2.0 5-door auto gearbox delight, which is sitting out in the court now. Immediately wanting to take it for a spin, we succeeded in getting to my parent's house (where K had to print some college work) and back home as we were both shattered.

Having set aside this afternoon for a fun-run (in the car, not of the charitable, ambulatory kind) to bed it in and find out what she can do, we were both excited when we set out. Expecting to do my usual round of the country roads, flitting through all the different road types to give us a really good sense of what she can do, we set off about 3 o'clock for an adventure.

Come 4.45 we were sat in my parents' kitchen nearly falling asleep after just an hour and a half of driving, covering a fairly meagre 50-odd miles. Surely I can have more fun than that?

But no, I remind myself, I can't. I have to accept that I can't and find something rewarding and relaxing to do with my time at home on the sofa.

So, now K and I have the study sorted and the bookshelves up, with our wonderful new library formed from the merging of my collection and hers, I've decided I will simply have to get cracking on going through the host of titles K's already been through and catching up on some literary culture.

I'm not sure quite how well that's likely to go, but it's got to be worth a try. If I can't improve my body, at least I can exercise my mind.

For those of you who wish to keep track, I'm just finishing off Stephen King's Carrie and I'll let you know what's next.

April 2007
(7 Months)

Low and up?

Monday 2 April

This is going to have to be a relatively short one (I can hear the cheers already), because I don't have the energy to sit at the computer for long this evening after heading back across to Oxford this afternoon for a progress check.

Last night I reached my lowest ebb that I can remember for a long time – I honestly couldn't remember a time when I've felt worse in my head about how I felt in my body. The advantage of hitting an all-time low, however, is that there's only one way left to go.

Hopefully, in the next couple of days I'll be able to sit down and put into words the experience of the last couple of days, but for now suffice it to say that the bottom having been hit (stop giggling at the back), the upward spiral is now unfolding.

At Oxford this afternoon (which is a very comfortable drive in the new Mazda), my lung function was a pretty static 0.75/1.35 – not very impressive, but equally not too concerning, either. The docs made the, frankly not very difficult, decision to keep me on my current IV's (Gent and Cef for those who are marking the card) for another week and to get me back in after Easter to see how things are going.

I had more Gent levels done today, which is a fairly easy process of 2 blood draws spaced an hour apart to get a pre-dose and post-dose peak and trough level for the drug in my blood stream. Gent can have some pretty dodgy medium- and long-term side effects if given in too higher doses, so it's important to make sure levels are checked regularly.

The next 24-48 hours is going to be taken up with almost total rest, as I'm hoping to head to London on Wednesday to fulfil a prior commitment which means a lot to me and I really don't want to miss. Following which will be another 48 hours enforced bed-rest on Thursday and Friday, for which I've already cleared my diary.

Fingers crossed everything has now turned the corner and is on the up. Perhaps sometime soon my life might return to normal – or at least I'll get used to whatever my new version of normal is.

Courage

Monday 2 April

'Courage doesn't always roar. Sometimes courage is the quiet voice at the end of the day saying, "I will try again tomorrow."'

Mary Anne Radmacher

Sunday

Thursday 5 April

Followers of this blog will be familiar with the various ups and down I've experienced over the last months since I began writing, and friends and family of mine know about them from much before then, to varying degrees. So when I say that this last Sunday gone marks possibly the lowest point I can remember, it isn't a remark I make lightly.

More than ever, this entry in the blog is a personal one – one for me to look back on in the weeks and months to come as I look back over the trials and forward to what may lie ahead and to be able to see that I've come through worse than I'm going through.

SmileThroughIt was designed as a pithy phrase to help me remember that when it comes down to it, laughter really is the best medicine, and that taking the time to remember the levity and vibrancy that life gives us can turn a perspective upside down. Through most of the things I've experienced in my life it's an ability to laugh at myself and situation that's really pulled me through, and having family and friends who share my often bleak and black sense of the humorous that helps beyond words.

But sometimes, even though part of you knows that you can fix it all with a grin and a giggle, your body and mind won't let a smile cross your lips; not the glimmer of a smirk or a corner of the mouth upturned.

This is how I found myself on Sunday night.

Sitting on the edge of the bed at half-past nine, four days after coming out of hospital to renewed hope and the excitement of a new car, I found myself fighting for breath with a new sensation of pain and exhaustion ripping through my chest and as I stared almost vacantly at the floor, I felt an overwhelming desire to give up.

It's hard to reconcile the feelings of joy I had at escaping the confines of the hospital last Wednesday with the hurried turnaround once I reached home. Aware as I was of the fact that I was by no means fully recovered, I was anxious to get back to something – anything – which even vaguely resembled normality: being able to choose what time I did my drugs, being able to sleep for hours during the day if I so wished, not having treatment times dictated to me by staff with a dozen other patients to see.

What I discovered, however, is that home can feel like more of a prison than any hospital ward. In the same way that the four walls of my hospital room started to feel reassuring and safe, home began to feel like a well-decorated prison cell, with a world of wonders on the outside.

I'm exaggerating, I'm sure – home is never really a prison – but as the weather turned warmer and sunnier, I just wanted to be outside. Coupled with our recent automobile acquisition, my sense of adventure began to take over and K and I began to explore the bounds of my stamina and the car's performance.

Had I been more disciplined with myself and stricter in keeping myself bed-bound upon my return, I doubt I would have landed in the position I did on Sunday night. But then, had I not landed there, I don't know if I'd be on the up-slope to recovery I find myself on now. Sometimes you need to plumb the depths before you feel the benefit of the clean-aired heights.

Sunday afternoon took the biscuit, really, as K and I set out for a pleasant Sunday drive around the countryside to enjoy the spring sunshine and run-in the new car. After an hour and a bit of driving, I began to feel the fatigue creeping in and by the time I got home after around 2 and a half hours out of the house, it was pretty much game over.

What alarmed me, and what caused the moment of pause on the edge of the bed as I got myself ready to sleep, was the new sensation within my chest that burst into prominence.

Back in the days when Emily had her knackered old blowers (not the shiny new ones she has now), she used to write in her blog about her chest throwing hissy fits and causing enforced rests and lie-downs. I thought I knew exactly what she meant, having felt the overwhelming tiredness and sense of exhaustion after over-exertion. But sitting on the end of the bed last Sunday, I realised that I hadn't even touched the sides of it yet.

I've had chest pain before, usually pleuritic, occasionally pneumothorax-related, but always of the same variety: a sharp, stabbing pain the side of the chest, usually around the lining of the lungs, where one can imagine a large chunk of infected tissue rubbing angrily against a chest wall which is struggling to keep it in check.

This, however, was something entirely different. This time it was a kind of internal stinging sensation which felt like the inside of my lungs had been rubbed raw with a grater and immersed in a vat of TCP. And unlike the pleuritic pain, there was no sign of it fading away with a few deep breaths.

As I laid in bed on Sunday night, with K lying next to me and sensing my discomfort and utter dejection, I tried to put into words what was going through my head. Sadly, I am not the same wordsmith orally as I am on paper, and in the heat of the moment, my vocabulary failed me.

I sat and stared straight ahead of me and desperately tried to recall a time when I'd felt lower – more hopeless and filled with sadness. For a second, a fleeting moment at my parents' house in the build up to Christmas after my hospital admission last November entered my head, but that had lasted just a few seconds and this decidedly not so.

The truth was, I was tired. Tired of the fighting, tired of the same old stories, the ups and downs, the scrapes and pickups, the ever-turning and tightening vice around my chest. I was tired and I just wanted it all to go away. Nothing anyone could say could make a difference – something K seemed to instinctively know and chose to observe.

Then the strangest thing happened. As I sat and contemplated the worst of scenarios, I thought about my brother and what he's been through. Not only the completion of 11 weeks of impossibly hard training and testing and fighting for the commando course, which he had just last week reached the end of and grasped with proud hands his Green Beret, which will go with him everywhere from now on.

But also the times he's fought through everywhere else: through his year out in Tonga, when he so nearly gave up and came home after just a couple of months, but stuck it out and had one of the most remarkable life experiences anyone can imagine; through his year at Sandhurst, fighting through test after test, performing top of his class, but never letting anyone know how truly hard work it was; right through to his running of the London marathon last year on a few week's training and the number of people he inspired to sign up to the organ donor register, all because he told them he was doing it for me: I still bear the medal he took home, framed on my wall with his inscription, "Live The Dream" underneath.

I thought of all of these things and I saw myself reflected in his eyes and I realised that I couldn't give up. What kind of message would that send out to my friends, my family, worst of all my Godchildren, my two fabulous, wonderful young boys who I vowed nearly a decade ago to watch over, guide and protect in the name of God? How could I possibly decide that enough was enough, just because I was tired and it was hard?

As images of my brother washed over me, seeing him at his lowest points of the last 11 weeks, fighting for strength through everything and finding it within himself to keep going, I knew that I had to keep going too. What's more, I knew that if my parents had passed on to him the ability to keep going and never give up, then I must have the same genes flowing through my body, too. If one of us can, I've not doubt in my mind whatsoever that the other can, too.

Sunday 1st April 2007 will go down in my mind and my history as the lowest point I ever reached in my battle through life so far. But when I look back on it, it won't be with pain or disappointment, but with a profound sense of pride and pleasure that not matter how dark it got, I was able to see the tiniest, remotest speck of light at the end of the tunnel – and I will make it there. Sooner or later.

Easter. Tired.

Monday 9 April

Traditionally, for my family at least, Easter has been a family-focused time – a chance for the four of us (plus significant others) to get back together for a weekend and catch up. Since I've moved out of home, it's always been a weekend I've returned to Mum and Dad's for the large majority of to sit and talk and eat and drink.

This year was, by necessity, pretty different, able as I am to manage no more than a few hours of doing anything other than sitting quietly on a sofa or in bed. It's been pretty tough to have to force myself to ignore my instincts and natural predisposition to surround myself with family and instead make sure that I conserve the little energy I have into doing the most important parts of the weekend.

Those were, by turns, a family photo shoot (it having been nearly a decade since the last one and Mum was obviously getting itchy for some new smileys on her wall), a family dinner on Saturday evening to celebrate Easter an my bro's passing his Commando course, then Easter Sunday spreading our time between our two family's respectively, spending an hour or so with each trying to avoid exhausting myself.

I can't say it's been my best Easter – being limited to only doing what you can manage without making your chest scream at you is hardly a resounding indicator of a brilliant time for all, but I think we've managed to make the best of a bad lot and enjoy what we could of the weekend. And after all, time spent with loved ones should always be about quality not quantity – right?

Today has been a different story all together. I was pretty tired last night – a step up from exhausted but still struggling – and hit the sack pretty early, only to be woken after a couple of hours feeling tight and breathless and having to haul myself out of bed to do some physio and nebs.

What annoyed me more than anything, though, was that the whole thing woke me up and kept me up until gone half past three in the morning. By the time I finally fell asleep at 4am, I had just 2 hours till my alarm to get up and do my drugs, after which I managed little more than a fitful 30-40 minutes here and there until I finally gave up and got up just before 12.

As a result, I've spent the whole day completely wiped out and unable to consider doing anything at all, really. Mostly, I've been lying in bed and trying to relax and not focus on how completely shattered I am. I've not really succeeded, though.

My mind is pretty blank right now, if I'm honest – I'm

struggling to find any words to string together today, mostly because I think all my conscious thoughts have migrated to sunnier climbs where sleep comes in glorious 8-hour stretches without interruption and leaves you feeling fresh, bright and alert.

Right now, I'm none of those things.

Still trucking

Wednesday 18 April

It appears, having just flitted over to the CF Trust's message boards, and by looking through my inboxes, that I've had people rather worried by disappearing from my blog for the last few days. Oops.

I assure you, everything is fine. Certainly improving.

To tell the truth (not sure why I needed to add that, since it hardly pays to lie to oneself on your own blog….) I was bumming myself out, which is why I stopped for a bit.

Far from reminding myself to SmileThroughIt and keep on finding the positives in the darker times of life, I found that every time I started writing a post on the blog in the last few weeks, it's only been to say either that I feel like crap or that nothing's changed for the better. Even the times when things had changed for the better, the change seemed so infinitesimal and pathetic that it either wasn't worth mentioning, or served only to heighten my despondency about how I've been doing.

It's been weird to find myself trapped in a vicious circle of negative thought, and not something I've been used to in life. Most times, my dark periods inhabit the odd spell of a week or so before things conspire to kick me up the butt and show me the way to carry on. This latest downturn has been different, though.

I don't know if it's the increased fear of mortality (or, "Am I gonna kick it?" as I prefer to call it) or the impairment to my quality of life inherent in having sunshine blazing through the windows but not enough energy to leave the apartment and enjoy it, but I've been lost in a mire of negativity for the last few weeks from which I seemed to have lost the map that usually provides my guide.

Sure, I've had good moments – I've managed to share Easter with the families around me, I've shared a little laughter with friends, I've even managed a trip to Borders (hurrah!), but there has been an overwhelming sense of good, old-fashioned, Dickensian melancholy hanging over me throughout.

It's not that I entirely lost perspective on the whole thing: last week I was sitting a the funeral of a young girl who's been an almost constant fixture of my working life for the last six years, since she's been coming to the MK Youth Theatre sessions since their inception. Sitting in the packed church among many young people experiencing their first distressing taste of grief, I realised that the very day I hit my lowest point – Sunday 1st April, as documented here previously – her Mum, Dad, younger brother and Grandparents were waking up to a new world without their beloved daughter. How could I complain about pain in my life when held up against the pain of a parent outliving their child?

I've still appreciated each day I've been given, but it sticks in my proverbial craw (I've never really known what that means, but it seems to fit here, anyway…) that "making the most of it" is limited to sitting in the chair at the bay window using the bright sunlight to read by, as opposed the to dim interior light all through winter.

Finally, though, after weeks of dragging myself through the rough parts of every day and persevering in ways I wasn't even sure I was capable of, I seem to have made it out the other side.

That's not to say things are all bright and rosy, but I have at least got the energy to pop over to my 'rents and enjoy the fresh air and sunshine if I want to, or to sit in the study and surf the 'net a while without completely exhausting myself and having to collapse into bed.

I'm able finally to contemplate looking at the next issue of CF Talk, which has been sitting unattended on my desk for nearly 2 months now and is in dire need of completion. I'm able to think about the other writing projects I was looking at before and see if I can rekindle the spark that was there before. I'm able to focus my mind on something other than how my chest is feeling or whether or not I should stay in bed rather than move to the sofa.

I've one more negativity-hurdle to overcome, and that will be over after the weekend.

This Sunday sees the Activ8 Youth Theatre show at MKT take place, an event which was to have been my first opportunity to get stuck in to directing a short piece for the Youth Theatre and to benefit the CF Trust. If I'm honest, I saw it as something of a swansong with them, after acknowledging the likelihood that my involvement is being compelled by my chest to end.

Rather than a happy ending, though, it's going to be an

extremely tough one to get through. Not just physically, although I can't pretend that that's not going to be a challenge in itself, but because I've ended up having almost nothing to do with the finished product. Three weeks' of rehearsal in a 12 week term doesn't amount to a contribution, in my mind, and the work I had hoped to see up on the stage is now more likely to bring me down than uplift me.

I wanted so much to make this something to remember – an event that showed the Theatre's support not just for the CF Trust, but for the whole Youth Theatre, and a true showcase of the talent that's been nurtured through Activ8 over the last half a decade. And don't get me wrong – it is still very much all of those things.

But it doesn't feel like it's anything to do with me. I feel like a passenger, an outsider, something akin to a "consultant" who's seen parts of the process leading up to performance and had a little input, but not someone who forms part of the "team" whose talents are being showcased.

I know that people will shout me down and will be quick to try to dissuade all of my fears and make me feel a part of it, but I can't get passed the fact that I've not been there for them or with them for pretty much the entire term. This is their show and their showcase, and it's nothing to do with me any more. That saddens me, and it's going to be hard, but nothing will stop me being their to support them.

I am trying to keep my air of positivity and move forward from here – and I know I will continue to progress – but I also know that this weekend is going to be a really tough one to get through.

Thanks to everyone for your good vibes, your love and prayers over the last few weeks. They really do make a difference, and they have helped me enormously. I shall endeavour to keep up with my more regular out-put of the past, as I will endeavour to keep myself looking up and not down, forward and not back.

Keep on truckin'.

They did it!

Tuesday 24 April

And Sunday's show was spectacular – with a capital Spec.

Undaunted by a day spent running here there and everywhere trying to fit in as much technical work as possible and still have a chance to rehearse their pieces, all of the groups absolutely shone and truly showed the talents with which Suzanne and I have been working for the last 5 years.

In the whole process of seeing all of the kids and young people on stage, I even managed to forget all the things that were most bothering me about my input (or lack of it) over the last few months and actually take in and appreciate what a huge achievement this show has been not just for the groups involved, but for the whole creative team.

That's not to say the endeavour didn't come without it's price – two days of being laid up in bed not able to do anything more than stumble to and from the bathroom and occasionally as far as the kettle for tea seems to be a pretty high price to pay, but then if it gets me through the rest of the week with no ill-effects then maybe it just proves that I'm learning to listen to my body.

Physically, I handled Sunday really badly. Intent on showing my support to the oldest group by being their for their rehearsal in the afternoon, I completely overlooked the fact that the scheduled break between tech and performance almost never materialises. Rather than getting an hour to take myself back home and recover/carbo-load for the evening, I instead found myself staying at the Theatre and "working" through it.

The quotation marks aren't meant as a self-depreciating qualifier on the day's activities, but rather an acknowledgement that for most of Sunday, I was a passenger. Here and there I lent a bit of a helping hand, but really there was nothing to be done that wasn't a) already covered by someone else, such was the level of organisation or b) physically impossible for me to do.

Strangely, this last fact didn't seem to perturb me as much as I expected it to. It did cross my mind a couple of times that this time last year I'd have been running all over the place and doing whatever needed doing, whereas this time I was simply sat on the side lines watching others do the running, but I somehow managed to section it off from the rest of my thoughts.

I suppose it goes back to the train analogy I first wrote about here, and I clearly unconsciously managed to avoid getting on the train of negative thought and instead kept myself where I should be, making the most of the opportunity afforded to our wonderfully talented bunch of youngsters.

The last two days have been pretty tough, and I've certainly felt it on my chest, but I'm really hoping that I've handled it well enough that it's not going to be a major set back. The problem with my cruddy lungs, though, is that you just never know.

But it's another successful MKT production under my belt, another fantastic learning experience, and there is a world of possibilities still out there for me. Here's hoping I find one to pick up soon.

It worked!

Wednesday 25 April

Two days of lying in bed and doing *nothing* at all actually did the trick and I am now able to sit in my study and actually contemplate work.

I say "contemplate" because we all know (or at the very least we should all know by now) that I'm the world's number one procrastinator and can find a way to wheedle out my time sat in front of my computer better than anyone else in the whole wide, entire world.

As it happens, I have achieved a lot of "work" today by checking and sending emails. These consist largely of sending ideas out to people for possible projects/ideas for collaborations that I'm hoping to get off the ground.

The Youth Theatre experience has taught me that being house-bound and energy-limited needn't necessarily mean not doing anything at all, but rather that I need to find the right project and the right people to work with to make the most of what I have to offer.

So I need to find myself things to do whereby I can inspire and facilitate things for other people to pull off: kind of like a producer on a film – which is, interestingly, one of the projects I'm considering.

Like all good executives, what I need is to set up a situation where I can delegate work to the people who can handle it and can fill in for me when I'm not up to the task. At the same time, it should leave something on my plate to make me feel a) involved and b) useful. Being a base-touching point-of-contact is perhaps the ideal situation.

That may all be rubbish, of course, and in fact just be providing a very useful excuse to give me a reason to avoid sitting at my desk and getting any worthwhile writing done, but then I'd hardly be doing myself justice if I wasn't working hard to avoid working hard.

In fact, trying my best to avoid doing any work appears to be the perfect proof that I need that I must be well on the mend. If I'm not moaning about not being able to work, then I must be doing my best to avoid doing it when I am able.

Most people would think that ironic, I know. Lucky I'm not most people.

May 2007
(6 Months)

Lost plot (and momentum?)

Tuesday 1 May

It's been a bit of a gap again since I last posted – I seem to have lost my blogging momentum, although I have a feeling it's because the evenings are much harder for me now than they were. I used to write my blog posts right before I went to bed at 10 or 11 at night, but now I'm usually struggling quite a bit with breathlessness by then and sitting at the computer is about the last thing I want to do with my bed calling me.

Still, I'm sure I'll work myself back into a groove somewhere.

I had intended to sit here this morning and launch off into another rant about Allied Respiratory (yup, still rubbish) but I'm not sure I can summon the energy or the bile to do it proper justice. I'm doing so well at the moment in terms of energy levels, happiness and all-round doing-things-ness that it seems silly to waste any of it venting my fury at Allied. And it's such a glorious sunny day outside that I don't want to spoil it with grumpiness.

I will say, however, that yesterday I was not quite so circumspect or forgiving when they failed to turn up with my oxygen delivery for the 2nd working day in a row. Having expected it on Friday, only to have it moved to Monday (that's a weekend with no spare O2) and then pushed back another 24-hours yesterday, I was seething. Particularly as no one from Allied deigned to call me to tell me.

The way they treat their patients/customers/fools is completely reprehensible. When I phoned to ask about my delivery at 3pm and asked if anyone had been likely to call me to tell me not to wait in for it, I got a nice, curt, "No, I don't expect so, not at this time in the afternoon." Cheers guys.

Do they honestly think that just because I'm transplant-listed and dependent on 24-hour oxygen I don't have anything better to do with my time than wait around for cylinders of oxygen to let me leave my house? It's pathetic.

Anyway, I took it upon myself to draft them a letter expressing my regretful displeasure at the standards of the service they were offering and I eagerly await their response. Not that I'm expecting them to do anything.

But I'm not going to let that dominate things today (well, not unless they fail to deliver this morning and mean that I have to scrabble to find K an alternative lift to her appointment in Northampton which I'd not have enough oxygen to run her to). Instead, I'm going to enjoy looking out at the sunshine and contemplating the next move in my rather unhurried life.

The last week or so has been quite nice, as I've had nothing really to do or to focus on, having not come to any conclusion as to what I'm tackling next. I've just knuckled down to finishing off the next CF Talk, but most of the copy for that should be done by the end of the week.

I know, though, that if I don't pick myself a project soon, I'm going to drift off into a little no-man's-land of indecision and boredom and get into a vicious circle of boredom/tiredness/negativity.

The best thing about the last couple of weeks has been finally working out the ins and outs of my body as it is at the moment and finding the balance between activity and rest – knowing what I can and can't manage and how to deal with whatever exertion I do undertake without running myself into the ground. It's been a much longer and trickier learning process that last time I was doing it back in December, but I finally feel like I've grasped it now. Famous last words, I know, so keep your fingers crossed.

Now I'm off to sit and watch the clock tick round 'til Allied turns up with today's delivery.

At least I've got local News

Wednesday 2 May

Some days are easier than others, that's pretty clear after all the months I've been scribbling these bits and pieces for myself and whoever happens to be passing to peruse. But while a day may not have been as good as the day before it, at least you can rely on the laughably awful local newspaper to make you giggle through anything.

It is, quite possibly, the worst newspaper in the history of publishing – it would be laughed out of Fleets Street and probably still raise quite a few disparaging chuckles from Sesame Street. It's pathetic, lazy journalism with hardly a hint of any sub-editing. But boy, does it make me laugh.

Take today's issue, which landed on my doormat this morning. The lead story was about a pensioner who's been *banned* from his golf club for using his own buggy. Or at least that's what the headline leads you to believe. Actually, he's bought himself a golf buggy to save money on hiring one from the club and they've told him he can't use it because they're not insured for it.

Laughable health and safety procedures, yes, but hardly the totally-out-of-order disability-discrimination they're trying to make it out to be. Sure, I feel sorry for the old fella: it's not cheap to hire buggies. But honestly, it's hardly the meanest, nastiest thing in the world, is it? It's a bunch of silly rules that have upset a pensioner.

It gets better, though. How about the article (or is it just an advert) about the new flats going up in Bletchley? With over half still on the market, you too can share the AMAZING views of Milton Keynes from your living room window. It's even illustrated with a picture of the amazing view: IKEA. Well, IKEA, ASDA, the new footie stadium, downtown Bletchley and some trees. Not exactly the inspiring penthouse vista that you might have anticipated.

I'm consistently amazed and amused at the hilariously low quality of the rag (it really is a rag), and it's collection of "human interest" stories that get published every week. I suppose I shouldn't be railing against it quite so much as I have, on occasion, been known to use it myself as a voice of publicity for the various campaigns I get involved in. But even then they managed to spell my name differently in the main article than from the headline. Awesome.

I honestly don't know if it's just that MK doesn't have enough in the way of "news" to make it interesting, or if there's a genuine total lack of decent editorial leadership, sub-editing or reporting skills, but whatever it is, the paper is worth more as a source of entertainment than as a source of information on the city.

Oh the joys of having very little to do: you do get to see some wonderful things.

All right, I bottled it

Thursday 3 May

You know me – I'm really not a mean and nasty person, and they say you should be careful whom you tread on when you're going up lest you pass them again on your way down.

Since I very much hope I'm still on the way up, and since I very much hope that I've got lots more publicity left in me, I've ducked my head back below the parapet and removed all references to the exact publication I was referring to yesterday.

I know, I know, I'm weak and feeble and shouldn't give a flying one about what people think of me, but the way I look at it is this: in the coming months I'm going to be looking to do a lot more awareness raising of Transplant and Organ Donation and I want as many people on-side as possible. Surely a petty (albeit nicely amusing) rant about the quality of a paper's stories shouldn't get in the way of that?

At least now they're not likely to find it on a random Google search of the name and I shouldn't find myself blacklisted next time the wonderful Paula sends out an immaculate press release she's authored on my behalf.

I shudder to think of the low esteem some fellows writers and bloggers would feel about me reading this, but I suppose that's just who I am – I need to be liked by everyone because I'm a very insecure and shallow person. So there.

On the up side, I've had some great ideas for promotion and publicity as well as a few short films and other projects I might just have on the burners right now. Who knows what'll become of them – and I'm not going to detail them here just yet, because we all know what happened last time I did that – but we'll wait it out and see.

The sun took a long time to come out today. I'm hoping it does better tomorrow.

Maxwell – at last, good drama!

Friday 5 May

I've been wading my way through quite a bit of TV drama of late, spurred on by positive reviews in the press of all the new things like New Tricks, Hustle, Kingdom et al, and have found myself almost constantly disappointed.

There's just something terribly formulaic and dull about British TV drama where it pales in comparison to even the ropiest of American TV product. There's just a slickness and a freshness to the US output which I find myself yearning for whenever I park myself in front of the telly for the new "best thing" on our screens.

So thank goodness for David Suchet, Craig Warner and Colin Barr – the star, writer and director respectively behind Maxwell, last night's dramatization of the last days of the life of Robert Maxwell.

Not only was it brilliantly scripted and performed with a tour de force from Suchet, Barr's direction and the immaculate and very filmic camera work really set the whole thing apart from the usual hour-and-a-half one-offs that we get over here, and puts it in a whole different league to the dull, lifeless weekly dramas we get over here.

I don't know if it's to do with the time constraints imposed by low budgets, or a dearth of creativity within the industry at the moment, but every drama programme seems to follow the same visual formula and the same stodgy editing techniques which seem to be turning a very visual medium into a close-up-ridden copy-cat of a good night at the theatre, but sadly lacking the good scripts and – all too often – the performances.

I yearn for a bit of directorial freedom, to see talented people take the scripts that are there (which must be dramatically improved, if you'll excuse the pun) and turn them into their own films, not the cookie-cutter rehash of last week's episode.

I understand that within a series there has to be continuity, and that there's an accepted way of going about doing things, but when anything artistic reaches a status quo it rapidly loses merit.

It's no wonder Channel 4, ITV and Five are tripping over each other to buy up American drama for over here – and apparently making big mistakes while doing it, according to the press this week – because they simply can't rely on this country turning out enough drama of quality to fill their schedules.

If we could only produce drama good enough to entice and

intrigue and audience, perhaps we wouldn't see broadcasters relying on hideous grotesques in "reality TV" to fill their schedules and boost their ratings.

It's about time we had something to shout about, and Maxwell is certainly a stonking start.

Sympathise and duck

Monday 7 May

It's been, all in all, a pretty good bank holiday.

I was feeling a little run down at the end of the week – not sure why as I'm not sure I'd been massively active – so Saturday was spent very much in chill out mode not doing anything beyond reading the paper and sitting on the sofa.

Sunday I went over to Mum and Dad's for the afternoon to watch the end of the Championship footie season, willing on the Saints to their playoff place, which they secured thanks to a handy 4-1 win over Southend (was there ever any doubt…?), after which we had a gorgeous roast, shared with my bro and his other half. It was good to catch up with them, and nice to see them again so soon after the last time, since I've got rather used to not seeing my bro for pretty extended periods of time.

Today's been a bit harder, largely because yesterday took its toll. My Godson came up to visit with his parents, my mum having laid on her usual lunchtime spread for guests, and K and I popped over for food and games.

Sadly, my chest only lasted for about an hour after the meal before deciding that sitting on the floor playing loud, shouty games was not in it's order of the day, so set about making me feel decidedly uncomfortable with a dedication that really should be admired.

What really hit me today, though, is how some people choose to sympathise with you when you feel unwell. My problem at the moment is that when I get tired (which I do, very easily), I very much lose my ability to put a happy face on things.

I've thrived – as some of you will know first hand only too well – on always keeping not just a stiff-upper-lip, but one that's ever so slightly curled up at the edges; a mirthful demeanour no matter the inner "turmoil". Now, though, my reserves are depleted to the extent that any moment of flagging in the day means that the positive spin and happy vibes are the first energy-drainers to be lost.

What I think that means to people on the "outside" is that for the first time they are seeing me in a different light – I guess for the first time I look like I'm suffering. And boy do I hate it – there's nothing worse in my eyes than other people seeing how hard things can be.

I've no problem with telling people how hard things can be, as long as I can do it with a smile on my face and do my best to laugh it off in the process, but when people can *see* how much it sucks, that bums me out like nothing else and there's nothing I can do about it, because I don't have the energy to fake it.

What's more, some people seem to think it helpful to show/tell me how much they appreciate the shiteness of the situation. I know it's good-natured and well-intentioned, but when people tell you that they know it must be horrible, or say, "it must be really shit right now" – it really doesn't help at all.

I'm well aware of just how completely, head-screwingly, eye-gougingly, heart-breakingly pathetic my life can be on my bad days at the moment – I don't need someone to tell me it must be horrible. It is. I live it.

I know, too, that much of my reaction is just tiredness and not being able to rationalise the thought process, but it just seems like a spin-off of the affected sympathy you get where people try to explain that they know how you feel because they once had a cold so bad they couldn't breathe through their nose at all, and that the doctor thought that if it carried on any longer they might need *antibiotics*!

I know it's well intentioned, and I know people can feel awkward and that they have to say something to show their support, but please, next time you see me, don't tell me how much you appreciate how hard my life is: just give me a hug.

The funny thing is, I know that the opposite extreme annoys me just as much: the people who try to belittle what I'm going through by comparing it to other people's problems. The whole, "everyone has something to worry about," line.

Again, I appreciate the attention, but actually, frankly, in a game of "How cruddy is living in your world" Top Trumps, I think I would probably take some beating. So telling me that you've got a friend who's got an in-growing toenail *and* has to walk the dog twice a day *and* has to look after a child all the while needing to make sure they can Sky+ the football doesn't do a whole lot for evening out my perspective on things.

Like I said before, I know that much of this is tiredness, but the fact is that I'm a tired old grouch a lot of the time now, so I guess I'm thinking of this as a primer for how not to make me throw things at you the next time we talk. Or at least as a warning to duck once you've finished speaking.

I guess the whole thing comes down to the simple things in life. If in doubt, hug it out.

My life in a bottle

Tuesday 8 May

This is why I don't like tiredness. My mini-rant (was it mini?) yesterday has been playing on my mind all day.

I stand by what I say, because it is all incredibly annoying and occasionally morale-sapping, but at the same time I feel a bit petulant for having brought it up in the first place. I suppose it's the "suffer in silence" side of me coming out again.

Lest anyone get the wrong impression yesterday, I don't hate my life. I have a huge number of very positive things going on in my life and I'm surrounded by wonderful people. I enjoy every day (some more than others) and like to make the most of what I can do with each one.

Although I may not be able to do the things I did this time last year, and although I may get a little down about being in a different situation which places more demands on my sense of sensible-ness than it has previously, I still manage to do the things that matter most to me and living in this way has given me a wonderful sense of my priorities in life.

I received an email today from someone who had obviously got my address from the message boards and wanted to ask me a couple of questions about life etc. In my reply to her, I realised just how much of a positive thing being on the transplant list can be.

Rapidly declining health, or a low-health plateau such as I've hit at the moment, is wonderful for really hammering home what really matters in your life – what you choose to expend your energy on.

To use an analogy, a day's energy is like a bottle of water: every day you wake up in the morning and you fill your 2 litre bottle up to the brim with fresh water. Over the course of the day, the various things you do each require different amounts of water.

Make breakfast takes, say 100mls. Do some exercise and you've spent 500mls. Sit as your desk working for a few hours and it's a few hundred mls more.

When you get the stage I'm at, suddenly you've not only got less water – a single litre, maybe – but it also takes more water to do things. Cooking a meal becomes 250mls, which is 1/4 of your daily allowance taken up already. Walking anywhere, for even the shortest amount of time may be up to 500mls – half your day's worth gone. And on the worst days you can be doing as little as possible and still find that you've got a hole in the bottom of your bottle and you're leaking energy all over your shoe.

So when I wake up and fill my bottle in the mornings now, I know that my ration is that much less than I'm used to, that I need to make sure that the water I am going to be pouring out of the bottle goes in the most sensible of places.

Sometimes it's not even the most sensible place – sometimes it's just the place that matters the most. But you know that if you've only got a finite amount of energy for the day, there's no point wasting it on things of little consequence. It means you spend it on the things that really matter.

Yesterday, thanks to a busy weekend, I had a very small bottle of water. But I knew that the most important thing to me was to see and spend time with my Godson. I only manage a couple of hours before I ran myself dry, but those were two of the best, most enjoyable, most pleasure-focused hours that I've spent with my Godson for a long time – because I knew I was using my ration for him. It didn't matter to me that the rest of the day was a total washout and that I would be incapable of doing anything else: I was more than happy to use my ration on him and him alone.

The thing I dislike most about tiredness is that loss of perspective that it delivers – how it takes away your ability to see things in the light you normally see things. It's not about losing the façade, which I seemed so keenly aware of yesterday; it's about losing the bright side – losing the very positivity that drives me forward each and every day.

I try to keep my water bottle as full as I can and I try to replenish it as frequently as possible. But some things are worth emptying it out for – and it's when you realise what those things are that you really strike gold.

Is that a corner Allied are turning?

Friday 11 May

I say, sometimes a little bit of communication goes a long way.

Following my recent let-down from Allied, where I was left waiting for delayed delivery after delayed delivery, I sent off a "strongly worded letter" to them and got an almost immediate response.

Now, there's two parts to this story – a personal and a "professional".

No sooner, it seemed, than Allied had received my letter, they were in touch and full of abject apologies for the confusion and the misunderstandings. And, in fairness to them, it was a very genuine and "un-corporate" apology, too.

Having explained in my letter that I can't really carry their PD300 cylinders comfortably and really need the lighter weight PD430s, they straight away put me onto a fixed weekly delivery, commencing this Monday, of 6 PD430 cylinders to last me the week (which is more than enough) and they will continue to arrive every Monday unless I phone them to let them know they won't be needed.

I have to confess, I'm over the moon. To finally have access to the right amount of truly portable oxygen in quantities enough to last me a whole week of doing whatever I please is fabulously freeing. I'm looking forward to a new ability to do what I want by myself without the oxygen-planning issues I've had up to now.

What concerned me, though, was that my "solution" with which I'd been provided was a panicked stopgap to "shut me up" and get me off their backs. The cynic in me was squirming at the thought that if I were contented then I'd stop writing letters that get copied to the CF Trust and Department of Health.

It was important to me to make sure that it wasn't just me that was getting the best of the service, but that other people in my position who weren't so willing to speak up, or didn't know there were other options available, can get the best, too.

To my immense surprise, and no little pleasure, I discovered that far from "fobbing me off" with the appropriate organisation, the team at Allied are really keen to improve their service and get things working as they should be – and to involve me in the process.

Already I've been told about a new cylinder they've acquired which is not only lighter than the PD430, but lasts longer, too, and it is Allied's expressed intention to prioritise the CF community with them.

PWCF are, I think, a unique breed among oxygen users in that they are the youngest and most independent of the type of people who may need home oxygen therapy. At the same time, they are often the smallest and weakest of the lot, too, meaning that the "portable" oxygen tanks need to be pretty light to really be "portable".

Allied seem to have taken this on board and are working hard to identify PWCF among their patient lists to make sure they are the first to benefit from the new cylinders. All GPs who prescribe home oxygen are supposed to add a code to the order form to indicate the medical condition for which the oxygen is being supplied. Sometimes this doesn't happen and Allied are unaware of a patient's CF status.

Above all, communication is the key here. I am actually really confident that Allied are doing all that they can to improve things at the moment – and I honestly never thought I'd see myself writing that. But if they don't know a person's needs then they can't do their best to deal with them.

As with many things in life, communication is vital – making sure everyone's on the same page and that people can get the things they are entitled too, whether it be oxygen, money, services or anything.

Every good relationship thrives on good communication and this experience has taught me a lot about how little is needed to make a difference if you just talk to people.

No cards, please, it's my birthday

Monday 14 May

For those of you who are not on my email list (you lucky, lucky people) and who may be close enough to me for this to matter, here is a copy of an email I sent out last week proclaiming my up-coming 25th birthday:

"Dear one and all,

As I'm sure you're aware (ahem), the 25th of this month sees me notch up a quarter of a century on this planet. Whilst that may be an ambitious target for the English cricket team, it was one that at one time or another many have believed to be beyond me.

Thanks to brilliant medical teams from Northampton (as a kiddie) and Oxford (as a growed-up), I've celebrated many more birthdays than I may have otherwise.

Although I may not be a picture of health, I could certainly pose for happiness: I am surrounded by family and friends whom I love very dearly and who love me just as much in return (that's you, that is!). I'm blessed to be in a position where I don't really want for anything more than a new pair of blowers to enjoy your company all the more.

Because I consider myself to be so lucky and to be in need of so little, I have decided this year that I would rather put all of your love and good will to use and ask you to make a donation to charity rather than buying me anything or sending me a card.

I don't expect any huge sums, all I ask is that whatever you would have spent on me (even if it's just £1.50 for a card and a stamp), you instead donate to the CF Trust through my JustGiving page, where you can also leave me a birthday message. Like the ad says, every little helps.

For the traditionalists who still want to make contact on my birthday, you can email me or text me instead and save not only trees, but perhaps some lives too.

And if I've been far too presumptuous and you wouldn't have bothered sending a card, then that's fine, too. I still love you all the same.

With love and best wishes to all,

Oli

xx"

(Whisper it) I'm writing

Wednesday 16 May

Believe me, it's amazing myself as much as anything, but so far this week, I've exceeded my target of 6 pages a day three days in a row – how brilliant is that?

I've no idea where this sudden glut of motivation or inspiration has come from, but suddenly things seem to have developed their own sense of momentum and I'm rolling along at a cracking pace and really enjoying myself, too.

It's not just my new script that's coming on leaps and bounds.

Live Life Then Give Life is still going strong, expanding all the time and the team behind it has grown and solidified into a

[hard]core of people dedicated to improving organ donation in this country. It's a privilege to be involved with such a great campaign and group of people, who all work incredibly hard and really spur each other on to greater and greater things.

National Transplant Week, set up and run by Transplants in Mind (TiM) is in July and we're all working feverishly to see what ways we can come up with to publicise it and raise as much awareness as we can.

There's also the new issue of CF Talk, which is coming together really nicely and now sits with the designers, who are currently working their very particular brand of magic on it. I love the work our designers do on the mag and this is always the most exciting stage of an issue for me, where I hand them the copy and they come back a week or so later with some cracking imagery.

What's always really funny about the whole process is that they are fantastically open to comments and ideas on all of the stuff they do, but there's so rarely anything I want to change with the stuff they come up with it almost always goes to print identical to the first draft version I get sent through. I suppose it's a perfect illustration of a team working in harmony together to get all the elements looking their best.

I worry at the moment that it is almost always when things are rolling along at their best that the trip-ups tend to come. But at the same time, knowing the up-and-down nature of my health at the moment, it seems all the more reason to enjoy doing all of these things while I can without fretting about the "what ifs" or the "what's coming next".

I suppose it's something akin to parents trying to wrap their children in cotton wool. If you never allow your child to go out in the garden and play in the mud and put themselves at risk of germs and all the things children come into contact with then they may very well not get ill and stay more healthy than other children, but they also lose a large chunk of what it is to be a child – to explore the world and find out first hand that mud is mucky and worms don't taste very nice.

And so it is for me at the moment. I could easily shut myself away in my bedroom and rest 24/7, spending my days eating, sleeping and doing treatments. But I don't want to look back at this time pre-transplant when I've finally had my op and think of all the things I missed out on because I was too worried about what would happen next.

If a downturn is coming, then so be it – I'll take it on the chin and ride it out like all the others. I hope I can stave it off and continue to enjoy the good side of life. But whatever happens, it's not going to stop me doing the things that mean something to me.

Jinx?

Friday 18 May

I've never really put much truck in jinxes, or quirky twists of fate, but I'm struggling to convince myself that I haven't jinxed myself all over again.

It seems that whenever I talk about what projects I've got going on and what I'm getting accomplished and what I hope to achieve, I take a huge dip in the form the next day. It happened back in March/April when I was excited about pushing forward after Laughter for Life, and it's happened again this week, after I proclaimed my success at getting back to writing.

Ironic, really, I suppose, considering I wrote so specifically on the ups and downs of life and how I could cope with whatever was being thrown at me. People call it tempting fate, something I've never really agreed with, but am starting to question my conviction.

The concerning thing about times like this is that you never quite know where it's going. It's the same for most things in life, I suppose, but it seems all the more important when reserves are low and the littlest molehill can so rapidly escalate to the mightiest mountain.

The last couple of days I've been under the weather – nothing too drastic, just very tired, low on energy and slightly achy. My head is swimming a bit with a feeling like I'm getting a cold, but I know that it's more than likely just hay-fever, which I suffer from every year and always starts out feeling like I'm getting a cold.

So more than likely, there's nothing really wrong at the moment – my chest, although slightly more productive than usual, isn't causing me significant problems, and the only real "symptom" of anything wrong is a little glandular swelling, which is more than likely hay-fever related.

That knowledge, however, doesn't work to exclude the possibility that things could be on a downward slope. More often than not, in the past, all this would hang around for a few days and make me feel a little rubbish, then sort itself out and go away. Now, though, everything carries a greater significance.

It's hard, at times like these, not to worry about what comes next, but at the same time, my mind is bugged by the knowledge that the more positive I stay, the less likely anything is to take hold and drag me down for proper. I don't want to sound like a crazy "mind-over-matter" nut-job, but I strongly believe that your mind can influence your body in more significant ways than people always consider.

So I'm spending my time at the moment in bed, resting, trying to take on as many calories and possible and make sure that whatever has got me on a slow-down doesn't become something which puts me at a stop.

Rolling again

Tuesday 22 May

Happily, the jinx doesn't seem to have lasted too long, which is definitely a good thing. After a bit of a slow down at the end of last week and a weekend spent doing as little as possible, things seem to be back to where they were before I decided to blog-big about my projects and plans.

From now on I intend to only highlight imminent events on here, and to talk about everything else only once it's safely behind me. Which is odd, because I really don't believe in jinxes/superstition. As my brother delights in telling me, it's unlucky to be superstitious.

So, the last couple of days have seen me finally bite the proverbial bullet and really get my head into CF Talk to get it swept off to the designers. They do a fantastic job, but do insist on having FINAL copy before going to work on it, as they've found to their cost in the past that if people are still chopping and changing while they work then a certain turn or phrase or clever image in the text that spurs them on to create a funky look for the page can disappear and leave the reader bemused as to where the page-layout idea came from and possibly whether the designers were smoking something while they worked.

And I know for a fact that Tin Racer is a no-smoking facility.

The trouble with having to provide them with final-final copy is that I'm terrible for making lots and lots of little tweaks to the text for the CF Talk copy. Often, the copy we receive is too long for the format and needs to be cut down, but I'm always anxious that while

I may be cutting and re-jigging the article, I am never rewriting it. Because the whole idea of the magazine is that it is written by PWCF for PWCF, it's really important to me to keep the original author's voice on their work, and not edit it into one homogenous style throughout the mag.

What this means is that while I'm editing, I'm constantly making changes and adjustments to the articles to make sure I'm keeping the thrust of what's been written, as well as the original voice, whilst shaping it into an article that will fit within the space constraints imposed by our format and style.

It's not easy and it's one of the jobs that I always find myself trying to delay. This time it's been even tougher as I had a long spell out of the editor's chair going through my recent rough patch, which meant that I had to come back to look at all the articles again, having completely lost the flow I was in before I had to down tools and sort myself out.

Happily, though (and I do enjoy seeing that word twice in the same blog entry), I have now managed to sign off on over 3/4 of the copy for the new issue and turn it over to the guys at Tin Racer. All I have left to do is all the little mop-up pieces that come last, like the Editorial for the issue, the contents page and the competition page.

It's been a long time coming, but hopefully we'll carry a bit of momentum into the next issue and get it out quite quickly this time round.

Obviously, I'm looking at taking a long weekend off all work-related bits and pieces this weekend to make the most of my 25th Birthday, for which I have so far studiously avoided planning anything. It's a little sad, I have to say, to not be able to celebrate things properly, but I'm actually so glad to be here to see it and to be able to share it with all my family and friends, whether I get to see them or not, that it's not got me down as much as one might expect it to.

I'll be sure to chart progress of the other work I do manage to achieve this week on here once I've got there, but I'll hold back from jumping the gun and shouting about my plans for the week for now. I've learned my lesson.

It's finally here…

Thursday 24 May

No, not my birthday – that's tomorrow.

No, I'm being much more materialistic today: I've got my huge, lovely, big, fast, super-specially brilliant new Mac Pro sitting on my desk in the study just begging me to get creative (and, in a little voice, to play Championship Manager, too).

It feels like it's been an age since I ordered it but yesterday it finally got here and I eventually found it amongst all its packaging. Mind you, I think it speaks volumes about a product when even the boxes it comes in are cool.

It's only taken 24-hours of head-banging, shop-tripping, telephone-help lining to get the whole thing off the ground and doing what it's suppose to, but now it's flying at full mast, there's no stopping me.

Well, I say that, but I suppose if you're going to make the most of a state-of-the-art editing system, you really need some projects to edit. Which, I suppose, means I've got to get to work making some projects. But of course, I can't talk about those, because we all know what happens when I discuss my future plans on here.

I could instead go into incredible detail about how I've spent my day since 6am this morning (yes, I was up at 6 and no, I have no idea why) trying to puzzle my way around the various internet-connection problems I came across, or I could regale you with tales of the unbelievably complex and cool software I spent the afternoon installing. I could even slide in a witty anecdote about my trip to Maplins at lunchtime.

But I'm not going to. Because a) you really don't care that much and b) neither do I. The point is, I've got it, it's here, it's ready to go and now the fun can really begin.

Now, if you'll excuse me, I'm off to play Championship Manager until K gets home from college…

25's up

Saturday 26 May

With little fanfare, and no candles, I quietly passed into my 26th year yesterday.

Whether emailing all of your friends, posting a MySpace bulletin and blog piece count as "quiet" is perhaps a debate for another day, as I like to think it was peaceful and respectful.

My little idea of raising a hundred or so pounds for the Trust by asking for donations in place of gifts has blown me away ever so slightly. At last check, justgiving.com/oli25 was running at a massive £320, with pledges of more to come from a few corners.

It has truly over-whelmed me the number of people who have donated – especially people who I know wouldn't have been buying me anything anyway. It means so much to me that they donated something anyway; I've been really touched by everyone's response.

Thanks also to everyone who sent me birthday messages and good wishes.

I had a great day, being spoiled rotten by K all day long, with breakfast specially prepared fresh from the shop, all fresh and delicious, plus a spectacular act of rule-breaking in the most fantastic fashion including a furry orange book about the making of Avenue Q, the puppet musical I've become slightly obsessed with.

For the first time in a really long time, I've got new DVDs to add to my collection, including a few I've wanted to see for a really long time and a classic I really should have seen but have never got around to.

Birthdays are amazing things. They serve to remind you of all the joy you have in your life, all the people who mean something to you and to whom you mean something in return.

So many people complain so much about reaching another birthday – I guess fearful of the on-rushing of old age. I don't know where it comes from, other than an age-old, in-built fear of getting closer to losing something, whether it's your faculties or your life.

It's always struck me, though, that people look at birthdays the wrong way. Perhaps it's because I've been forced into a position where every passing year counts as a true blessing, but I don't understand why people choose to fear their birthdays rather than embrace them.

Every year of our lives brings new adventures. It brings new experiences, new people, new wonders we know little of when we celebrate the passing of another 12 months. Every day that goes by we learn something new, we grow as a person and we extend our life beyond what it was the day before.

Surely that's an amazing thing – so why don't people see it and appreciate it for what it is? Is it that every year that passes we slip into more of a groove of comfort wherein everything blurs together into one homogenous experience? Do we learn over time an inability to distinguish the wood from the proverbial trees?

The saddest thing in life is when a person stops seeing the beauty that surrounds them and the experiences they are open to. Childhood is seen as the happiest time of our lives, because that's when we take in the wonder of the world and see things for the first time – the time when we don't think we've seen it all before and are eager to take it all in.

Adulthood shouldn't be about getting bored of the same old things around us, it should be a time when we can use our years of experience and perspective to take hold of the things in life that really matter and put aside the thoughts of the things that don't.

We should take each passing year as an opportunity to do the things we want to do, go the places we want to go, see the things we want to see, but more than anything, to not let the world blinker us to it's beauty and ever-changing wonder simply because it's become familiar to us.

Tomorrow morning, I want you to look out of your window when you draw back your curtains and really notice the things you can see outside it. If it's dull and grey and there's rain falling down, don't let your heart sink, but turn your thoughts to the amazing way the falling water changes the way you see the street, the way the light falls differently. Take note of the things you see everyday, but look closer and find a detail you've not seen before.

And when you go downstairs and you greet your loved one(s), take a moment to appreciate what they bring to your life. Take a moment to think about what they've brought into your world that's made you who you are. As Alfred Lord Tennyson once wrote,

"I am part of all that I have met."

July 2007
(4 Months)

It all started with a sniffle

Tuesday 3 July

It had been my intention to sit down at some point and fill in the blanks of the past months with an epic, multi-post entry to tell my tale up to today (or up to whenever I got around to posting).

Luckily for all of you guys who are still bumbling across the site in the vain hope for a new entry, I've decided against it.

There are many reasons why I should and shouldn't give up a full account of the last 4-5 weeks during which time I've managed to post a grand total of 0 times.

Over the months since I started this blog just before Christmas, I've shared a lot of the ups and downs, highs and lows, peaks and troughs of everyday life and tried to use this site as a tool to force myself to keep a bit of perspective on the whole thing – life in general and my health. Sitting here now, after quite possibly the worst month of my life, it seems strange to say it, but I want to focus on moving forward more than raking over the past, even the not-so-distant past.

So, what you get is the shortened, edited, cut-down, weight-watchers version:

At the end of May, after my birthday, I was running pretty low, energy-wise. In the middle of this low, I managed to pick up a cold. Fighting the cold was one thing, but as is almost inevitable with CF, the amount of time and energy my immune system was expending on fighting the cold virus meant I had no defences left to look after things in my lungs.

Before you could say, "seriously guys, I don't feel very well," I had collected myself a roaring infection and an inability to extricate myself from my bed.

After a bit of family decision making, I returned to the warm and caring centre of the family fold for my Mum to switch back to nurse/carer role in looking after me 24/7.

Even that wasn't enough, though and within a week I was on the ward in Oxford, having spiked an impressive temperature and gathered the mother of all infection markers.

Levels of infection in the body are most easily assessed by measuring the levels of C-reactive Protein (CRP). Don't ask me what it is, I just know that it should, in a normal person, be in the 0-4 range and that in PWCF it's frequently around the 10 level, as we are often fighting low-level infection constantly. Anything over 10 gets worrying and 20-30+ is cause for proper concern.

When I was admitted to the ward, I was told that the labs doing my bloods had stopped their CRP count when they got to 160.

Now, while I should be monumentally freaked out by all of this, I still can't help but feel slightly short-changed as my good friend Emily once managed to mark up an impressively gob-smacking score of 400 – but they obviously like her enough to keep counting and not just give up when they get past "bloody high". Oh well, Em's always done things more impressively than me, anyway.

In the midst of all this, there were lots of antibiotics being hurled around, different combos being tried here and there and various other drugs being tossed in my direction.

Most upsettingly for me at the time was being put onto a short course of steroids, which at the dosage they were giving me all but removed me from the active transplant list – my one chink of light in a world of enveloping blackness was being blotted out and I had no control over it.

June has been a true nightmare month, in every sense of the word. From beginning to end I was struggling through every single day and at times it seemed like there was nowhere to go. It is, without doubt, the closest I have come to meeting my maker and there were times over the last few weeks when I have honestly believed that someone was waiting outside the door with a convenient bucket for kicking.

One of the reasons I can't take myself into much more detail than I already have is that a lot of the last few weeks is already a haze, my mind working it's magical ways to blot out the middle-ground of strife and tedium and leaving me with but a few key moments lodged in my brain.

Thankfully, most of those key moments are the ones that give me the spur to push onwards and upwards and to keep fighting for my transplant. There have been times in the last month when I've been in a darker place than I've ever been, but the knowledge that it's possible to pull back from that and to recover to some semblance of normality again is reassuring beyond expression.

That's not to say life is all sunshine and roses now – there's a lot of things that are still a struggle and my world can still be a lonely place at times. But I'm still here, I'm still fighting and I'm still able to laugh – at myself and others.

It's been fitting that over the course of my last battles I've not managed to post anything on here, because smiling was the last thing on my mind through most of it. Now, though, I've got something of my mojo back, and I'm revving up for the run-in to my new life.

Bring on the lungs, baby, I'm ready to roll.

Pointy hat with a "D"

Tuesday 3 July

So I'm back at the flat now, enjoying a wonderful, 2-person existence with K and my own space with everything in easy reach. ("2-person existence" meaning K and me, not 2 versions of me in a crazy Jekyll & Hyde kind of way).

Before I left the flat, we'd been trying, ever-so-hard, to sort out our internet connection, which had been thrown into disarray when we discovered that neither my nice new, shiny Mac Pro, nor K's nice, new, not-quite-so-shiny lap-top with Windows Vista-poo, would work with our current Broadband modem.

Don't ask me why – it's some kind of computer conspiracy between Microsoft, Onetel, PC World, Maplins and computer telephone helplines that would take years to unravel if anyone ever bothered to, which they won't because no one understands enough about things to unravel them enough to make sense of anything to work out who did what to whom and when and why and what.

It just doesn't work.

So, I went out and bought the doofer they told me to buy, thinking I was being very clever and techie and would sort it all out in a flash.

Sadly, the one I bought was, frankly, poo. Sometimes in life, you get what you pay for and what I paid for was a cheap piece of rubbish that no one on any helplines had heard of, not even the people on the helpline for the company that made the modem product that I'd bought.

So I took it back.

Fast forward through a month of not being at the flat (see other post) and I arrive back at the flat knowing exactly what I need to get and roaming the internet to find it, order it and get it delivered.

And today, it arrived!

So I leap (stumble) out of bed and run (walk) to the study, throw (plonk) myself down in the chair and busily set about slotting (ramming) cables into the various slots they may or may not fit. I do all of this with the authoritarian air of someone who knows exactly what they're doing.

To my delight, I turn on the computer and nothing explodes.

So, I jump into the software settings gubbins, which I now know inside out having messed around so much trying to make the other lump of rubbish work. I'm entering long strings of complicated numbers and letters and passcodes – sorting my DNS from my IP from my PPPOA and other wonderful collections of letters.

And my computer loves it! "Connected," it says.

It lies.

Nothing will come up on the web browser. Nothing doing. The light on the modem is red. I'm no rocket scientist, but even I know that a red light on a piece of technology is never a sign that things are all fine and dandy.

So I phone Apple customer support, who have up to now proven to be consistently clear, concise and totally helpful on all related matters to my purchase. Indeed, they are again.

We run through a number of things and they tell me that everything on the Mac is working perfectly and all the settings are as it should be. They suggest I contact my service provider as it's most likely that a) they haven't activated my account or b) the network is down.

I hang up the phone despondent. I've been on the Internet all morning on my old computer on the same account, so I know none of those things is true.

I phone the modem manufacturer's freephone customer service line. It's no longer in use – it's now an 0845 number, which I'll have to pay for. Nice.

I talk to a nice man in Delhi. He tells me everything on the router is working fine. The red light is because my Username or password is incorrect.

I hang up the phone despondent. I check and recheck the username and password I've entered. It's all correct.

I phone Onetel customer service. I may or may not be talking to exactly the same bloke I just came off the phone with. He tells me I need a load of settings to set up the modem. I tell him I have them and I've done that, but he takes 15 minutes reading them to me anyway.

He starts to read me my username and password. The username is 32 characters long and he's spelling it out letter-by-letter, then using the phonetic alphabet with it. I cut him off and reel it off to him from my notes. As I get to the end of the line of letters and digits, everything slips into a momentary pause as a sluggish dawn swims smugly across my consciousness and I realise that the '1' I've entered as the 27th character is, in fact, an 'L'.

If anyone wants me, I'll be the one in the corner with the pointy hat on my head.

The Black Dog

Thursday 5 July

Earlier this week I sat down with K to show her a film I thought she'd like that I'd caught on TV a while back and just picked up on DVD.

The Gathering Storm covers the year or so leading up to Winston Churchill's re-appointment as First Lord of the Admiralty in 1935, during which time he tries in vain to convince his Parliamentary colleagues that Germany is re-arming itself for a war which no one else in Europe is prepared for.

It's a fantastic film – an HBO/BBC co-production for television, not cinema release – with a marvellous central performance from Albert Finney and an eye-watering supporting cast.

What struck me, on watching it back again, though, was the reminder of how Churchill struggled with what the doctors called, "a certain melancholia" and what his family – most notably his wife, his adored Clemmie – called his Black Dog.

Nowadays, of course, it would be called depression and he'd be on all manner of pills and psychological couches to come to terms with things, but this isn't the time or the place for a detailed breakdown of my personal feelings towards today's current epidemic of depression.

I have, of late, felt myself under attack from the very same Black Dog as afflicted Churchill, I feel.

The analogy to a dog is remarkably accurate – it carries a life and a will of its own and it can come and go as quickly as the summer sun behind the clouds at Wimbledon. Like a dog, it can be docile and quiet one minute and turn unutterably savage the next: a constant threat hanging over you, but with no indication when or how long the next surge will come.

Today was very much a Black Dog Day. It seems at the moment that whenever my chest is less than perfect… hmm, no, that's not the right way to put it, given that "perfect" is something my chest hasn't been since my earliest years… but whenever my chest is a little worse than it was yesterday, or whenever I feel slightly more under the weather than I have been for the few days previously, the Dog attacks with a savagery I've never before experienced.

Yesterday was my last day of IVs for this course – normally a time of great celebration and a chance to enjoy a long, hot, refreshing shower (something I can't do with my port accessed, so I have to settle for half-baths which don't get my shoulder wet). This time round, however, I feel like I'm losing a crutch that I've been leaning and relying on to improve me.

I've been so used, over the years, to going down hill, having a course of IVs and pitching out the other end all fine and dandy, it's an alien feeling to come to the end of a course of IVs as I have the last couple of times and still find my chest almost as clogged up as it was before, albeit with markedly less infection and with much thinner and more "friendly" sputum.

I think there's a part of my brain which is still convinced that I'm not actually any better at all and that I should still be on the drugs, something which all medical evidence strongly contradicts. It is this nagging centre of the brain that I think is holding the leash for the Black Dog and sees fit to set him free at the merest hint of a downturn.

I've had a few really good days since I arrived back at the flat almost a week ago. I've been getting stronger and feeling more upbeat than I have in a long time. So it's all the more arresting when the Dog attacks as he did today.

As if lost in a cloud of darkness that envelops all around it, I found myself losing touch with myself and veering off down a course of negative thinking that I normally nip in the bud in seconds. And where I sit at the moment, once the cloud does descend, once the Dog has its teeth into me, there's nothing can be said or done to clear the air or shake it off.

Strangely, the fog I found myself in for most of the afternoon suddenly lifted this evening. I strongly suspect it's down to a fillip in my physical state, whereby my chest deigned to allow me out of bed without making all kinds of disagreeable noises and causing problems.

What I need to find is something that will disconnect my mind from my body – to keep my mental state separate from that of my physical. Because let's face it, if I start to bottom out at the first sign of a little physical hurdle, I'm going to be fighting through far, far too many mental battles when I should be focusing all my energy on my physical ones.

Anyone know where I can buy a muzzle?

National Transplant Week

Thursday 5 July

As you may or may not know, next week is National Transplant Week, throughout which various things will be happening to raise awareness of organ donation and suchlike.

Tomorrow morning I'm being interviewed by BBC Look East and the piece should run as part of their 6.30pm main evening news, all things being well, so those of you in the Eastern region, keep your eyes peeled for that.

With luck, I'll have more media stuff going on throughout the week, too. The local papers will pick up my story again, I hope, and also perhaps local radio, too.

Nationally, look out for Emily on Richard and Judy during the week, as well as a friend of mine called Robyn who will take Emily's place on the GM:TV sofa as resident PWCF awaiting transplant – naturally I'd have been up for it, but I'm not a pretty girl, so I think that ruled me out…

So keep your eyes peeled in your local press for pics of attractive young people sporting their Live Life Then Give Life or their I'd Give You One T-shirts – and spread the word about organ donation to all around you.

Look East (at me!)

Friday 6 July

One of the joys of finally being off IVs is not having the alarm blare at 8 o'clock every morning to get you up and out of bed to do your morning dose. Annoyingly, my body seems to have seen fit to re-set it's internal clock to keep raising me from my slumber sometime near or just after 8am anyway, as if I'll miss out on something important if I don't. Regardless, it's still nice not to be woken by an alarm, I suppose.

I had the BBC round today to do an interview for Look East, the local news bulletin for the Anglia region. It was only a 2-man job, nothing big, with a reporter and a cameraman and took less than an hour from top to tail.

Interestingly, I didn't feel even a touch of nerves today, which I normally get before any of the interviews I do, so I am forced to assume that my brain and nerve-ometer have come to the conclusion that once you've done live Radio 4, taped local news is nothing to be bothered about.

Not that I'm complaining at my head's somewhat pompous stance – it makes interviews a whole lot easier and less tongue-twisty if you're not feeling the nerves beforehand. And in fact today I felt I gave on of the best interviews I've done – I covered all the bases clearly and succinctly and gave them lots of material to cut around, depending on what angle they wanted to take.

I was even pretty pleased with the final version which went out on in the 6.30pm programme tonight – it managed to put everything across well and didn't rely too heavily on the kind of news-package clichéd coverage that usually gets shot for PWCF, although we did have to have the inevitable nebuliser shot.

The rest of the day has been spent trying to chill out and rest up in the hope of making it to Birmingham for the Live Life Then Give Life event in Victoria Square in the afternoon. It's frustrating not to know whether I'm going to be able to make it or not yet, but I can't commit to anything when I have no idea how I'm going to feel from one morning to the next.

Most of the afternoon has been fine, although this evening my chest is feeling a bit tight and grumpy, so it's anyone's guess how

I'll be in the morning. I'm hoping that it's just a bit of tiredness creeping in and that once Neve takes over the legwork of breathing for the night, I'll be set for a trip out tomorrow. We'll have to wait and see.

Brum

Saturday 7 July

So it turned out that my chest decided not to try any last minute histrionics and I did make it up to Birmingham today.

I'm sure there will be much amusing cross-bloggage between myself, Emily and Emma on the subject, but since I appear to have got here first, I'll be popping my smug face on. Or possibly reflecting on the fact that they clearly have better things to do with their Saturday nights than sit in front of their computer detailing their day. Ho hum.

Today saw the beginning of National Transplant Week, which runs until next Saturday, and to mark the occasion the Live Life Then Give Life team assembled in Victoria Square in Birmingham to create the world's biggest Loveheart (you know, those little hard sweets with "Date me" or "Sexy" written in the middle).

The idea was to create a 1 metre wide version, which, when finally calculated, required a massive 70kg of icing, which all had to be rolled out, dyed, plastered together in a neat round shape, then have the heart-shape and letters spelling out the organ donation line phone number placed on top.

Due to the hugely limited reserves of energy I have now, however, most of the fun of the day was off-limits to me, with my arrival timed to coincide with the completion of the finished Loveheart around 3pm, when we hoped to have some press along to mark the occasion.

Mum and Dad drove over and collected K and me just after 1pm and we headed up the M1 to Birmingham in really good time, car loaded down with my newly acquired wheelchair, plenty of spare oxygen, a snack-box of energy-boosters and spare bits and pieces like paracetamol, which I've found immensely useful in recent weeks for calming hyper-active chest flaring moments.

I have to confess that I was pretty nervous going out of the house today. Things can change so rapidly from moment to moment with my chest at the moment that the prospect of traveling quite so far from the relative comfort and safety of home, where my bed and Neve are always to hand, concerned me. The prospect of getting into difficulties in a car on the motorway filled me with a kind of nervousness I've not experienced before and it really threw me off.

That said, it was a really wonderful afternoon – everyone there was so fun and friendly. I saw a few faces I'd met previously at Laughter for Life and met a few people who I've only had contact with via email and message boards up to now.

It was fantastic to be out in the open air and having some fun with people, compared to my usual life at the moment of sitting around at home doing hardly anything at all. The daily grind of nebs, physio, more nebs, resting, nebbing, physioing and on and on in a loop is brought into focus by a break from routine like today.

My chest behaved admirably. Once we got home it gave only the mildest of complaints, letting me know that it had done quite enough for the day, thank you very much, but not ranting and raving about it as it sometimes deems necessary.

I've been pretty spectacularly tired all evening, but have forced myself to stay awake so I get a good night's sleep tonight, which I'm now assured of, so I'm going to whisk myself off to hit the hay and catch up on other things tomorrow.

Thanks to everyone who helped out today, and to everyone who popped down to say hello. We made an odd sight in the centre of Birmingham, standing over a giant sweet in various random states of hilarity and occasional fits of giggles, but we made contact with a lot of people and passed on the message of organ donation, which is what this week (and our campaign) is all about.

Hooray, not rubbish!

Sunday 8 July

Woke up this morning later than I have been – all of 9.30am – fully expecting to feel worse than horrible and was surprise (and delighted) to discover I didn't.

In fact, I felt as good if not better than I had the previous morning. No complaints from me on that one. I was a little bit more chesty than I have been, but I think that's down to not getting as long a session of physio in last night as I would usually do, largely due to being so shattered from the day.

I've spent the day on the sofa doing next to nothing – watched the British Grand Prix and then realised that all through this season I've sat and watched races, only to remember with a quarter of the race to go that I really don't like F1 anymore because it's so chuffing dull. When the only time cars overtake each other is when one of them stops for petrol, you know you've got a problem with your sport, surely?

I remember the olden days when the cars used to drive quite close together and every now and again one of them would try to get past another one *in a corner* – oh, the memories. I still have no idea why I sat through all 60 laps of today's GP other than using the excuse that I was deliberately trying to do nothing.

My dad has it right – he Sky+'s most of the races, and then zips through them at x6 speed, which is much more interesting.

To break from the sporting tedium, we sat and watched The Queen this evening, which was entertaining, but nowhere near as grand as it's been reported to be. Helen Mirren is outstanding, but the script is *incredibly* clunky in the first 10-15 minutes where the filmmakers are clearly working over-time to make sure that all the Americans who want to watch the film are up to speed with how our country works with the monarchy, the Prime Minister and all the rest of our constitutional gubbins.

It's hideously badly handled, although I suppose the defence would be that it had to be shoehorned in to make the film make sense to the foreign markets. I still think there are other ways of doing it, though.

The cast are generally very good, although some veer towards the bad side of impressionism and caricature, and the idea of a peering into the Royal household at such a difficult time is intriguing, even if some of the scenarios they come up with stretch the bounds of believability a little.

It was worth seeing to see what all the fuss was about, but I wouldn't rush out to pick myself up a copy (our copy being a LoveFilm rental).

Hoping for an early night tonight, although with my brain running the way it does at the moment, I'll be wide awake again come 8.30 and it'll take me till midnight to feel sleepy again.

British Rail Sunday

Monday 9 July

It would appear that my Monday was, in fact, a delayed Sunday (or a British Rail Sunday, as I prefer to call it), bringing with it as it did all of the slowed-down, energy-less deflation that I was expecting to get as a hangover from my Brummie exertions.

I haven't been feeling completely rubbish, but it was certainly a *lot* harder to get up and out of bed this morning than it has been for the last week or so.

A good session of physio once I had managed to get up and about seemed to sort things out, but I took the day very easy anyway, spending most of it on the sofa watching the extras on my King Kong DVD (having been totally addicted to the superb production diaries) and getting through 3 episodes of the first season of Entourage, a show which managed to sneak under my radar but which is brilliantly my kind of thing, following as it does the path of a Hollywood actor and his close-knit bunch of friends. Aspirational TV, I guess you could call it.

Once my batteries were sufficiently DVD-charged, I did manage to plonk my butt down in the study and get some work done, reviewing pages for the new issue of CF Talk and responding to some emails which have been hanging around for my attention for a while.

Also had to tune in to Richard & Judy this evening to catch the ever-wonderful Emily turning on the charm for Mr & Mrs daytime (or is it prime-time?) TV, along with her charming and incredibly open mother, Mrs T. Using footage from the various interviews they've done with Emily over years, pre- and immediately post-transplant, I have yet to see a more convincing advert for the benefits of organ donation than seeing the contrast in Emily in those films.

The thought of the immense and immeasurable ways in which my life could change with just one phone call is at once hugely exciting and tremendously saddening. It is impossible to see into the future and to know what lies in store for me, but the thought of such amazing, intangible possibilities sitting so close but so very far from reach is a hard one to reconcile in one's mind.

It's a process in which I feel like a terrified passenger, willing the runaway train to stay on track and ease into the station set for new life, whilst all the while knowing that one little bump will send it hurtling off the rails.

How do you live your life from day-to-day with something like that hanging over your head? I'm not sure even I know, except to say that if I wasn't living it, then there'd be no point waiting for the transplant, I guess.

So, for those of you who are in touch with the Big Man Upstairs, now's the time to get on your knees, bow your heads or do whatever comes most naturally to you when you pray and ask Him to bless me with a second chance. And for those of you who don't believe, well, maybe He'd like to hear from you, too.

Annual Review

Wednesday 11 July

Boy, annual reviews are depressing.

I've never liked the yearly MOT, ever since it was my only trudge over to Oxford every 12 months as part of my shared-care arrangement with Northampton Paediatric Unit (not an uncommon arrangement for PWCF, especially children), when it was marked with endless hors of waiting around and pointless questions from a doctor who you see once a year but spends their brief meeting with you asking the sort of intimate question you'd struggle to find the courage – as a child/teenager – to answer your own doctor about.

Seriously, how many 14 year-old kids are going to sit in a consulting room with their Dad and answer anything but "No" when the doctor says, "Do you smoke"? Obviously, I never have, but there are those – even with CF – who do, and it is critical to their on-going care that the doctors are aware of something like this. Asking in front of Dad is not the way to go about finding out.

As the year's have gone by, and the process has moved from being an annual schlep to Oxford to being just another clinic appointment with my adult team at the Churchill – and one that's marked by a good deal less waiting and a good deal more friendliness – it's taken on a paradoxically much more unpleasant feel to it.

If progress were marked on a chart – and with many areas of CF, it actually is – the over-riding theme of annual reviews is to watch the graph slip-sliding ever so slowly downwards in an ever-decreasing mountainside style.

This year, I suppose it reached it's nadir – there isn't a whole lot lower to go, and compared to last year, things look pretty ('scuse the French) shite. It's hard to stay upbeat and positive when you're looking back at a set of results which at the time were immensely disappointing, but for which now you'd give your proverbial eyeteeth.

(By the way – can anyone tell me what eyeteeth actually are and why they're called that? It's dead confusing. Answers on a postcard, kudos as a prize…)

There are moments of levity in the experience, though, things I suppose I must cling to, although all of them come firmly in the category of "if you don't laugh you'll cry".

Take the psychological survey, for instance, an 8-page document quizzing you on how CF affects your quality of life (or QOL as they like to put it), with the kind of inane multiple choice answer boxes like A Lot, Not Much, A Bit, Not Really.

"Does CF affect your day-to-day life?", "Does CF prevent you from doing the things you want to do?", "Does CF affect your relationships?". A monkey could answer these for me right now.

What did make my nurses laugh, though, was my minor fit of pique whereby I simply crossed out the entire section devoted to "social life and socialising". I wish.

I now have to wait a few weeks and head back for an ultrasound scan and then to see my doctors, who will have all of my results and can sit down and take me through them. Can't wait for that day – it should be a barrel of laughs.

Anyway, I've had enough of bleating about the awfulness of annual reviews, my chest and my life at the moment – I'm going to go and plonk myself on the sofa in front of a good movie and forget about everything. Until I remember it again…

I'm ok, really

Wednesday 11 July

It's been pointed out to me that my last post was a touch to the darker side of happiness and light.

In the spirit of remembering the title and inspiration of this blog, I wanted to post to clarify that I'm not living a world of utter blackness with no mirth or merriment whatsoever.

I'm not going to edit or delete my prior posting, because I stand by not only what I said but also the sentiments expressed in it. However, I wanted to add that I can still see the funny side of life, swinging as I do from mood to mood like a restless teenage monkey trying to impress the girls with his feats of daring in the tree tops.

To illustrate the fact, I've just giggled my way through nearly all of Punch Drunk Love – I don't mean I watched nearly all of it, I mean I was giggling at most of it, but not some parts (the bits that weren't funny), because those of you who know me will know I can't just watch a bit of a movie, it's all or nothing. You will also notice I've lost none of my pedantry in the process, either.

Still, I've just giggled my way through most of Punch Drunk Love, which would be a great illustration of my current access to the fun-sensors of my brain, were it not for the fact that only a very few people can I imagine extracting the same bizarre glee as I do from this quaint, weird, surreal little movie.

I would encourage all of you to go and seek it out to see what all the fuss is about (check out my ego too, thinking that my little mention in a blog counts as "all the fuss"), but I'm fairly sure that 90% of you would not only not see the same thing as I see in it, but in it's place see something incredibly dull, surreal and very, very odd.

In fact, I think you might lynch me.

Anyway, I just thought I'd write and say, honestly, I'm OK, really. Kind of.

Thick and fast

Friday 13 July

The funny thing about not doing very much is that when things do happen in your day, it makes them seem like a much bigger deal than perhaps they would seem on another day.

On the other hand, the ups and downs are coming in so thick and fast at the moment that I don't really know what to do with myself at some points. Most weeks seem to end with an interesting good news/bad news summary for the week, although I try not to dwell on that too much lest the knowledge that the week contained more of the latter than the former start to drag me down again.

Then you get days like today, when the good news/bad news cycle suddenly notches up a gear and starts flying along quicker than a steroid-powered rider in the Tour de France.

I woke up this morning just before 9am, a good average morning wake up time, feeling pretty good. After doing my nebs and physio, I'd noticeably slowed down a good chunk and was feeling a distinct lack of energy. Immediately, my head starts to worry about how much of a struggle today is going to be.

Luckily for me, I didn't have that much time to dwell on my

thoughts because for three quarters of an hour between 11am and 11.45am, the phone didn't stop ringing. If you want a clearer demonstration of a good news/bad news day, you'll have to search long and hard. Although it was really bad news/good news. The phone calls went as follows:

- Lisa, my nurse from the Churchill in Oxford calls and tells me that the result from my Glucose Tolerance test in my annual review was high, a possible indicator of the beginning of CF-related diabetes (CFRD), more on which later, but suffice to say it didn't put a smile on my face. She's going to try to find me a blood sugar testing kit for me to monitor my sugars for a couple of weeks before my next clinic visit on 2nd August to see what's going on.

- Mum phones. Tell her why I'm not sounding over-joyed. She tells me not to worry about the GTT. Immediately, it makes me worry. Mum only tells you not to worry when there's something to worry about (or at least only says it in that tone of voice where she doesn't sound entirely convinced there's nothing to worry about). Tells me my Grandpa is up for the weekend if I want to come over and I'm left to ponder if I'll have the energy to make a trip to Mum and Dad's to see him.

- Emma calls to tell me that the Daily Mirror want to run a feature on me and Robyn, who is also currently waiting for a double lung transplant and also has CF, and is currently the face of National Transplant Week. She asks if I'd be interested. I know it's not really a question because she knows how much of a media monkey I am. She has to check with Robyn, too, but will get back to me.

- Emma calls again, Robyn's on board, so she gives me the writer's details.

- I phone the Daily Mirror writer and talk to her a bit about donation and things. The spread will form part of their One in a Million campaign, through which they're aiming to sign up a million potential organ donors. We arrange a proper telephone interview for Monday morning and I pass her Robyn's details.

- K phones from work after I text her about the Mirror piece. She's excited (she tends to be more excited than me about pretty much everything, for which she thinks I'm rubbish) but can't talk for long, so I don't tell her about the GTT results.

The thing is, I don't really know what to feel about the possibility of CFRD. What confuses me is that the perception of people being diagnosed with diabetes is that a massive blow and in some ways the end of life as they know it. Just think how many "Oh God, I've got diabetes" stories you see in medical dramas and other TV shows. Just this week, K and I watched an episode of Brothers and Sisters, the new Channel 4 show, in which the family's life crumbles around a daughter's diabetes diagnosis.

But at the same time, I know plenty of people – many of my friends – who have diabetes and CFRD and it makes no apparent difference to their lives. There are countless stories of people doing all sorts of things through diabetes – take Steve Redgrave, who won an Olympic medal while dealing with it.

So it seems like it shouldn't be that big a deal, but at the same time I think my mind has been programmed into thinking it's a nightmare.

I certainly don't relish the thought of yet more drugs and treatments and things to think about during the day, but as Lisa said on the phone today, it may explain why recovery times seem to be longer at the moment. Perhaps getting my blood sugars under control – if indeed they are out of control, which we still don't know for sure – will open the door to a more full-on recovery and bring back other little aspects of life I'd given up on for the time being, like popping out to the shops.

I suppose the biggest problem with having not very much to do all day is that it gives you a lot of time to dwell – to think on things for far too long, when in an otherwise active life, you'd have busied yourself with something that takes your mind off it. When you feel so short of energy that you can't engage with anything, your mind is free to take itself off to all sorts of places you'd rather it didn't go.

So I'm deciding for myself tonight that I will go to bed not focusing on the "maybes" of dubious GTT results, and instead relish the thought of *finally* getting to match Emily by hitting the National Press. OK, I'm a long way behind her in media stardom for now, but I've got much more in my tank yet. Just you watch…

A desire to do

Saturday 14 July

What seems to consume me more than anything else at the moment is an overwhelming desire to "do" something – anything really. I spend so much of my time sitting around, either watching TV or surfing the internet looking for articles and information which may interest, entertain or educate me that I just crave the normality of "doing" something.

It doesn't help that my favourite films and TV shows are ones showing people with high-powered, mile-a-minute jobs that demand 100% attention from them at all hours of the day. I think I'm a frustrated workaholic. There's so much I want to be doing which I just can't do because my energy reserves are lower than an Iraqi oil refinery once the US has taken it's "share" from the depot.

It's one of the sillier frustrations with my life and I suppose it's only natural when one is confined within the same four walls 24/7 with barely a break for air. I guess it's also the attraction of being well enough not to have to think about whether I've got enough energy or if I'm well enough to do a job or make a trip or take a meeting – a pleasure I've not enjoyed for a good few years now.

When I think about it, my situation now isn't all that different to how it was a few years ago it's just that all my timescales have telescoped. Whereas when I was at work I had to think about whether I had enough energy to do something on both Tuesday and Wednesday, I now have to wonder whether I can do something at 10am *and* 11am. All that's changed is the timescale and the size of the task.

When you look at it like that, it takes away a touch of the rougher side of life. It's all too easy to dwell on the things you miss most when you're pretty much invalided out of life. But making the fight seem familiar somehow lessens the blow and makes things more comprehensible, even if it doesn't necessarily make them any better.

It's all about perception – something I know I've written about on here more than once – and the advantage of perception is also its curse, namely that it's easy to have when you're feeling OK, but it's the first thing to abandon you when you start to slide backwards.

Here's hoping I can cling to this little slice of perceptive thinking for at least a few days and keep myself in an upbeat mood. I much prefer me when I'm like this.

Clean hair, no breath

Monday 16 July

My days seem to get more and more roller-coaster-y by the week.

Take today:

Woke up this morning and no sooner had I taken Neve off and got out of bed than I was struggling for breath and feeling distinctly uncomfortable, not helped by a significant amount of back pain, a repercussion I'm sure of sleeping in a slightly more propped up position last night.

With regards to my sleeping habits, it seems I can't win. Going to bed breathless, as I did last night, demands a more upright sleeping position, or at least having my head and chest raised a little further than I would otherwise choose to sleep. While this eases the breathlessness and causes less problems with waking up coughing in the night, it plays havoc with my back, which I think ends up slightly unnaturally curved. But I digress.

I managed to struggle through some breakfast, which I have to admit was a bit of a chore, and I laboured my way through sorting out and taking my nebs before taking myself back to bed to read, where I felt most comfortable, both for my chest and my back.

At 11.30am, I spoke to the lovely journalist feature writer from the Mirror for about 45 minutes and far from ending up breathless, I seemed to get stronger as the interview went on – completely bizarre and totally the wrong way round.

It was a great interview, covering a lot of my life and progression over the last few years up to talking about the present day and the Mirror's One in a Million campaign. It was funny talking to a journalist and constantly second-guessing how she was going to write it up; I was very wary of not saying something which she could infer to mean something else.

Asking me what I thought about people who hadn't signed up, I was trying to explain how frustrating it is that so many people are in favour of donation without actually signing the register, but without saying it's frustrating, as the last thing I want is to be portrayed as accusing the country of not caring about organ donation or other people's lives. She asked me if I felt "let down" by those people and I had to hastily back-track over what I'd said to make sure that wasn't the impression I was giving.

I'd never say I felt let down by people not signing the register, but it does seem like such a waste that there are people who's organs could be used that aren't simply because they've never taken that step to make people aware of their wishes.

That said, there's an awful lot more to increasing organ

donation than merely signing up more people to the donor register. The Sunday Times ran a front page piece talking about the Opt-Out system yesterday, which on paper is a great idea for increasing the number of organs donated. But in practice, it still requires a huge investment in the NHS infrastructure and we still need to look into the education and training of NHS staff to make sure that the system is optimised. Simply changing the way in which consent is acquired won't be enough.

Back from my rather lengthy segue, I found myself feeling much brighter after the interview and managed physio and nebs before heading to bed for a bit more rest and reading.

By mid-afternoon, I had recovered sufficiently to get out of the house for half an hour to run an errand with K, which was a really nice change of scene. Although I was tired when I got back, it was nice to get out and enjoy a little bit of the nice weather.

This evening, things have swung back a little the other way. In preparation for the photographer from the Mirror coming round tomorrow, I decided to have a shower to wash my hair and boy was that a bad idea.

The problem with a shower over a bath is that it's very hard to wear oxygen in the shower, with wires hanging all over the place and water running over your face, and even harder to wash your hair with specs over your ears, so I tend not to wear it. Tonight's shower was, I think, one of the single most uncomfortable breathing experiences I've ever had.

It's not that I was dramatically out of breath – not panting or gasping for air – but more that I just couldn't seem to get enough air into my lungs to keep me going. The whole thing from start to finish probably took me about 3 minutes and it was horrible. By the time I finished I had to climb out and sit down in the bathroom for a good 10 minutes to recover myself. Not nice.

Still, now I'm fresh and ready for the snapping man and I have very little to do between now and then, so I can try to make myself comfortable and chill out a little for the evening. Hopefully my breathlessness will be under control tonight, so I can sleep in a more back-friendly position, but we'll have to wait and see what my chest rollercoaster throws up for me tonight.

Media Whirlwind

Wednesday 18 July

Crikey, what a busy few days it's been around here – I'm exhausted (although feeling much better for having spent most of the day tucked up in bed).

After my interview with the lovely Mirror lady on Monday, I spent the day not doing too much thanks to strangely wavering energy levels. However, we were starting to get wind of the rumour that Professor Liam Donaldson, Britain's Chief Medical Officer, was to announce his intention to push for an Opt-Out system of organ donation in his speech on the current state of the NHS.

Indeed, by Monday evening, two members of the Live Life Then Give Life campaign had either been interviewed on BBC Radio 5 Live (Jen) or been booked for silly-o'clock in the morning on GM:TV (Emily – "friend of the show").

I woke on Tuesday morning and stumbled into the lounge to flip through my recording of GM:TV (as if I'm going to be up to watch her at 6.20 in the morning – I love her, but not that much…) and catch her 2 (yes, two, she's THAT important) appearances on the show – well, technically two shows, as they switch presenters halfway through.

Calm and collected as ever – in fact, more calm and collected than the presenter at one point, who looked like he was about to jump up and hug her – Emily talked through all her experiences and the tale of her transplant, which I think she now has lodged away in a part of her brain which runs on autopilot when someone says "So, you waited two years for a Transplant, then what happened…?".

Then, no sooner had I caught up with our little missy's escapades than I had 5 Live on the phone wondering if I'd go on their show in 20 minutes to discuss what Liam Donaldson had just said about Organ Donation.

Now, being the intelligent, media-savvy gent that I am, having graciously bitten their hand off to get on the show, I thought I'd use my 20 minutes for research and go and check what Prof D (as I like to call him) had said.

What 5 Live had failed to tell me was that he had *literally just said it*. Like, as they were talking to me, he was talking. The upshot being *nowhere*, not even the newswires, had *any* of the text of his speech nor did anyone appear to be showing any coverage of it.

Reassured that he had, in fact, called for the Opt-Out system to be introduced, I jumped onto Matthew Bannister's phone-in show (but as an invited guest, you understand, not just Joe Public calling in from his car on the M6…) to put across the perspective of someone awaiting transplant.

Which I did. It was fun. I was quite good.

And so the day moved on and I sat about and read a bit and watched telly a bit and ate some food and did other sitting-about-type things with not a care in the world (almost).

Until just before 6pm when I get a call from a very jolly sounding young guy at the BBC saying, "My you've been busy today, I see you did 5 Live earlier,". I didn't have much of a response other than to say, "Er, yes."

"Would you be free to do News 24 at 9 o'clock from Northampton? We'll send a car."

Well, clearly, being the media-monkey that I am, I nearly fell out of my chair, but it turned out I was sitting on the sofa, so I just sort of fell sideways onto more cushions, which is a lot more pleasant than falling off a chair. And less painful.

Strangely, though, I didn't bite his hand off this time. I asked for 10 minutes to make a couple of phone calls before I confirmed it with him.

You see, I was wondering to myself whether or not this was a sensible idea. 9pm is quite late and Northampton is more than half-an-hour away. That meant that at the best guess I'd be out of the house until at least 10pm, and I know that my chest often starts playing up in the evenings.

Was it sensible to go gallivanting off of an evening, when I'd had a rocky couple of days anyway and didn't know how my chest would react? Should I be letting my thirst for stardom over-rule my sensible medical head?

So I phoned Mum, because she always agrees with me and I knew she'd tell me that it wasn't a good plan and that I was being a very sensible boy staying at home, even though it felt a bit deflating. I got her on her mobile in Tesco, where I could hardly hear her. I managed to get through and explain the situation.

"Brilliant – you should absolutely go! It'll be brilliant and you've got nothing to do tomorrow so you can stay in bed all day."

Right. That rather changed the perspective on things. So, my angel and devil still warring on my shoulders, I spoke to Jolly BBC

Guy again and accepted his offer, arranged the car to get me at 8.15 and sat and waited.

When you've done as many radio interviews as I have now, both in the studio and on the phone, both live and pre-recorded, you tend to get a small smattering of nerves which remind you you're doing something cool but don't get in the way. When you do TV pre-records like I've done a couple of times, there's no nerves, because you know you can keep going over and over the same thing until you're happy with what you've said.

When you're doing *live* TV – for the *first time* – on the BBC.... Well, that's a whole other bucket of kippers.

And when you've got 2 hours to sit and wait and work yourself up, that's an even larger vat of cod.

Suffice to say that by the time I was perched precariously on a semi-stool in front of a lonely looking video camera in the corner of the main office at BBC Radio Northampton, listening to News 24 down an ear-piece far too large for my ear, waiting for the presenters to talk to me, I thought I was going to throw up. And I was thinking how stupid I'd look to the gallery of TV Directors and Producers watching my video feed if I just leant forward and spewed on my feet.

Still, I managed not to, which is nice, and I turned out to be reasonably coherent in the interview. I only know that because I watched it back when I got home. The adrenaline rush was so huge that I can hardly remember any of the interview itself from being live and have no idea what I actually said.

All I do remember is stumbling through my last answer after my ear-piece pinged out of my ear halfway through, leaving me with my mouth moving and words coming out whilst my brain is busy screaming, "I hope they don't ask me any more questions because I'm not going to be able to hear a thing!". Turns out that my mouth is pretty good when left to it's own devices, because I somehow continued to make sense and moments later heard an ever-so-faint, "Thanks for coming on" somewhere vaguely in the region of my left ear and I thankfully realised the interview was over.

For what it's worth, it was 10.30pm by the time I got in and I've slept through a lot of today, or sat in bed reading, but it was definitely worth it. I loved doing it and am still totally addicted to the media. I think it may have inflated my ego a little much, though, because far too many people have been far too complimentary about it.

Still, just to inflate myself a little bit more, the feature piece on me in the Mirror is going in tomorrow (Thursday 19th July), so I'll get to see that, too.

If you're going to check it out, be warned that being a tabloid piece, and being part of the One in a Million campaign that the Mirror is running, it's likely to focus a lot on the negative side of things. I've not seen it, so I don't know for sure, but from previous experience I'm sure it's going to be a heart-string tugger, so if you're feeling fragile, steer clear.

Dropped

Thursday 19 July

So how many phone calls/emails/texts have I received today to tell me I'm not actually in the Mirror? OK, actually only about 5, but that's not the point.

You work feverishly to have such a rubbish quality of life that it merits the attention of a national newspaper, manage to persuade your nearest and dearest that they should be happy to pose for a picture for millions of people to see when they normally balk at a family snap, tell the whole world (possible exaggeration) that you're going to be in the paper and then it turns out you're not.

Feeling foolish? I certainly am.

Honestly, they really did call me to tell me I was going to be in it today. I won't say they promised, because that would be a lie and also, let's face it, who expects tabloid papers to keep their promises nowadays?

Still, they are a very friendly bunch (the two of them I've actually spoken to, and the lovely photographer who came round), so I'll not hold it against them and I'm sure it'll go into an issue soon. The trouble being, of course, that by the time I know it's in that day's paper, it'll be too late to let most people know. You win some and others get away from you, I guess. (There must be a more pithy way to say that…)

I've spent today almost entirely in bed again, still catching up from the whirlwind of Tuesday, but still grateful for the chance to do what I did and very much glad I didn't opt-out – thanks Mum!

Although there's no official statistics yet for the number of people signing up to the organ donor register recently, I've been reliably informed through a source that there was a huge boost in numbers attempting to sign up through the organ donor website and the telephone line.

Once official figures are confirmed, I'll be sure to pass them on here, but on initial inspection it looks like through National Transplant Week and the hubbub of Prof D's announcement earlier in the week has really driven home the message of organ donation and its importance.

This is no time for complacency, though, and we must continue to encourage as many people as we can to sign up to the register. The Opt-Out system, even if it does get through Parliament (which it failed to do just three years ago), more than likely won't be in place for at least another couple of years. Without more people signing on to the organ donor register, people like me, Robyn, Jen and thousands of others face losing their lives for the want of a donor.

Although the press spent a lot of time and energy focusing on the Opt-Out portion of Prof D's report, the full text reveals a true grasp of the infrastructure, education and training needs of the transplant system if it is to improve, not just the need to find more donors.

It's encouraging to see that all the necessary issues have been flagged up and that hopefully they will receive the attention they urgently require. As the system improves so, hopefully, will donor rates and less people will die needlessly waiting for their second chance.

I'll leave you with the most pertinent section of the report, from our current position. If you haven't signed the register, take two minutes and do it now. If you have signed the register, why not use the two minutes to send an email to someone who may not have and encourage them not to wait for Opt-Out, but to use their autonomy and Opt-In.

"Increasing participation in the NHS Organ Donor Register is critical to improving the current poor position. Targeted campaigns, including options at the time of issuing of drivers' licences, at general practice registration and in the commercial sector, such as via the Boots Advantage Card application, have led to an increase of people on the NHS Organ Donor Register. Such ways of increasing sign-up should continue to be devised and applied."

I said that

Friday 20 July

It's interesting when you do interviews for newspapers, because you never quite know how they're going to turn out. My experience up to now has been limited to the odd local newspaper reporter giving me a buzz on the phone and doing a bit of a catch-up to expand on a press release they've received and the ensuing article rarely bares much semblance to the truth, or to what I said.

What with the perception of the tabloid newspapers in this country for sensationalism and tarting things up, I wasn't holding out too much hope of seeing my views expressed in the article due in the Daily Mirror.

Imagine my surprise, and yes, my guilty and grudging admission that I was wrong, when I opened today's Mirror to find not only a brilliantly written appeal for organ donors through their One in a Million campaign, but also the bare minimum of sensationalism in my story. Every quote that is attributed to me, I actually said – that's something I've never experienced before!

It's great to see organ donation being pushed more and more into people's consciousness. As I said yesterday, we need to keep encouraging people to sign up and make a difference. In fact, if everyone who said they supported organ donation actually signed the organ donor register, we wouldn't need drastic measures like the Opt-Out system.

Weekend

Monday 23 July

It's been an up-and-down few days (when isn't it, these days), but more up than down.

The trouble is, this evening I feel so tired and my back is causing me so much bother that try as I might, I'm struggling to pin-point the highs and lows of the last few days.

A definite high was seeing K's big niece, little niece and nephew, all of whom I haven't seen for ages. It was nice to see their dad, too, although even nicer of him to go get us a paper (thanks, Rob!).

I managed a good hour or so of fairly sedate entertainment, leaving K to do most of the running around and baby-chasing as little Jack set off exploring the wonders of the un-baby-proofed apartment. Having palmed off the high-maintenance duties to K, I settled myself with a game of chess and a bit of a story book/CBeebies magazine, which is much more my kind of pace. Although chess with a 1-year-old knocking about is a far more defensive game.

The rest of Sunday was gainfully employed resting, although we did pop over to my 'rents for some food in the evening. The trouble is it's such a long way away now (yes, 20 minutes' drive is a long way now) that to avoid being a dangerous, half-asleep driver on the way home, we literally only get to swoop in for food and then run away. I know parents are parents and they don't mind things like that, but it does bother me how anti-social we can be.

I suppose it's one more thing to look forward to post-transplant: those long, leisurely Sunday lunches which start at lunchtime and roll on to dinner time with a good deal of laughing and chatting in the middle. Another thing to add to my "To Do's".

Saturday was very quiet, resting up at the promise of baby visits on Sunday, and expecting a slightly fuller day of visitors were it not for the odd drunken mishap changing plans around. (No names.)

Today started really well after a bad night's sleep. I woke feeling surprisingly spritely and sat reading for a while before showering (*with* my oxygen!) and doing physio and finally getting through the few pieces of copy I had to write to finish off this issue of CF Talk. We should now be at a final proof stage, which I should receive in the next few days, and I can check it, correct the mistakes, sign off the whole thing and get it out.

This afternoon has seen a bit of a down-turn, with my chest getting a bit tighter and me more breathless, with a slow onset of not only a headache but a good deal of back pain, too.

As I write, I'm about to whisk myself off to bed to see if I can settle myself and sort it out, before trying to get an early night's sleep for a change. I could really do with a good, long night's kip. Here goes...

My mini library

Tuesday 24 July

I've come to the conclusion that if I'm going to be sitting around on my rump for the greater part of the passing days, then I might at least put the working parts of my body to good use and exercise my eyes and brain by learning some new stuff.

So in a spirit of adventure, I have embarked upon devouring the full 800-odd closely-typed pages of a biography of Churchill written by a man so famous that his name eludes me and shall continue to do until I clamber into bed this evening, seeing as I'm not inclined to rise myself from my typing post to go and check it now.

(The thought has just occurred to me that I could check the author's name on Amazon, and even provide a link to said biography, save for the very important fact that it would interrupt my flow and my stream-of-consciousness would become merely a trickle.)

It's heavy going, for sure, and I'm only managing about a chapter a day – any more and I don't think I'd take any of it on board – but it's fascinating stuff. He was quite an impressive bloke that Churchill, not just bowler hats and cigars, you know.

I'm also working my way through the Alastair Campbell Diaries, which are just as fascinating, albeit in a very different way. They're much more easy to read and digest, too and being in daily-diary format (my personal preference for historical/biographic material) are much easier to pick up and put down.

I say easier to pick up, actually they're mildly hard since they're about the same number of pages, but in hardback not softcover, making Alastair Campbell more weighty than Churchill and I bet that's not something oft said.

Given the political bent to my current reading, I have developed something of an obsession with it over the past few weeks and have additionally to my real-world reading, spent a lot of today online learning all about the parliamentary process and goings on in the Houses of Parliament.

They say you learn something new everyday, which is undoubtedly true, but by my judgement, I can after today go for the next eight and a half weeks without learning a thing and still hit my average for the quarter.

Other than that, I've not done much today. Harefield tomorrow – I'm going to lobby them with my newfound political powers to bump me up to the top of the list and get my butt-sittery days behind me.

Foot in Mouth

Thursday 26 July

I like to think that I'm a nice guy – I'm friendly, jocular (wow – now *that's* a pretentious sounding word when you put it down in black-and-white), fairly unimposing generally and keen to get on with people. I'm also always keen to make a good impression when I meet people.

Imagine my dismay – nay, my horror – at putting my foot so spectacularly in mouth that I could almost taste my kneecaps. Not only that, but doing it with one of the lovely, friendly, wonderful and caring transplant coordinators, in whose hands – more or less – my life may rest.

The coordinators at Harefield (there are 4 of them) have changed around over the last year or so, meaning that I've actually only met 2 of them in person. I've spoken to all of them and know them to talk to, but it's still very different meeting someone in person.

So it was a delight to meet one of the disembodied voices at the clinic I went to yesterday. In fact, she even shared my sentiments, telling me, "It's nice to put a face to a name – to finally get to meet the person you know down a phone line."

How lovely. Being the self-depreciating chap that I am, I countered with a swift, "I'm always a bit disappointing, though."

Only I didn't. The first word didn't actually appear to emerge from my mouth when it should have been the most prominent part of the sentence, leaving merely, "Always a bit disappointing."

It was one of those wonderful moments when you realise you've sunk yourself so deep into a giant well of not-very-niceness, when your stomach lurches and your brain races to catch up to say something to hurriedly recover the situation, but all the while you just know that nothing you can say is going to make it sound any better.

I drifted off into a daze of internal arguments with myself of how best to back-track, while the vast majority of my head is telling me not to say anything more as I'd only get more and more David Brent with every passing word.

By this time, of course, I look like I've just hurled and insult and shut up shop – even better! Not only do I knock the lovely lady down, but then ignore her completely.

I tell you something, my brain is in a LOT of trouble, not to mention my mouth for running off and starting the whole escapade before it's communicated properly with the up top.

Cringe-worthy introductions aside – and ignoring the fact that I spent the majority of my trip to Harefield yesterday waiting (appropriate, I suppose, given the subject of the visit and the hospital) – it actually went rather well. I think they could see that I'm no where near as well as I was last time I saw them and probably consider me a more important/urgent case than perhaps was their perception before they caught up with me for my review yesterday.

So, provided the mortified coordinator (who shall remain firmly nameless) hasn't sent a memo round telling everyone that I'm the last person on earth who should be given a second chance, I'm hopeful that my habit of getting through things almost exactly 6-months behind our Emily means that I'm due my new blowers any day now.

We can but hope.

Third time (un)lucky

Saturday 28 July

I'm not entirely sure what day it is today. I'm fairly confident it's Saturday because there's more sport and less Richard and Judy on TV, but as far as I'm aware it could just as easily be Tuesday week.

I've suffered something of a lack of sleep over the last few days and my body clock is so far out of synch I could be in Australia. All thanks to my third aborted transplant call.

Aborted call, false alarm, non-go-ahead shout, call it what you will, it was my third foray down to Harefield in the middle of the night to be pricked, plugged and prepped for an op that never came.

This one was, however, at least mildly entertainingly different, being as I was a "back-up" recipient for the first time in my 3 calls. The previous two times it has happened, I've been right ready to receive the lungs when it was decided they were no good. This time, I was second in line to someone waiting (at another hospital) for both heart and lungs, which obviously come best as a package. Should there have been anything wrong with the heart or should there have been any reason the other recipient was unable to go ahead with the operation, I would have received the lungs.

This meant a very different thought process for me from the last times I was on ward F East, nervously waiting to be told if they were good enough or not. This time, I was convinced from the moment I spoke to the T-C, Julie, at just after 11pm that it would not be my night. Which lead, inevitably, to a *very* boring 5-hour wait in a room on the ward to be told that I wouldn't be heading to theatre.

The saving grace of the whole night was the comforting knowledge that the heart had been fine and the heart and lungs were being transplanted into the original recipient on the list. Not only did it mean that at least someone's life was being transformed in the early commuter hours of Friday morning, but that the organs of a lost loved one were being put to the greatest use possible and that perhaps in days or weeks to come their family may draw some comfort from that fact.

As it happened, all the whole experience meant for me was an entire night with no sleep whatsoever, which in turn lead to sleeping from 7.30am (when we finally arrived home in the morning on Friday) until 2pm and sitting through the rest of the eternally-dragging day feeling beyond terrible, hardly able to lift myself from the bed to drink some water, let alone contemplate eating or doing anything more energetic like watching TV.

It was pretty horrible, to be honest, and a mark of how much my body now struggles to cope with the unexpected. Without a night's sleep to rest up and repair some of the daily damage, my body was truly struggling to cope and wasn't backward in coming forward about it – it was making more than sure I knew about it.

Things are better today, after a sensible night's sleep, although the tiredness is still pervasive and I could do with a kip every half-hour. I'm sure after another day in bed and another good night's sleep I'll be back where I was before.

And at least this time I managed a whole 6 hours at Harefield without mortally offending someone.

Not angry any more

Tuesday 31 July

You know that noise you make when a sigh turns into something slightly more expressive, your lips vibrate and it comes out a little like a horse sneezing when you feed it? I just did that and got spit on my keyboard. That's pretty much the day I've had today.

Some days you wake up and you just know it was a bad idea to even think about having a day today. Much better to just curl in a ball on the bed and forget about life for the next 24 hours until it's the next day on the calendar and you can expansively cross it off with an enormous flourish. That was my day today.

Some days, no matter how little you do, how hard you try, how many physio sessions and nebulisers you do, how much resting and relaxing you do, your chest still won't listen and insists on reacting as if you've just come running full pelt down the Mall at a sprint after the other 26.1 miles of the streets of London at a similar pace. That's been my day today.

Luckily, the anger has subsided, replaced this morning by a heavily-weighted black cloud which hung around like flood waters in Gloucestershire and only shimmered to a dissipated mist in mid-afternoon when my big bro descended on the flat for coffee and a catch up.

Of course, it's all relative, these mood swings, as it was partially my brother's return to town that had brought on the downturn in the first place. Before you get the wrong idea, I love my brother very much and I love having him around. It's more the reminder of how far downhill I've come that bothers me.

It used to be that when my bro swung into town it was cause for a family night out – a nice restaurant, everyone else getting drunk, me as designated driver, a chance to catch up on gossip, share stories and take the mickey out of Mum for not making any sense.

But this time all the fun will be had without me, the stories shared around a 3-seater table instead of 4. And it's not that I begrudge them that, nor that I would want them to come over to mine and have a take-away or do something at Mum and Dad's, because whatever it is, I know I'm not up to it. That's what really pulls.

Tonight the anger and frustration has ebbed away into a dull resignation. There seems no other way of putting it than propping your head in your hands and sighing with that little bit extra expression where your lips vibrate and it comes out a little like a horse sneezing when you feed it. If only I could spell it.

August 2007
(3 Months)

A Good Day

Thursday 2 August

I was back in Oxford today for the second half of my annual review and surprisingly, given the distinctly non-positive vibe that I've been getting from recent hospital visits, I actually came away feeling good today.

The diabetes tests looked clear – or at least not significantly abnormal; my blood sugars remained pretty much within the normal range consistently for the last couple of weeks while I've been measuring them, which was a good start.

Even better, though, was my conversation with my consultant, the ever-wonderful Dr Bennett, who is encouraged by my progress since June.

I've been more and more breathless recently and it's started to impact more and more on what I can and can't do (as you're no doubt aware if you've been following along). Raising it with the team today I was fully expecting downcast looks and a feeling of, "that's pretty much where you are now," and facing a determination to put up with it and keep fighting.

To my immense pleasure and surprise, Doc B felt that it's something we can tackle, given the right effort and application and can aim to improve my breathlessness and stamina and bring my quality of life back up.

Looking at my health in general since my downturn in June, she suggested that although I'd had a really bad month and the infection had hit me very hard, it was encouraging to see that my lung function had pretty much returned to what it was pre-exacerbation – about 0.8./1.3 (actually dropping slightly to 0.7/1.2 today, but I was expecting that, and to go on IV's, anyway). What this indicates is that the infection, whilst making me seriously ill, doesn't appear to have any lasting impact on the conditioning in my lungs.

What has been affected, clearly, is my exercise tolerance and muscle mass, both significantly weakened by spending the whole month in bed and by not being worked on in the four weeks or so since. It is Doc B's belief that if we can work out an exercise plan, with extra oxygen support as necessary, and work to improve my cardio-vascular fitness, there's no reason we can't combat the breathlessness.

This was all news too me – good news, to be sure, but news all the same. I had resigned myself, I think, to the downward slope of things ahead and didn't really think there was much of a way around it. So it feels pretty great to be told not only that there's potential improvement around, but that the docs actually feel like it's achievable.

Clearly, it's not going to mean a massive turn around, but if I can raise my tolerance levels enough to manage a trip out of the house a little more often, maybe a stroll around Borders once in a while, it'll make a big difference to keeping my spirits up.

It's doubtless going to be a really hard slog and I don't quite know how I'm going to deal with it at the moment. I've never really pushed myself hard through exercise and I've no doubt that whatever program I'm given, whilst laughably pitiful for regular mortals, is going to be a hell of a job for me.

But when you're facing the months ahead that I'm facing, I suppose motivation should be too much of a factor – after all, my entire life right now is focused on stretching things out as long as I can until that call comes. If doing 5 minutes of step ups a couple of times a day is going to help achieve that, I can learn to tolerate the gasping and rasping that comes with it.

A Great Day

Friday 3 August

You know, living from day to day gives a weird perspective on life. I've said it before and doubtless I'll have plenty of opportunity to say it again in the future, but this bumpy road called life certainly throws up a few of those Yank-loved curveballs.

Today, I've done hardly anything more than I have done for the last three weeks – I took K to work (possible on a good day, not an exceptional event), I worked on the computer (and have just remembered the one thing I had to do that I forgot to – hooray for me), I had a cup of tea with my Mum (she was having withdrawal symptoms, so had to swing by on her way off for the weekend) and went for a bit of a drive in the sunshine when I picked K up from work, which is about the only difference to my days of the last month or so.

But I did all of this while feeling absolutely brilliant. My chest felt open and clearer than it has in ages, I only stopped to grab my breath a couple of times in the whole day. At no point did I get overwhelmed by tiredness and I didn't have to have a snooze after my afternoon dose of drugs. It would not be an over-statement to say that today I've felt amazing.

It's all relative, I know, and compared to "normal" people, or even to how I was six months ago, it's probably not much cop – I'm certainly not bounding up staircases or thinking about giving my oxygen the heave-ho – but to spend a day without the burden and weight of lugging around a stroppy chest and cloudy head has been truly indescribable.

(There's an irony here about an entire blog entry trying to describe something that I can only describe as indescribable. Maybe there's a hint at how I can cut down my word counts, too…)

I'm also aware that this feeling may not last for long. By tomorrow, the updraft could have floated away on the breeze and I'll be gliding gracefully back down to sofa-dom, but interestingly I think it's made me appreciate and enjoy today all the more. I have so many truly rubbish days these days that to have even a sniff of a good one is beyond compare.

If it goes a little way to making this journey a little smoother, to making me a little happier, to making these blowers last a little longer, then I can plough through the rough and enjoy the hell out of the smooth.

Tonight, aided by *Happy Feet* (go rent it now, it's brilliant) and the unmistakable rhythm of life, my heart and my head are vibrating with the energy of the world and an old African proverb has just sprung into my head:

"If you can walk, you can dance
If you can talk, you can sing."

Let the sun shine, let the music play, let the world spin on and don't let it stop. In the words of a much wiser lady than I, "This is my life and I choose to love it".

Nothing at all

Tuesday 7 August

It's been a gorgeous few days here in the haven of middle England that I call my home – sunny, hot, beautiful skies and all the other things that come with summer, but no wasps, bees or semi-naked men parading their non-tans. No, wait, that last bit's not entirely true...

Still, I've been feeling great and much perkier than I have for a long time. The steroids are clearly doing the trick and have certainly ramped up my appetite, which can only be a good thing. The IV's are having an impact, too, I'm sure, although not as marked, largely due to the fact that I didn't wait for a full-blown, raging infection to get started on them this time and they're doing brilliantly at damping down what is already lurking in my lungs, as opposed to being deployed as a reaction-force.

Yesterday I had the pleasure of being well enough to take myself over to Mum and Dad's to have lunch with my bro before he shot off on holiday to Bulgaria for a couple of weeks. Clearly travel with the Army isn't enough for him, so he's off to see some of the Eastern European summer before he shoots off on more international travel masquerading as "training exercises".

It was really nice to be able to drive myself to the other side of town, hang out for a couple of hours and drive myself home without feeling more exhausted than someone who's really exhausted from doing something really exhausting all day. Nice metaphor, huh?

I've been trying to actually get some work done while I've been feeling good, too, but somehow I seem to have achieved nothing in that area. I think I've been enjoying having a clear head and chest so much I've either been out and about "doing" things or been surfing the net catching up on all the mildly brain-working sites I like to browse but often don't have the brain-energy to absorb them.

I think tomorrow I might ban myself from the Internet and do a bit of project focusing for a while. Although having said that, I know I've got a physio appointment in Oxford to go over my exercise regime in the afternoon, so I'll probably convince myself that I should be allowed to relax and surf the net in the morning because the afternoon will be hard work.

I've got to admit, though, it's really nice to be in a position where I'm chiding myself for not working enough, rather than sitting feeling crappy wishing I could get up out of bed or off the sofa to do some of the things I want to do. I just need to use that feeling to inspire me into actually getting something done...

94%

Wednesday 8 August

I'm now mid-way through my course of IV's (provided I'm only on for 2 weeks, which is always a big "if") and I was back up to Oxford today for a check on how things are going, some mid-point bloods and an exercise session.

As I mentioned in my post about my annual review here, the docs think that if I can get myself doing some exercise and building some of the muscle mass I've lost over the last few months, I'll stand a much better chance of keeping my lungs ticking over for a while longer than they may first have predicted.

Apart from the exercise (which I'll come to in a bit), the most amazing thing to come out of today were my oxygen saturation levels – the amount of O2 that gets transferred into the blood stream to be carried around the oxygen. I know I've been feeling brighter and fitter over the last few days, but nothing prepared me for the physio clipping the monitor to my finger this afternoon.

Normal sats levels run between 99-100% and back when I was off O2 and doing well a couple of years ago – and for a good while before then – I used to run fairly steadily about 96-97%. Recently, even with my constant flow of 2 litres of oxygen per minute being shoved up my nose, I've usually topped out at 89%. That's pretty low. OK, very low.

Imagine my surprise, then (I seem to say that a lot on here, so I guess all you guys who stay with me and continue to read this must have a pretty good imagination by now) when I perched on the bed on the ward today and saw my sats hit 94% at rest for the first time in well over 4 months.

I was totally gobsmacked. I have to admit it was totally beyond my wildest dreams that I could or would recover the function that I'd lost, having convinced myself I'd waved it goodbye for this set of billows. Even my physio seemed a little startled by it, but she said she didn't see why we couldn't maintain or even improve them with the right exercise programme.

Obviously, it's not exactly Olympic standard – I don't even need any gym equipment, unless you count the beautiful, girly-pink dumbbells they had me using for my bicep curls – but it's something which gets my heart-rate going and will hopefully strengthen some of my core muscle groups and increase my general exercise tolerance.

The programme consists of a "cardio" set (in quotation marks as it's not exactly pushing my maximum heart-rate) to build endurance and "weights" set (in quotation marks because all but one of the exercises actually uses body weight and nothing more) to strengthen my arms and legs, the areas which take the biggest hit during any period of inactivity.

The endurance set is a very simple 5-6 minutes of step-ups onto a low stair, broken up into 1-minute reps with 30 seconds recovery in between. The aim is to increase the time by 30 seconds every couple of days until I reach a comfortable but taxing plateau, repeating the set every day.

The strengthening set consists of several different extension exercises, including leg-lifts, quad stretches, hip movement and arm/shoulder lifts. The idea is to do 3 sets of 8-10 reps of each of the exercises three times a week – so Monday, Wednesday and Friday, I should think.

I'm actually really psyched about being presented with something that I can do to help myself. For so long now I've felt like a passenger on this ride. I know that doing nebs and physio everyday is a big part of fighting off the avalanche of attackers busying themselves in my chest, but this finally feels like I have a chance to do something to take the bull by the horns and drag myself back up the slope. (And on the way up I'll find some more weird metaphors to mix, too).

It remains to be seen just how good I am at staying motivated when things get tough and I'm tired, aching and stressed out, but everything has to start somewhere, so it might as well be on a high. If I can just help to turn this into a habit, then maybe it'll become as second nature to me as nebs and physio are at the moment.

Needless to say, I'll be doing my best to use the blog as an exercise diary, so I can be applauded or chided as necessary to spur me on.

(PS – for the record, my lung function mid-IV's is at 0.8/1.5, which is actually better than it was at the END of my previous set of IV's)

Step forward fitter me

Thursday 9 August

I'm off to a flying start. Well, I suppose it's more of a stepping start, really, but isn't there an old Chinese saying, "Every great journey begins with a single step?" and I did, like, at least 30 and a half steps today, so I must be really well started on my great journey, even if I do have to go back and start again because I forgot my GPS and Satnav.

I woke up this morning with both my thighs telling me in great detail how they'd been brought rather rudely out of retirement yesterday without any prior warning. I suggested back to them that they might want to get used to it because there was a lot more where that came from and oddly enough they just laughed at me. Even my legs don't have any faith in me.

I didn't let it deter me, though. I resolutely soldiered on with my day – I did my morning IV's, I ate my breakfast, I sat on the sofa and read a little and I sat at the computer and surfed a little. Extremely strenuous, clearly. I also slipped back to bed to read for a bit and then do some physio and then I had some lunch. They were still moaning, mind.

In fact, I think my quads had only just stopped giggling and been lulled into a nicely false sense of security when I took the bull by the horns (yep, the same one as yesterday) and marched to the bedroom to pull out my little yellow step from under the bed.

I think I may have to work on the phrasing around my exercise equipment, or come up with a cunning euphemism for it because, let's face it, "little yellow step" is a bit pathetic isn't it? Maybe I'll christen it Goliath.

So I dragged Goliath from under the bed and I set myself up in the door frame to the living room – facing a bemused K sat at her desk "working" while trying to keep a straight face, clearly – and set off into my routine of step-ups.

10 and a bit minutes later I'd completed my prescribed 6 minutes, with 30 second breaks between rounds, and was feeling it,

too, but happily hadn't keeled over or gone dizzy. I quickly knocked back a glass of milk (fluid replacement AND calorie booster rolled into one, easy, cow-born package) and hoped that foot and mouth isn't a problem in pasteurized produce.

Goliath was kicked (sorry, hauled) to one side to wait for his return tomorrow and I sat, slightly sweaty, on the sofa with a smug look on my face with K muttering approval from behind her laptop in the vaguely-guilty-sounding voice of someone who knows they ought to be doing something similar, too. (Exercise-wise, that is, not sitting smugly on the sofa.)

Hurrah! One day down and I can feel the habit forming already. Well, kind of. OK, maybe it's not the habit I feel so much as a vaguely uncomfortable stretching of the quads, but I still did it – and did it unprompted, too.

I'm actually now so scared of people with large sticks (thanks to the comments on the previous post) that I think I've got motivation enough to last me till winter.

The big, shiny, happy birthday blog

Saturday 11 August

Tonight I am a tired boy, but it's OK to be tired because all of my energy has been expended on being wonderful and making sure my beautiful, doting, life-enhancing and gorgeous other half enjoyed the most fabulous, spoil-some birthday in the history of ever.

I even got up 30 minutes early this morning – that's a whole half of an hour, that is.

Imagine, rising from bed in tip-toe quiet fashion so as to leave the birthday girl to her beauty sleep, nipping out to the Tesco on the corner to pick up some nice, fresh croissant and fruit juice, sneaking back in and setting out all the breakfast and presents and celebrations to look lovely for when she wakes. And all before my morning IV's, too.

Of course, it doesn't always work as seamlessly as planned. Tiptoeing out of bed is all well and good, but it's hard to muffle the enormous, alarming "BUZZZZZZZZZZ" of the oxygen concentrator as it kicks to a start in the morning. I've heard teenagers make less noise when parents have tried to rouse them from their slumber during school holidays.

Still, the advantage of the concentrator in the bedroom is that while the alarm may be startling, once it's on and running the mid-level hum it generates masks out most of the noises created by banging around preparing breakfast spreads and makes sneaking out of the house a whole load easier.

Of course the easiest way to win someone's affection on a birthday is to buy them presents, so this was something I took care of some time ago and in copious quantities. I say some time ago, but being a boy what I mean is ordering them on the 'net last week. I don't want to give you some illusion of forward planning anywhere akin to the levels K works at, where she has already started assembling gifts for Christmas and people's New Year birthdays. Forward planning in my world consists of remembering that there's a day you need to remember at some point this week. This month if you're lucky.

Still, said assembly of presents appears to have been appreciated and it was brilliant to be able not only to entertain my Mum and Dad for a mid-afternoon visit (yet more presents – including ice creams for everyone: they can come again!) but also to make the self-powered trip over to K's parents' for a little birthday tea party with most of her nieces and nephews.

As delighted as I have been over the last week to be enjoying something of a return to previous heights, there's nothing that quite reinforces the value of having at least some state of health than being able to do things without having to second-guess yourself or your body.

A couple of weeks ago I wouldn't have even deigned to consider seeing both sets of parents in one day, let alone driving us all the way to K's 'rents. To be able to do it all today and to make the day so special for her is a one-in-a-million feeling and it really rams home the importance of making the most of the good days when they come along.

But enough of me – today has all been about K and making her the happiest girl she can be. I'm fairly confident we've managed to achieve it between me, our families and our ever-generous and wonderful friends.

K really is the other half of me – she's the light to my dark and the sweet to my sour, but I know that I'm just as much to her. Everything we share we share together (which is meant in a much less, "well, duh," way than it came out…) and everything we go through we go through together. Neither of us will ever know the physical struggle the other faces, or feel each other's pain, but we will always know that wherever we go and whatever we do, we have someone with us no matter what.

Happy birthday, gorgeous, don't ever stop those happy feet.

Another late-night Harefield excursion

Wednesday 15 August

I don't have much to ramble on about this morning, I'm tired and I don't think my brain is working properly.

I got another call from Harefield last night, around 6pm (the Tx-coordinator actually interrupted the end of Neighbours, the cheek!). It took me a while to grasp what she was calling about as I'd phoned her earlier and thought she was returning my call, so I was merrily chattering away to her about this, that and the other before she manage to slip into the conversation that she wanted me to go down.

It was a very different experience this time, although I can't quite put my finger on why. Feeling completely serene (at least for my part), we drove the back roads so as to avoid the rush-hour motorway traffic and got to the ward just before 8pm, where I slowly went through the battery of tests they perform to check your suitability.

For the first time on any of my calls, I saw one of the surgical team, a really nice German/Austrian doc who talked through everything with us in immense amounts of detail, which managed to be both petrifying and completely reassuring. Not quite sure how that works.

The combination of it being early evening rather than late night and the collection of tests and assessments being strung out over a longer period of time all seemed to help the time pass much quicker than on previous calls.

By 11pm I was showered, shaved and scrubbed in my gown, lying in the bed ready to go, waiting on word from the team. Almost to the second around 11.15pm I started to feel the nerves kick in and then they somewhat ran away with me. It's a strange kind of fear that I felt, centred largely on not knowing what I was going to wake up to.

Strangely, I don't have any fear of dying on the table, or post-op, nor do I particularly fear any of the rest of the process, but what bothers me is not knowing how it's going to feel and what I'm going to see when I come round the other side. Everyone reacts totally differently to the op, so it's impossible to judge by anyone else's experience how it's going to be, which in turn means there's nothing I can do to prepare.

As nervous as I was, though, I was confident in myself and my decision to go ahead with things and still excited at the prospect of my new lease of life.

Unfortunately, the coordinator came in just after midnight and let us know it was a no-go. They had apparently all had very long discussions about the suitability of the lungs, but in the end they'd had to err on the side of caution and decided it was just to dangerous to transplant them in their current state. It was odd, though, as the coordinator seemed almost as gutted as we were – I think everyone there was convinced that this was our time.

I felt completely gutted, in a very literal, physical sense – it felt like I'd been hollowed out in my stomach and left gaping. The three previous false alarms had been disappointing, but have never caused such a swelling of negative emotion in me. The journey home was a long, tough one last night.

Of course much of an adverse reaction to things like last night comes through pure tiredness – lack of sleep does all sorts of odd things to your emotions and thought processes. I know that things have to be 100% right for me to stand a decent chance of coming through things, so I know the docs are doing their best by me. I know also that they are thinking of me and will get me up whenever they can.

I still feel tired and flat this morning, but I think it just needs 24 hours of bed rest and I'll be back on all-cylinders again. Apologies for typos in this, spell checking is lower on my priority list than sitting doing nothing at the moment.

Still going…

Thursday 16 August

After almost a full 24 hours tucked away in bed sleeping off the after-effects of our 3am bedtime from Tuesday, I was back up to Oxford today to finish off my IV's and see how the exercise program appears to be working.

First of all, though, I had the morning to spend with one of my best friends who I've not seen for an age, who came around with her shears to attack my unruly barnet, which she did with considerable gusto, even tipping a small vat of bleach onto my head for 45 minutes.

To be honest I'm not entirely sure I like the result, but the thing with Lea's haircuts is that in all the time she's been doing my hair (which is about 6 years and counting now), I've never actually liked the cut or colour for the first 24 hours. I think it's because it's nearly always pretty drastic, so I'm not used to the sight that greets me in the mirror. But without fail a couple of days after I've had it done, I always LOVE it. I'm odd like that, but there you go.

We've kind of got used to each other now – she'll finish and stand back excited and happy, cooing and purring over her handiwork and I'll stare at myself in the mirror and um and aahhh over it for a while and generally be unenthusiastic. Then in a couple of days' time I'll do my hair in the morning and be straight on the phone to her to tell her how much I love it. Legend, she is.

What's more, she's one of those fantastic friends who you can go for months without seeing but pick up from exactly where you left off as soon as you're back together again. We had such a great time this morning; it really helped lift any of the remaining fug from Tuesday night.

Oxford was good again. With the steroids being tailed off – reduced by a third in the last week, and with a noticeable energy reduction – I was expecting to see a pretty big difference in the workout session with Lou the physio today. So I was pleasantly surprised again (and pleasantly surprised to be pleasantly surprised again) to get through an 8-minute step-up workout with her and see my sats stay in the optimal/safe 90% range during exercise and rising back to 93/94% at rest afterwards.

The next couple of weeks are going to be the real test of the plan's long-term prospects as I drop the IV's and begin to slowly wean myself off of the steroids. If I can keep my appetite up and give myself enough fuel to run through the programs I've got, then potentially I can keep my chest feeling stronger and clearer for longer and avoid the usual post-IV dip.

The motivation is still there, even if the energy levels are more variable. It's just a case of trying to find the right moment in each day to get the most out of my chest without leaving me exhausted for the rest of the day. It's another of those slow learning processes, but at least it's got very positive benefits to aim for and a real sense of achievement to top it off if it works.

The end-of-IV checks included looking at my lung function, which has stayed at a fairly stable 0.8/1.4, which is good if unremarkable. Mind you, I've not been over 0.8 for more than a year now, I think, so it's probably safe to say that's pretty much my ceiling now, so as long as I'm staying there and not dropping, we know things are going OK.

Although the exercise program is unlikely to improve my base lung function, the hope is that it will help out with the oxygen flow round my body and help reduce the breathlessness. We'll have to wait and see if the theory holds true, but for now, it's time to plough onwards.

Mañana Mañana

Sunday 19 August

It has occurred to me of late, rather alarmingly, that I may be turning into a middle-aged woman. Not in any real, physical sense, you understand – I'm not that weird, yet – but rather in what I like to call my "Mañana Manner".

For years I've observed that strange phenomenon in women who feel a little over-weight to protest over a long, languid Sunday roast of a dozen or so courses with free-flowing wine and truffles to finish that their diet starts "tomorrow". So many "tomorrows" are there in the world of middle-aged women that it's a wonder today ever happens at all.

Losing weight is obviously not an ideal goal for me – being the svelte 52kgs (that's 8st 2lbs in old money or 114lbs to our American cousins) I am at the moment – but I have found the "Mañana Manner" creeping into other areas of my life ever more prominently as I continue to enjoy something of an "up".

For weeks now, I've been promising myself that I will get back to the screenplay I abandoned half-finished at the back-end of May, when I was whizzing through my 6-page-per-day target almost non-stop. My birthday upset the balance at the end of the month, and then my prolonged "outage" set me even further adrift. Now, I seem to find excuse after excuse to avoid putting myself in front of the screen to finish off a piece of work I'm actually pretty happy with.

Last week didn't help, turning as it did into one of those run away weeks which sweep you up from the start and end up dumping you at the weekend with hardly a moment's pause for breath (paradoxical, I suppose, since I have hardly any breath to pause for). An aborted call in the middle of things didn't help, but I honestly could not tell you whether or not the last three days really did have their full 24 hours or if someone decided to switch us on to fast forward for a little while.

You know the sort of thing I mean: when you go to bed on Monday, wake up in the morning and it's Sunday and although you know you've been busy all week you can't for the life of you think of the things you've done.

So it was hardly a struggle to continue to find reasons not to get back to my desk, although I'm getting pretty good at that now.

It started innocently enough as a case of writer's block – reaching a mid-point in the story which needed a kick and not being able to work out where it should come from. I can't, however, really cling to that as a reason not to have confronted it in the last couple of weeks, since I sorted that problem out in my head a good couple of Monday's back.

It is much more a case of the intrusion of the "Mañana Manner" on my writing habits: I can't possibly start writing today, I've got to finish this chapter of my book first. I can't possibly start writing today, it's the middle of the week and I shan't be able to write tomorrow, so what's the point in getting into the swing of things, just to lose the flow again? I can't possibly write today, it's nearly the weekend. I can't possibly write today, it's Sunday. I can't possibly write today, there's a small black-and-white dog lurking outside my study window. I can't possibly write today, the sun isn't quite bright enough to echo the mood of the piece I'm trying to create and I'm not going to be able to find the right "zone".

It's remarkable how creative one can be in forcing oneself not to be creative.

What's more, it amused me as I thought these things through to myself as I washed-up (yes, washed-up – if that's not a sign of improvement, I don't know what is) that for someone who can procrastinate so spectacularly well around doing something I'm passionate about, how is it possible that I manage to park my butt in front of my computer to bang out nearly 1,000 words of blog most days of the week? I think my priorities may be a little skewed….

Still, the most important thing is that you've got something to read to waste 5 minutes of your day. After my transplant I'll have plenty of time to do things for myself, for now I choose to put you, dear reader, first. I'm that sort of a giving kind of person, me.

I love Studio 60

Thursday 23 August

I have an unnatural love of Aaron Sorkin. It's really not very becoming for a man of my age. I have a kind of giggly schoolgirl relationship with everything and anything he does. Oddly, though, not many people actually know who he is.

Most people have never heard of him and fewer seem to have seen his TV shows. The only thing most people know him for is *A Few Good Men*, the Tom Cruise/Demi Moore/Jack Nicholson movie, and even then most people only know it when they hear Nicholson bellowing, "You want the truth? YOU CAN'T HANDLE THE TRUTH!"

He wrote that.

He went on to create and write the immensely underrated *Sports Night*, which ran for 2 seasons and 40-odd episodes in the States a decade or so ago, starring some proper actors who went on to big things in *Six Feet Under* and *Desperate Housewives*, but never really took off. It got buried in the schedules on ABC1 over here a couple of years back, but I don't think anyone noticed it.

After that he hit the big time (at least in the States) with the unbelievably brilliant *West Wing*, probably my all-time favourite TV show and multi-Emmy award winner. Sadly, English audiences never really took to it and after the first series was broadcast to critical acclaim but rubbish ratings on Channel 4 it got shifted and bumped around the schedules on E4, More4, Another4, Someone Else's4 and other such channels.

It was, however, consistently the best thing coming out of the States for 3 seasons, dropped a little in the 4th just before Sorkin left. It carried on for another 3 seasons and was cancelled last year, ironically after its best season since Sorkin left.

So what did he do next? The master wordsmith, the writer I most admire, the man, the myth, the legend went and created Studio 60 On The Sunset Strip – a behind-the-scenes comedy-drama about working on a weekly live sketch comedy show for a fictional US Network.

It's inspired, sublime and completely riveting – I love the whole thing to pieces, even before you add in to the mix Matthew Perry (ex of Friends) in a role that let's him loose with his very real talent, and two of the West Wing's best regulars in Bradley Whitford and Timothy Busfield.

The only problem with watching the series unfold week-by-week on More4 as it is at the moment is the horrible knowledge that comes from following TV production in the United States. You see, Studio 60 is SO good that the network (the real one, not the fictional one) pulled it after one 20-episode series.

Bummer.

Which leaves the tantalizing question of what it did wrong to get cancelled. All shows have their bad weeks, especially when you're working in the American system where they write the shows as they go (as opposed to the UK where all but the longest series like Dr Who or Robin Hood go into production with all of the scripts in almost final form), but Studio 60 has so far, in 5 episodes, hardly hit a bum note.

Did the American audience just not go for the show? Did they just not carry on watching? Or does it suddenly, mid-season, get completely rubbish.

I'm a Sorkin addict – I'll watch anything he does because I think he's one of the most talented writers on the planet. And I know I'll keep watching this to the bitter end (and you know already that the ending's going to be bitter), but it's kind of turning into car-crash TV, to be watched with your fingers over your eyes from behind the sofa. Because you have to imagine that for a show this good at the start to get cancelled after a single series, something BIG has got to go wrong with the quality of the output somewhere in the middle.

Ah well, you can't win 'em all. And even if it does get rubbish, I've got 115 hours of The West Wing on my DVD shelf to give me my Sorkin-fix.

A week in revue

Saturday 25 August

This week I have been going through good days and bad days alternately almost by the book. The annoying thing about it is that I've yet to put my finger on a reason why one has been good and the next bad, other than attributing it to the regular seesawing of my chest.

Pleasantly, the ups and downs of my chest have not been matched in mood, which makes a nice change having spent so long over the last few months with every butterfly flutter of the lungs causing a storm in my brain. This week has been pretty positive, all things considered.

I saw my bro on another one of his flying visits and we managed to get a good family night in while he was back for all of 24 hours, as well as catching up over coffee the next day, both or one of which I wouldn't have been able to do the last time he was home.

I've also started to roll along (well, nudge gently) a couple of projects that have been sitting quietly on the back burner for a while.

Today I sat down with a couple of friends to go over some ideas for a short TV spot for the Live Life Then Give Life campaign, which we're hoping will serve as a pilot to create a series of them to spread the word about organ donation through the website and other internet video sites.

They've taken themselves off with our discussions and brainstorms to draw up some storyboards, which I'll then hopefully go over with my co-director on Tuesday with a view to getting them shot as soon as possible. The advantage of not knowing how your health is going to hold up from day-to-day and week-to-week is that there is a bit of motivation to try to get things done quickly while you're feeling good and not sit about on your butt waiting for this, that and the other to fall into place.

Of course, we all know that blogging about it is usually the kiss of death to most of my projects, so we'll just have to hope that this is the one that breaks the cycle.

I had a long chat to the co-ordinator of the My Friend Oli campaign this week as well. Bizarrely, although we've exchanged emails and messages, I'd never actually spoken to her before. It became clear pretty much straight away, though, that we're VERY similar people and that if we're not careful we'll spend all day on the phone to each other.

When we did talk business, I discovered that the campaign is actually WAY bigger than I thought it was and looks like it's going to be all over Durham this year. We'd really like to introduce it at other Uni's too, but although we've had great support from other Chancellors (after Bill Bryson wrote to them about it) it doesn't seem to have materialised into support from the student body – and that's really what we need, as it needs to be co-ordinated from the inside, so to speak.

It's nice to have a few things on my plate, but not to have anything that's too demanding, that's pressing too hard for my attention or causing me to lose sleep. I seem, for once, to have struck the right balance. Let's hope I can keep it and not find myself flailing down towards that safety net again…

Sunday I'll fly away…

Monday 27 August

I know that, technically, the tense of the title is wrong, since it was yesterday and not next week, but it was such a fantastic pun which came to me in my half-dead stupor in bed last night that I just couldn't let it go, grammatically-challenged although it may be.

Anyway, to the point – I had the most amazing day yesterday, flying down to Ipswich to see my Godfather and his family. Yes – flying. To Ipswich. The only thing more remarkable than taking a helicopter down to visit friends and family in Ipswich is that someone who can afford to own a helicopter and fly his friends and family around would choose to live in Ipswich.

I love flying – I've done it a few times at school when I was a cadet in the RAF. The only reason I signed up, in fact, was that I heard you got to go for a buzz in a Bulldog – which, for those of you out of the loop on these things, is flying in a type of small, 2-man aeroplane, not unnaturally interfering with a canine.

Helicopters are so much more fun than planes, though, since they are infinitely more manoeuvrable than their winged cousins. The float serenely up into the sky – well, as serenely as you can with two engines and four blades shuddering around above your head – and whisk you much quicker than you'd imagine to wherever you want to go.

My Godfather lives in the middle of Nowhere-outside-Ipswich, which is a very quaint little village, which does, in fact, have a proper name, but navigation is much easier when you just fly straight into his garden. Road names are rather arbitrary.

They have recently been redoing their house – and by "redo" I mean gut and rebuild, basically – and I could go into immense detail about the 6 bedrooms, 5 en suite, chill-out room, grand staircases, floor-to-ceiling mirrors, televisions behind pictures on the wall and double-pool spa-complex with gym hidden behind a wall of mirrors at one end, but actually I think all you need to know to create a picture in your mind is the fact that you can land a helicopter in his back yard.

There are 2 things you notice about the East of England when you fly over it from anything ranging between 500 and 1,200 feet (we yo-yoed a little bit, for fun and frolics): 1) East Anglia and Suffolk in particular, is incredibly flat and boring to look at, endless miles of monotonous fields and the odd semi-major road and 2) there are more stately homes or Very Big Houses than you can shake a big stick at. Mind you, your chances of finding anything as interesting as a big stick in the landscape of Suffolk is close to zero.

Monotony aside, it's a wonderful experience flying over everyone's heads, seeing your shadow chasing across the fields below, spotting the rich areas by counting the number of swimming pools and tennis courts per *x* number of houses. Helicopter is the way to travel. Even a comparatively boring 40 minute ride like ours was about 100 times more interesting than spending 40 minutes on the M1.

I could fly all day – even over Suffolk. I do it a disservice by knocking its dull flatness, because anything is fascinating from the air – watching the roads wind around the countryside, spotting the big houses, fields being ploughed, small country airstrips (of which there are far, far more than you would imagine).

Although we weren't quite high enough to see things properly, there were times when you could even make out an interesting lie of land that would appear to indicate the presence of an old fort or similar – like being in a live episode of Time Team.

All of which is a very long-winded way of telling you that we spent the day with my Godfather and his family in Ipswich, which I completely and dearly loved every minute of. The fact is, without the convenience of flying pretty much door-to-door (we did have to drive 15 minutes to an airfield at our end), I'd never have been able to go.

It was a really, really wonderful day and it left me completely drained and shattered. Today's been spent almost entirely in bed and tomorrow will probably largely be, too, but it was totally worth it. I've not spent time with them for absolutely ages and K's never met my Godfather before, although she had met his wife, who's one of the world's greatest people when her scathing eye is trained on someone other than me. Luckily yesterday, her husband was around to deflect most of the attention, and I had K there so I didn't have to endure the "when are you going to find yourself a decent woman" conversation, either.

In fact all she had to complain about was my lack of visits recently, which I assured her I'd make up post-transplant by using her house as my rehab centre. For one thing, it's got a better-equipped gym than any NHS hospital and a good deal of private city-gyms too, I suspect.

It was great to get away for a bit and catch up with people I love to pieces and see far too infrequently. And to have the luxury of flying there and back, well, that just takes the biscuit.

Stuffing knocked out

Wednesday 29 August

Sunday may have been a great day, but I'm certainly paying for it now. Three days on and I'm still shattered and my chest is tremendously upset about something, though quite what its problem is I don't know.

I feel tight, I feel tired and I feel pretty unhappily breathless, too – a great combination for poor K as she has to put up with a very grumpy Oli (for a third day in a row, too!).

I don't know if it's all Sunday-related or if part of it is the curse of the project-mention in the blog, but something is conspiring to give me a really rough ride this week and I don't like it.

I was supposed to go to Oxford today for an exercise sesh with the physio, but there is no way my body is going to put up with 2 1/2 hours in a car and half-an-hour's worth of treadmills and step-ups.

As if to rub the proverbial salt in, I've also not been sleeping at night now, either, which just makes the daytimes seem worse. It's all one-thing-on-top-of-another and I know it'll sort itself out soon enough if I just keep resting up and keep my calorie count high, but it's a real b*stard to go through right now.

I suppose the lows are always harder to deal with off the back of big highs, too, since you've had that much further to fall, but I'm doing my damnedest not to let it get me down. The trouble is, I just don't have the energy to be up.

It's a funny thing, that. Being "down" takes no energy at all – it's almost like a default position, whereas being "up" requires an investment of energy, even if it's just a small amount. I think that's skewed, someone should write and complain.

Still, there's nothing better than writing a post on SmileThroughIt to remind me that I'm supposed to be SmilingThroughIt, so I'm off to search YouTube for videos of stupid people falling off logs and bumping their face.

Hyper-something, hypo-something

Thursday 30 August

The good news is my tiredness seems to have lifted, mostly. The bad news is that I woke up this morning with a roaring headache and couldn't shake it for most of the day.

I've noticed that being chronically ill gives you a bizarre form of semi-hypochondria: every little tweak of a muscle, snuffle or sneeze suddenly seems laden with horrible possibilities.

Take this morning's headache, for example. More likely than not, it was a simple, common or garden headache of the type we all wake up with from time to time. To my slightly addled brain, however, it could be a recurrence of the old CO2 headaches I used to get before I started on my NIV overnight. The issue there being that since I'm now actually using overnight NIV, it would imply that my lungs have deteriorated further and the NIV isn't working hard enough to clear the CO2 from my lungs while I sleep.

The chances of this being the case – considering there are no obvious other signs of major chest complaint (no significant drop in lung-function, no increase in volume of sputum etc.) – are pretty low, but it doesn't stop my brain working the scenarios over in my head almost constantly.

Most importantly, I guess, is the fact that I can see my slightly skewed look at things and take a bit of a step back from it. I'm not fretting my head off about it, but it is still playing on my mind a little. I'm sure I'll sleep soundly tonight and wake up tomorrow with no problems at all, and I'll feel foolish for even letting the thought cross my mind. But when you're sitting on such unstable ground, you get a little hypersensitive.

I shall be trying to get back into my exercise regime again tomorrow, having missed almost a week now through tiredness. I shall also be attempting to get back into the screenplay again, having failed to match yesterday's 10 pages with any pages at all today. I'm a bit hit-and-miss, me.

On the plus side for today, K's little 2 year-old niece and 15-month old nephew (I'm sure I'll have got that wrong now, I bet I get shot for it, too) came over for a visit today, which was just gorgeous as they were both in such fantastic moods. Even though I was feel really rough with my head banging and pretty short of breath, I managed to have a lot of fun. Luckily, I could play mostly sat down on the sofa or the floor and not move around much (I left policing duties to K and their Mum, who would race after the little one as he crawled off at top speed to reek havoc in other rooms).

I spent most of the time being either a fairy or a ballerina. I'm not quite sure what that suggests our niece thinks about me, but I'd like to think it means she understands that I've got a wonderful imagination, just like her.

Even when you're feeling tired and rough, there's something truly infectious about children's laughter – it reminded me what I used to love about working with the Youth Theatre. Having a child's simple outlook on life is so rare and so delightful; to focus 100% on what's going on right now with no thought for the history or what comes next.

With two children as gorgeous and laughter as infectious as theirs, it's impossible to say I've had a bad day.

September 2007
(2 Months)

Headaches: The Return

Monday 3 September

Like all good sequels, Headaches have come back with a vengeance, making sure to be bigger and better than before.

Having thought myself a chronic hypochondriac before the weekend, three straight mornings of horrible, horrible headaches have convinced me that it's not just a little something to make me paranoid, but that there's definitely something up.

Unfortunately, I have no idea what it is.

The headaches would appear to be CO2 related (as with last time), which would suggest that Neve isn't doing enough work, or isn't working efficiently enough to clear it off while I sleep. However, the headaches are also coinciding with an uncomfortable amount of neck and back pain, too, which may mean that it's not anything to do with my O2/CO2/Neve settings at all.

I spoke to my physio at Oxford today, who suggested adjusting my NIV settings for the night and seeing if it made a difference (it didn't last night, but she recommended trying it again tonight) and then said she'd arrange for the docs to see me tomorrow. I was supposed to be joining her for an exercise sesh tomorrow, but that feels a little way off at the moment, so we figured we should use the appointment to get myself checked over by the team rather than wait for my clinic appointment on Thursday – if I am coming down with something, we need to make sure we nip it in the bud ASAP.

It's a little demoralising looking at the prospect of another 2 weeks of IV's less than 3 weeks after I finished the last course, but

I've got so little room to play with now that it's no longer an option to just "wait and see how things pan out".

The worst part of it at the moment, really, is not knowing what they are or what's causing them. If I were sure of their origin, it'd be easier to gear myself up for a fight to get rid of them, but until I know where they come from, it's just a case of sticking them out. They are usually gone by the early afternoon and then I don't feel too bad.

Whatever is causing them, it's a pretty safe bet that it's all been kicked off by the seeds of an infection knocking around down there, so antibiotics would appear inevitable. We can only hope that something obvious presents itself in the next 24 hours or that once the antibiotics take care of the bugs, everything settles back down to normal. Fingers crossed, anyway.

That's settled

Wednesday 5 September

After waking completely breathless, despite still being on my NIV (which is quite hard to be breathless on) and finding myself standing in the bathroom fighting for air and trying to cough and clear my chest at the same time, it became apparent that my sleep/breathing/NIV difficulties were, quite simply, down to a big ol' infection which I've obviously been brewing for a good few days now.

Horrible as it is and horrible as I feel, it's good to know the causes of all the disruption in my patterns. I went to Oxford yesterday not looking for answers, but knowing that "all" I needed was a swift course of antibiotics (hopefully the same ones as last time, otherwise things get complicated with sensitivities and allergies) and some extra physio.

Monday night was the worst night I've had in quite a while – waking at 1.30am with breathlessness and a large mucus plug on my right side and the complimentary headache which comes with it all, I then spent the rest of the night trying to find a comfortable and non-distressing way to sleep, which I managed for short, 20-minute spells on-and-off for the next 5 or 6 hours. Needless to say by the time I got up I was more exhausted than when I went to bed.

In Oxford I was pretty spectacularly monosyllabic with my team – which curiously meant I think they knew exactly what was going on; they know me pretty much inside out now. I felt really sorry for them, though, because I was so exhausted and feeling so sorry for myself that I really wasn't much cop as a human being yesterday – offering hardly anything beyond the necessary replies to medical enquiries.

Still, I escaped the dreaded thought of ending up on the ward (which would just about have finished me off, I think) and came home with my first few doses of IV's to draw up and the promise of my full delivery arriving some time later today.

The only minor hitch of non-planned IV starting is that I didn't have time to get a preparation dose of steroids down me, which means I'm in for a couple of days of joint and muscle pain as my body reacts to the IV Meropenem before the oral pred kicks in properly. I've also now got a nice collection of ulcers on my tongue in protest at the toxins being shoved into my blood stream. Can't blame my body really, can you? I think I'd protest, too.

Reacting to IV's is pretty much a standard response for me and is weirdly reassuring, because if my body is feeling it then you can bet that the bugs are, too. It may take a little longer to kill them off, but I know things will turn around soon. It means having to put up with a few days of tiredness (which was there anyway) and soreness, but at least now there's the knowledge that things will start to improve by the weekend, rather than merely a looming sense of something not being right.

I'm off to do today's first session of physio, then to take myself back to bed to sleep off my morning dose, in time to get up and repeat the dose and do another physio session. I do love being on IV's…

NOTE: For the stats-lovers amongst you, my Lung Function yesterday was 0.6/1.1 (that's roughly 15/20% according to this site), my sats were 90% – not very impressive. My weight, however, was a massive 53kgs (fully clothed), so I guess that's my silver lining.

Back on track

Friday 7 September

I'm in a very weird situation with my body at the moment.

On the one hand, it's reeling from the effects of the infection and is suffering the usual IV hangover that comes with the first few days of pumping extremely high doses of pretty hard and powerful drugs into your system. On the other hand it's simultaneously feeling a huge surge of energy and general boost that comes from having large doses of steroids crammed in on top of everything.

It can't decide whether to be super-tired or super-energised and it's seemed to settle on some sort of manically-driven half-way house, where I feel like I can take on the world if only I could have a 10 minute cat nap first…

Still, the main thing is that whatever's happening, it's definitely doing the right thing. Without a doubt I feel hugely better than I did earlier in the week, tiredness aside, and I know that if my appetite is returning (or back with a vengeance) – even if it is steroid-related – then I'm definitely on the mend.

I've never been particularly good at recognising (or acknowledging is a better term, I suppose) the signs of an on-coming infection, so I'm quite pleased not only that I picked up on it properly this time, but reacted in the right way by getting myself to Oxford as soon as I could and not just waiting around for my next appointment, by which time it could have taken much greater hold and really started to kick my butt.

I was back at Oxford yesterday for a physio session, which is also a cunning ruse on the part of the team to give me a quick, unofficial once-over to see if there has been any improvement. They think we don't know these things, but we really do. Still, cunning or not, it was reassuring to know that the team all felt I was looking better. Being multi- rather than monosyllabic must have helped.

Strangely, this period of minor health-hiccup has coincided with a bright spark of inspiration and I've finally broken the back of the script I've been working on for the last few months. I'm now 70 pages in, about 20 pages from the end – at a guess – and it's all coming together beautifully. I actually can't wait to sit in front of the computer and bash out the next six pages each day and often feel like I could do more, had I the alertness to keep focused for long enough.

Still, I'm hoping to have finished my first draft by the end of the weekend and to have redrafted within the week. The stages between my first and second drafts are very quick – it's pretty much a read through and polish with a couple of additional scenes, at which point I'll then sit and work through it much more slowly and may seek out a couple of opinions from people who will give me good, honest notes.

Funnily enough, a great friend of mine for whom I am nominally writing the script, happened to text me on Wednesday to see how I was doing (health-wise, not script-wise) and it was the same day that the whole things became clear and concise in my head, so maybe there's a spooky little connection thing going on in my head there, somewhere. Whatever it is, I'm really enjoying it.

The dude at the window

Monday 10 September

I'm in an advanced state of "how to deal with the dude at the window?".

For reasons un-bloggable, the living room is currently out of bounds, so I'm holed-up, not unhappily, in the study, surfing the 'net a little to catch up on some of my favourite, but not every-day sites. Whilst I browse, the familiar clinking bang hits the wall and the half-creak, half-screech of a man climbing a ladder grows ever louder in my ear.

Sure enough, milliseconds later, armed with cloth and long wipey thing which has no discernable purpose beyond making it look like they're actually doing something, a man appears at the window.

So now I'm stuck in that awkward zoo-like state of strangeness wherein you don't know if it's appropriate to turn and acknowledge him or just to ignore him. You're perfectly well aware that he's there and he knows that you're aware of it, too. But where do you look once you've turned to look at him?

If you do acknowledge him, in what way and for how long? Obviously, being in a first-floor flat, opening the window for a quick "how do you do?" isn't going to be a warmly welcomed idea, and communicating through double glazing is hard enough when you can wave and shout and point at things, but given his donkey-on-a-pole status with buckets, chamois and wipers everywhere seems a likely impossibility.

Is it rude to ignore someone who's closer to you than it's natural for one man to be to another if they're not considering amorous relations or celebrating a sporting triumph? Does the pane of clear sheeting between you justify the pretence of ignorance?

I figure that most people opt not to acknowledge their window cleaners if they have something sufficiently distracting to legitimately hold their attention away from the window (say, writing a blog or performing micro-surgery on a wasp unlucky enough to die slap-bang in the middle of the desk). This conclusion leads me to believe that if I, being so occupied, were in fact to turn to acknowledge the presence of the ladder man, I would in fact so startle him as to risk his ability to maintain his balance and thus his position some 3 metres off the ground. Not wishing him to become too prematurely reacquainted with the earth, I decide on grounds of health and safety to ignore him completely and settle back, contented with my caring and considered manner in dealing with the problem, into constructing my witticisms.

For some reason, though, I can't escape the feeling that he's just climbed down and moved on the next window whilst muttering to his mate, "That miserable git up there has nothing better to do than pull the wings off flies and yet he can't even muster up a wave while I clean his bleedin' windows."

Still here…honest.

Sunday 16 September

Just a quick note to all the regular readers who may be getting a little antsy at the lack of updates. Full story and update when I can get online properly.

All queries should be addressed in writing to Why Can't Sky Sort Out My Smegging Broadband, The Stupid Annoying Lazy Bunch Of Muppets c/o Sky or seriouslyhowhardisittosendoutamodem@sky.com.

Emails and blog messages welcome, but I won't read or reply to them until I a) get my broadband up and running or b) get back over to Mum and Dad's to check the accounts again.

Current mood: flippin' furious.

Current status: disconnected.

Current bun: yes, please.

Stay smiley.

I wouldn't read this

Thursday 20 September

I feel like I should be doing a great big week-long catch up here, but I don't seem to have the impetus to go back over the whole of last week and work out what happened or didn't. I seem to remember largely feeling pretty knackered, thanks, no doubt, to the

IV's.

The good news is that they really did the trick and we got on top of the infection before it could develop properly. My CRP at the start of the course was at 89, which had reduced to just 33 after 7 days, which is good going. The extreme fighting going on is probably the major cause of the tiredness, too, alongside the drug doses.

I also feel like I should be entertaining you all with a blow-by-blow account of my troubles with Sky, but I think I'm so tired of all this malfunctioning technology and maladjusted people on the end of helplines that I can't even bring myself to muster up a random thread of expletives to describe the situation.

The IV's finished on Tuesday and I was up at Oxford yesterday for a quick post-IV once-over. The best news of the 2 weeks (and recent past) is that my weight is now up to a rather impressive 54.4kg – the heaviest I've ever been. I'm hoping that I can keep it on and keep adding to it even as I slowly start to reduce my steroids. My lung function had improved greatly, too, back up to 0.8/1.3 after dipping down to 0.6/1.1. It may not sound like much, but when you consider that's a 25% drop in lung-function, it goes to show why I may not have been feeling my best.

I have continued, on-and-off, to look at and sporadically work on new projects and a couple of old ones, although clearly a lack of Internet access is a bit of a hindrance to most productivity. Of course, being offline and having nothing else to use my computer for, you'd have expected, I guess, that I would make some significant progress on the screenplay. Rather impressively, however, that's not the case at all, and it's sitting just as untouched today as it was when I lost the Internet connection 10 days ago.

Only I could manage to ignore a chance to turn a technological disadvantage into an advantage – looking the misguided gift horse in the mouth, as it were.

There's not much else to add, really – I suppose it's been a bit of a boring week or so, or certainly that anything interesting that has happened seems far too long-winded for me to dredge back up right now. I'm still tired.

Ho hum, let's keep rolling along and see what tomorrow brings. Sorry for being boring today.

It's all gone dark

Sunday 30 September

I've taken a real step back over the last week or so, not so much physically (thank goodness), but mentally.

I'm all too aware that moods change on a regular basis and that it's more than possible to be up one minute and down the next – that changes in the tone of life are rarely long-held and that normality will be restored with time. But right now things just seem more difficult than they have been for a while.

I'm not entirely sure what kicked it off, although I suspect it was accelerated last Monday when I didn't go to the cinema. It seems like a strange non-event to become a catalyst for a wave of negativity, but it seems to have encapsulated a lot of hang-ups all in one go.

I was supposed to be going to see a flick I've wanted to see for a while with a friend of mine who had the week off, who then had to cancel as he'd promised himself to another mate for his birthday all day and couldn't swing the time for the movie. It wouldn't have been much of an issue in the past; I'd have just gone along on my own. But I realised that I had neither the strength nor the confidence to face going to the cinema by myself any more.

From there, things descended down what I suppose is a fairly inevitable path of reassessment of what's going on in my life and unpleasant realities creeping into my consciousness again.

All of a sudden my inner-eye has switched focus from what I am still able to do with myself from day-to-day to what is now beyond me. All I seem to be able to focus on is what I can't do rather than what I can. And there's a lot more things that I'm unable to do than things I can still do.

Everyone has these periodic reassessments of life – where you find yourself taking stock of where you are and how it compares to last year, how it compares to where you thought you'd be, how it compares to where you want to be. And everyone inevitably faces battles against what they expected and what they find – it's the way life works that we almost never find ourselves in precisely the position we would like to be in.

Still, I can't seem to shake the dark cloud that's descended on me again, dragging everything around me into a mire of misinterpretation and moping. I don't like this me, I don't like being so downbeat about everything and struggling to appreciate all of the wonderful things I've got in my life. But try as I might, I can't see the light through the dense forest of overwhelming bleakness.

Even the simple joys of spending time with K's nieces and nephews have been taken away this week as they're all coming through the early-autumn cough and cold season.

I'm trying so hard not to let myself get beaten down by the hard stuff and to enjoy the good stuff that's still around but I just feel so bitter and resentful and angry with the world sometimes, but I've got no outlet for it. I don't have the energy to shout and rant and rave and let it all out. I don't have the energy to take myself off for a cathartic drive around the back roads like I used to. I don't have the energy or the inclination to do anything to help myself out of my funk and it makes me even more angry – with myself and with my situation.

It's a vicious circle and I know that I'm helping to perpetuate it by allowing myself to wallow in my unhappiness. I just don't know how to take myself out of it at the moment – I can't see the proverbial wood for the trees and I can't remember what cleared my head of this fog last time.

The one hope I do cling to is that I know I've been here before – I know I've felt this bleak, dark blackness and I know it's gone away, so I know it's beatable. I just can't remember how. And I hope like hell I'll find the trump card soon.

PS – I've mixed so many metaphors here you could make a cake, so I apologise. It's not the kind of post I feel like re-reading to spell-check or clean up, though, so we'll just have to live with it.

October 2007
(1 Month)

Losing the me

Friday 5 October

So it's been a rough week. My mood over the last five or six days has been up and down more times than Billie Piper's trousers in an episode of Diary of a Call Girl (which, by the way, is so atrocious I beg none of you to waste 30 minutes of your preciously short lives giving it your attention).

It's a struggle to keep yourself moving forward when you don't know how you're going to feel, physically, mentally or emotionally, from one moment to the next. Right now, for instance, I'm feeling strong, confident and happy. Had I written this earlier this afternoon, it would have been a completely different story.

Therein lies the problem, really – how do you deal with a physical and emotional state that's ever-changing from hour-to-hour?

If I was feeling permanently down or upset, it would give me something to focus on, something to seek to improve or seek help with. If I felt permanently tired and exhausted, or chesty and rubbish, I could get on the phone to my team in Oxford and get them on the case. But I don't feel permanently anything, other than permanently changeable.

The plus side is, of course, that with all the downs come all the ups. I know that when I'm feeling miserable, I'm more than likely only a couple of hours away from feeling OK again and when I'm feeling chesty, I'm only a physio session and a nebuliser away from being comfortable enough to make a cup of tea.

It's the endlessness of it that's starting to wear thin, though –

the relentless ride through peak and trough which starts to grind away at the inner reserves one builds up over time to deal with the regular lifts and dips of life.

I feel like I'm slowly losing a sense of "me" – like I'm losing touch with the essence of who I am because I'm being subsumed by a constant need to "cope", to get by, moment-to-moment from each new challenge to the next. I don't have room to let myself breathe (no pun intended), to stop and just plateau.

I don't know if maybe there's a sense of a time-pressure that still hangs over me, like I need to make the most of things while I can in case the day never comes when I get carted off to theatre for my new lungs and new life. Since, physically, I'm seeming to be able to support myself in doing a little bit more at the moment, is the frustration coming from not being able to do quite enough to satisfy myself that I'm making the most of things.

If I'm honest, I don't think that's true at all, but there's so much going on at the moment that I'm not entirely sure what's right, what's wrong, what's real and what's imagined. I can't put my finger on anything that's making things better or worse and I can't identify what it is I need to do to stop these endless fluctuations of mood and manner.

I suppose, though, that no one does. I'd be a rather remarkable person if I knew to solution to all of my problems. Finding the way out of the mind's maze is the journey that makes the end all the more valuable. But when you're staring at a hedge with no sense of direction, it's not much comfort to know it's a shrubbery for learning.

All Spruced Up

Monday 8 October

Nothing really changes in my life these days – it's getting harder and harder to find something new to write about that's not just droning on and on about how hard things can be, or what minute fluctuations my chest is taking at the moment. So I figured that if I'm not up to making sweeping changes in everyday life, the least I could do was to give the blog a bit of TLC.

So here we have it – the all-new SmileThroughIt, courtesy of the lovely people at Wordpress (for all your blogging needs!). Hopefully, it makes the whole thing a bit easier to read – I was surfing the other day and saw the page for the first time in ages and noticed just how SMALL the font size looked on the front (I only see the "back end" of the page, which is all fresh, clean and white, totally different to the published version). It also, I hope, makes it easier to navigate the old posts, or the most recent posts, as well as seeing when I've published.

Anyway, as far as the "me" update goes… well, nothing's changed really.

I say that, of course, but there have been things going on. It amused me last week actually, when I was catching up via text with a friend of mine who's got himself cooped up in the Big House (read: hospital) and he was asking what I'm up to at the moment. I said I'm not doing anything these days, not really up to much.

Apart from still doing CF Talk. And the work I've got going with Live Life Then Give Life. And talking to the campaigners behind My Friend Oli. And the odd bit of writing.

I suddenly found myself looking back over my text wondering what, indeed, the Roman's had ever done for us. (Apologies to Monty Python). In fact, said friend said as much in his reply. Told me I clearly didn't have time to work, even if I *was* up to it physically.

So yes, I think to myself, nothing ever changes around here, but I'm still finding myself pretty busy. Saturday was a blessed day of nothingness, somewhat of an oasis after a busy week, which had been draining not just physically, but not helped by the mood swings and negativity flying about.

Sunday we popped over to K's 'rents to say hi and for K to raid their loft to try to find some old books of hers to help with her college course. K being K she's decided not to do the simple, middle-of-the-road, easy-as-the-proverbial-pie kind of project that they expect their students to do, but rather to launch into a semi-professional study which, all things being well, she is hoping to then go on and get published if we can find the right journal for it. The only thing is, it means she needs to wrap her brain back around the statistics info she learned way back when. I am, naturally, completely useless for this as I can't really count much higher than 10 and ask me to do division and I'm stuck beyond halving something.

While we were there we were, I think it's fair to say, attacked by our tiniest niece and nephew. I think it's also fair to say that they're not going to be the tiniest for long. The little one is nearly as big as his sister now, despite being 13 months younger. In a reversed nod to Animal Farm, he's just discovered Two Legs Good, Four Legs Bad – it's so much easier to cause havoc when you have your hands free to grab, hold and throw things while you move. His sister, meanwhile, is mostly contented jumping on her Auntie K and me.

Today I even managed to venture across town to pick up my own prescription, something that I've been relying on Mum and Dad for, although when I told Mum I'd done it tonight she told me off for not asking her to do it (you can't win sometimes).

Just writing all this down, I'm starting to realise not only that my life is still pretty full and varied, albeit in a different manner to that which I was used to, but also why I started this blog in the first place. More than just a place to air my frustrations, or my minor triumphs, I began writing these posts nearly a year ago in the hope that putting it down in words might help remind me that life's not as bad as all that and if I only take the time to look around, I'll see all the wonderful things I have in my life: my family, K and her family (my second family, really), my friends: a network of people who never let me forget myself. More than anything, maybe I've reminded myself to Smile Through It.

Why can't the day begin at 6pm?

Tuesday 9 October

That's what I want to know.

It's all very well this daylight hours stuff, with your mornings and your lunchtimes and your "after" noons, but wouldn't it just be better for everyone if the day started at 6 o'clock in the evening?

OK, granted, the answer's probably no, but I wish it did. 6pm is the time of the day – not before, not after – when my body decides it's OK to be human. For weeks now my daily routine has consisted of playing passenger on the journey my chest takes from grouchy in the morning through surly at lunchtime to grumpy in the afternoon, before it settles down and lets me get on with things from the time the first news headlines are read out.

The problem being, of course, that by six in the evening, there's no "things" to be getting on with. Anything even remotely related to the "real" world is out of the window because "normal" people go home at 5 o'clock, the inconsiderate beggars. Anything creative is pretty much pooped on because just when you get into your stride, dinner turns up – not that I'm moaning about dinner, you understand, since it's about the most I manage to eat all day at the moment, so I need it all the more.

What I'm left with, then, is basically, the ability to sit and watch telly without feeling rubbish. I suppose, really, I should be happier than I am that I get any sort of grace period in the day from feel awful, but I am starting to resent the fact that the very time everyone else is shutting down for the evening, I am just starting to rev up.

I'm even working against K, who, like everyone else, is all ready to snuggle down on the sofa whilst my body's telling me to get up and do something useful. About the only useful thing I've managed to find to do is the washing up, so at least the kitchen looks all right. I guess.

Thank heaven for small mercies, they say, and I do, everyday. But sometimes you do just want to bash "they" in their stupid mouths for being so flippant about such bloody annoying things.

I'm not ranting, really I'm not, it's just that if I was going to be granted a window of energy in the day, I'd rather choose sometime when I might be able to make some decent use of myself, or even just be able to have a coffee with a friend or visit a shop. (First person to mention 24-hour Tesco gets a spatula somewhere it shouldn't live.)

"They" also say beggars can't be choosers and I suppose in these days of low energy and even lower expectations, I can't really moan about being afforded three hours of feeling vaguely normal of an evening.

Not when there's so much other great stuff to moan about.... But that's for another day.

Wonder of wonders

Thursday 11 October

Today, I have felt good ALL DAY.

It's a mystery where it's come from, and I don't harbour much hope of it lasting into the weekend, such is the nature of my up-and-down life at the moment, but damned if I haven't enjoyed it today.

I woke up this morning after a good night's sleep (which is rare enough) not feeling horrible. As I plodded around the flat after rousing myself from the bedroom, I waited for the inevitable on-set of hideousness which usually hits about 20-30 minutes after I get up, but it never seemed to materialise.

I had the smallest glimmer of a headache after doing my morning physio session, but I hurriedly popped some paracetamol and ibuprofen and by the time I'd done my nebs it had passed, never to return.

We were joined, late morning, by our little niece and nephew on a spur of the moment visit with their mum. There's really no better way to start your day than with the fun and laughter of a pair of adorable children. I even had enough energy to police the tiny terror as he rampaged his way around the flat – a job that's normally delegated to K or his mum.

In fact, he didn't cause too much chaos being mostly occupied as he was with emptying the fruit bowl and putting it all back again, before deciding to re-home most of its contents around the living room. We're still finding oranges in the most unlikely of places and I'm sure we had a lime earlier, too. His main occupation after fruit-picking was wall-drawing, but we managed to get away with just the mildest hint of blue in the hallway, largely down to the grown-up party-poopers who kept spoiling the fun.

Once they'd gone – with the elder of the two climbing backwards down the stairs (all 18 of them) on the way back down the car park, cheered on by her little bro who would doubtless have been counting them down if he had any concept of numbers – we had time to chill a bit and grab some lunch before I ran K to the docs for a quick hello. From there, since it's just down the road from her 'rents, we stopped in for a quick cuppa, which is lovely because it's a good 20 minutes from our place and we don't get to do it very often.

When we got home, another of our friends popped over, enjoying his day off, and while K busied herself baking in the kitchen, we sat through Fantastic Four: Rise of the Silver Surfer. It was awful. Not just not very good. It was abominable. Like the snowman, but with less fur.

Mr S, who brought it over, had refused to see it at the cinema on the basis that he was sure he wasn't going to like it, so thought it would be amusing for the two of us to sit through the DVD together on the basis that we'd both spend most of the film shouting obscenities at it for being so rubbish. We, unfortunately, share a few friends who suffer under the delusion that it's actually quite good and would be very upset to hear us bad-mouthing it all the way through, so this afternoon proved very useful for both of us.

Seriously, though, it's AWFUL. Don't touch it. Not even for the kids.

Since then, I've managed my neb and second physio session and nebs (lots of those, these days) and am still – touch wood – seemingly going strong. Dinner shortly, then a catch up on last night's telly, methinks, before hitting the sack for what I hope will be another bonza night of sleep.

You never know these days how long the ups are going to last, but I seem to have perfected the art of making the most of them when they are around. It's good to feel good.

Tenterhooks

Wednesday 17 October

I don't like the change in the weather and I don't like the on-set of autumn/winter. The change in seasons brings with it, every year, an abundance of new colds, flu's, viruses and other horribleness and it makes life that much more worrying when you're desperately trying to keep yourself well enough for a life-saving operation.

Yesterday I developed that odd feeling in the back of your throat, the little tickle-come-small obstruction you feel when you swallow which often prefaces the on-set of a cold or sinus infection.

If I'm honest, it's petrifying. The last time I was unwell with any sort of cold/virus-type thing, it lead to the worst chest infection I've had for years and my body very nearly gave up the ghost. If it were to come around again, if the tickle becomes a cough, if the cough becomes a cold, if the cold becomes something else, it doesn't really bear thinking about right now.

Try as I might, though, I can't escape the thought of it. If someone tells you not to think about elephants you can guarantee that they'll be singing, dancing and tooting their way ear-to-ear for the rest of the evening. An impending cold is very much the elephant in the room.

I'm suddenly hyper-aware of every creak and tweak my body makes, each breath that feels shorter becomes a worry, each cough that feels irregular concerns me. I'm doing whatever I can to get food, drink or any kind of calories down my neck in the hope of giving my body the energy it needs to nip this in the bud before it takes hold.

It's impossible to know if any of it is likely to work – it's impossible to know right now whether it is even the start of a cold or just a strange feeling in the throat. It's impossible to know anything at all, really, which is, again, part of the problem I suppose. I'm waiting through each passing moment to see what my body's going to do, to see if I've done enough to see it off. I'm on tenterhooks.

The one morsel of comfort I'm dragging from deep within my reserves of pluck and fight is the fact that as bleak as it seemed to get last time, I pulled through it – I fought my way out of it and afterwards I enjoyed some of the best fitness I've had for the last 12 months or so. Should I be facing the same fight again, I can only keep telling myself that I've been here and done that, and I should really look into getting a T-shirt.

It is inevitable that the ups and downs of life on a waiting list as fluid and unquantifiable as transplant are going to be increasingly hard to bear – each trough will reach deeper than the last and each peak will seem higher, whatever the physical stats may show.

Without fight, though, where would we be? Without the need to push ourselves forwards, to fend off the onslaught of the outside world against our frail bodies, how would the human race have come as far as it has? How would we all make our way through our day-to-day lives? My fight is no more than anyone else's, merely against a different enemy, on different ground, with different markers of success and failure.

I suffer the slings and arrows of outrageous fortune, and I choose to take arms against a sea of troubles, but I know that without the help of the transplant team at Harefield, no amount of personal opposition will end them. All I can do is to my own self be true, and keep fighting the fight till the clarion call of a new life comes my way. (With apologies to Mr Shakespeare).

Good news/Other news

Friday 19 October

The good news is, I don't have a cold. The news-that-isn't-really-good-but-considering-how-bad-"bad"-could-have-been-really-can't-be-counted-as-being-bad (phew!) is that my body is keen to make me perfectly well aware of the fact that's it's been working very hard thank you very much and has decided to tell my legs, head, arms, neck and just about everything that's not a vital organ to stop working for the time being. Essentially, my body is currently the French rail system.

Still, compared to dealing with a cold, I can definitely put up with feeling a bit tired and finding tea-making a chore. If I had to spend the next week in bed doing nothing and seeing no one, I would happily accept it for not having a cold. As it is, I am hoping to be able to make it over to my 'rents tomorrow night for the rugby, although there is the slight hitch that I may expend so much energy on screaming at the telly (judging by the semi-final), I may not be able to drive myself home.

(I'm acutely aware that the end of the last paragraph will have been hopelessly lost on my American cousins who look in here, so for translation's sake: there's a World Cup (think "world series" which actually involves other countries) going on in the sport of Rugby ("Football" without the nancy-boy pads and tea-breaks every 30-seconds) and England (that's us) have made it to the (Grand) Final, which is somewhere akin to the Texans making the Superbowl (i.e., so outlandish at the start of the competition that if you'd suggested they might do it, people would have either laughed in your face or had you committed).)

I've made a deal with my body – limbs and all – that I won't do anything at all during the day tomorrow besides rest and refuel so that I can enjoy the game in the evening, and that I will do the same on Sunday so I can enjoy a meal in the evening with my bro, who's deigned to reappear from the far side of the world where he was "working". I use the term "working" very loosely, as he mostly seemed to spend his time sitting up a mountain finding it hard to breath. Heck, I do that in my own living room – I don't try to call it work.

The only possible barrier to the deal on Sunday is that the Saints are live on TV, but judging from our performances so far this season they aren't likely to be causing me a great deal of excitement or giving me much cause to scream at the telly. More likely I'll be slumped in resigned resignation (it's doubly bad, you see) as they let another 2-goal lead slip away and wave good-bye to another 3 points at the hands of some woeful defending while George Burley makes excuses about us "playing well".

Still compared to spending the weekend lying in bed with snot dribbling out my nose, my throat closing up in protest, my chest kicking off in a major way and the beginnings of the mother of all chest infections, I think I can handle any sporting disasters coming my way.

It's all about perspective, see?

Coming? Going?

Tuesday 23 October

I'm not really sure at the moment, if I'm honest.

My body and my mind are all over the place and I can't decide what to do with myself from hour-to-hour, let alone day-to-day.

Frustration is playing a key role in whatever I am doing at the moment, though, driving me to distraction.

For the last week or so I've been sleeping incredibly badly – not being able to get off to sleep and then waking every hour or so until the early hours when it tends to increase to a whopping 20mins of sleep at a time. It's been driving me bonkers. Also, of course, it's left me with very little energy to do anything with myself all day.

Once I'm tired, I'm also absolutely horrible to be around. I'm sure most of us aren't at our best when we're lacking a bit of shut-eye, but I know that when I'm sleepless I'm at my very, very worst. For all the days K's spent laughing at me and with me when we both get the giggles when we're tired, I'm sure she's now found out that when I'm really tired giggles are nowhere to be found.

Lack of sleep also causes more and more worries as well. I'm well aware of the fact that it's when our bodies are at rest that they repair themselves and set themselves up for another day. As you'll know from the more recent blogs, I'm also increasingly aware of the frailty of my body and the desperate need it has to keep itself ticking over. Missing out on crucial rest time bothers me big-time because I know how precious a resource it is.

More than all of that, though, the more tired I am the more frustrated I get with myself and with the things around me. My energy levels are so low that doing anything other than sitting and surfing the 'net causes me to feel like I've been running around a football pitch for hours. Without the rest it needs, my chest will start to moan and complain if I do much more than make a cup of tea and I can really feel my auxiliary muscles working overtime just to keep the oxygen flow going through what's left of my lungs.

I've been struggling for the last couple of months with pain in my back and neck where the over-worked auxiliary respiratory muscles are tensing up and causing all kinds of different, unpleasant aches and pains, which in turn makes it harder to sit properly or carry myself as I should, which only then serves to exacerbate the problem with my back and neck muscles. It's the very worst of vicious circles that no one seems to have identified a way out of yet.

There are so many things I'd like to be doing with myself at the moment, projects I'd like to be working on, writing I'd like to be doing, but it's the most I can do to get through a day without going mad at the moment. My brain certainly doesn't feel switched-on enough to achieve much beyond the occasional email. I don't think I've had a creative thought-thread for a couple of weeks now, which really gets me down.

Still, it can't all be doom and gloom – there are good things in the world. (Best not get on to last weekend's sport if I'm looking for sunshine, eh?).

My bro was back for a couple of days over the weekend, which was really nice – he's away so much doing this, that and the other that it's been really good to see him and catch up a bit. He seems really happy in what he's doing, which is so good to see. I get a real kick out of seeing my family and my friends doing things they really enjoy – I suppose it's a kind of vicarious pleasure that I've lived with for a while now and I have always felt it most strongly for the things my bro gets up to. If he's happy, I'm happy for him. And he's always happy, because he's that kind of bloke.

I know I could be doing a lot worse, too. My chest isn't 100% – an understatement of rather dramatic proportions I suppose, but then everything is relative – but it's holding on there for the most part. It could be much worse and I could be properly laid-up, which I'm not, so I should really not be complaining too hard.

When frustration bubbles up it's often hard to see the good for the bad – the wood for the proverbial trees, as it were – and it's all too easy when tiredness attacks to let it drag everything down with it. Positivity is a precious resource in and of itself, so I suppose what I really need is just the energy to go and mine some more of it.

More IVs, but it's OK

Wednesday 24 October

I'm in the mood to write a really witty, random, stream-of-consciousness blog tonight, but I can't because a) I'm knackered and b) I'm knackered. Also, I'm pretty knackered.

(Incidentally, when I say "in the mood" what I really mean is "tired" since all of my best stream-of-consciousness is always written when I'm tired. But not this tired.)

(Incidentally, it's just occurred to me that I can remember the very lesson at school at which I learnt how to spell conscious and consciousness. Odd, isn't it? That and "immediately", although they were different lessons. In fact, the teacher who taught us "immediately" taught it to us with a rhyme and to this day I can't type "immediately" without the tune going through my head. Weird, huh?)

Anyway, the knackeredness (yay, new word!) is caused largely by Oxford trip today, coupled with start of IVs, which I really should have predicted but thought I could get away with. My wonderful physio set me straight, though, and made me see the better of kicking off today as opposed to Monday, as was my wont.

For all you stat-monkeys out there, today provided a L-F of 0.7/1.2, Sats of 90% and a weigh-in at 54.4kg. All of which is really not that bad, really. But with increasing morning headaches, poor sleep and a newly-discovered need to turn Neve up just a trifle over-night, it made sense to kick off some IVs and head-off whatever may be on its way before it decides to settle in for the winter.

First dose this afternoon went fine and dandy, steroids started with them, so expecting huge appetite to kick in sometime in the next few days, too.

Can't think of anything more to say. Immediately — it's such a nice song.

Let's welcome…

Friday 26 October

…the IV mood swings and energy dips, Ladies and Gentlemen!

Like all good antibiotic courses (or at least all of my regular IV courses), it doesn't take long to start really messing with your body in as many ways as possible.

So far we've got: random tiredness springing up out of nowhere; random waking-upness springing out of nowhere; unquenchable thirst; over-bloating from taking on too much water; dry mouth; raised appetite; sore limbs/achy legs; irrational dip in mood; irrational spike in mood; regular-season, common-or-garden tiredness. Although so far (with plenty of wood on hand to touch, knock-on, slap my head against etc.), I've managed to avoid the usual mouth-ulcers and other symptoms.

I have delighted, however, in spending 2 days doing pretty much nothing at all, including going back to bed after my a.m. dose and sleeping through practically the whole morning. The one thing you can guarantee about IVs is that if they make you feel tired, sleeping is the most wonderful counter to it.

I appreciate that might sound a little "well, duh!" obvious, but it the kind of situation I'm in, it's actually not a given that sleep helps things. A lot of the time, the tiredness I feel isn't actually helped out by sleeping an extra 3 or 4 hours, like you might expect. It's a kind of false-tiredness that's more a complaint from the body about having too much work to do than anything else.

On IVs, though, it's a different story. The tiredness is much more a sign of the things starting to work and almost begging to be given more down-time in which to do their stuff while not having to concentrate on boring things like day-today operations of eating, drinking and sitting upright. What that happily means for me is that the next few days will be spent fitting in 12-14 hours of sleep in every 24 and actually feeling refreshed for it when I'm not sleeping.

IVs are pretty rubbish, so grabbing hold of the positives is pretty important and it wasn't really until today that I realised how much the sleep-inducement of IVs can actually help-out, so I'm going to cling to that for the next few hours while I try desperately not to drop off from exhaustion while I wait for my next dose. That's the other problem with IVs – if you sleep at the wrong time, you can guarantee that it'll come back and bite you on the butt and keep you *wide* awake just when you want to be getting the best of your shut-eye.

Anyway, moving away from all the boring medically-stuff, K and I picked up the 3rd season of Lost on DVD this week. I say picked up, I mean had the nice people at Play.com deliver for us. We were both hooked on the first two seasons but then missed out on the 3rd when it switched from C4 to Sky One, so we've been itching to get our hands on it for ages now.

Finally, we're back on the wagon – or off it, I suppose, since we have kicked-off a major addiction which is currently managing to over-rule just about everything else in the world apart from sleeping, eating and doing doses of IVs. In fact, it's ideal really, because if I'm going to be making the most of these IVs I really do need to be doing as little as possible, so Lost is keeping me in check, glued as I am to the sofa for endless back-to-back episodes.

The trouble is, we'll be through this season in no time, and then we'll be lost without Lost. So I'm thinking we might have to find some new old TV to catch up on in DVD box set format. US TV comes in such handy little 40 minute chunks that it fits perfectly into little treatment slots like gaps between nebs and physio and doses of IVs, so it's ideal for life at the moment. I think we may be getting through a lot more soon.

But first it's back to the island to unravel more of the might mystery…. It's sooooo good!

Today makes no sense

Monday 29 October

Today I am tired. Today made no sense. I think it's because I'm tired. But really, it made no sense.

I woke up this morning at 6.30am – that's really early. Luckily, it's not dark, because the clocks have gone back. So I woke up in the light. But it was still really early. I didn't get much sleep last night. It was past midnight when the light went out and I then spent the next hour or so getting to sleep, where I then spent the next four or five hours dozing and waking every hour or so to readjust my position because either a) Neve was coming off my face, b) my shoulder was hurting because of the port needle or c) I was lying too much over on my chest and giving myself breathing trouble.

I woke up grouchy. I don't think many people wake up at 6.30am happy, but when you've slept badly two nights in a row, coupled with not sleeping long enough two nights in a row, coupled with being on really high doses of the most drowsy-making drugs in the world (with the notable exception, perhaps of sleeping pills, which I suppose really ought to win the most drowsy-making award and if they don't then they should really have a different name, or get their makers sued under trades descriptions) then it's pretty hard to wake up at 6.30 in the morning without being grouchy.

I did my drugs. This involves (at the moment) doing about 10-15 minutes worth of injecting solutions from a syringe down the tube then connecting up a big bubble-thing that works like a drip, but in a different way. (That doesn't make sense, does it? If it works like a drip, then it must be a drip; if it works a different way then it's not like a drip, is it? Told you today didn't make sense.) That takes an hour to go through, then it's a couple of quick syringe squirts and hey presto, all done.

So the whole shebang took me up to about 8am. Every Monday morning, I have a delivery of portable oxygen cylinders to give me enough to move around for the week when I want to go out. Invariably, the delivery driver arrives at 9am. Looking at the clock, tired and grouchy, I decided I didn't want to go back to bed for an hour just to get woken up as I settle into a nice sleep to have to get up and answer the door. So I try to occupy myself to keep myself awake until 9.

Dutifully, the lovely Brummie gent turns up and drops of my new cylinders and whisks away my old ones. Following which I retire to bed for a catch-up nap, aware that I have to be up no later than 11.30 to get ready to go to the hospital for a physio appointment and drug-level check.

I clamber into bed and strap on my Neve-mask, only to discover that the condensation in the mask has done something – I don't know what and boy, do I wish I did – which makes something on the mask make a really loud, annoying clunking sound every. Single. Time. I. Breathe. In.

Annoying? Slightly. Grumpy-making? Exceedingly.

After, oh I don't know.... 5 minutes of trying, I give up and clamber out of bed, thoroughly bad-mooded for the day. I wash the mask up, in an effort to have cleared whatever the problem is for tonight, and sit myself quietly on the sofa to start reading Ian McEwan's Atonement, which I've finally wrestled from K and am keen to get through before having the whole story spoiled for me by people who've seen the movie.

Bizarrely, all the time I'm sitting reading, I'm perfectly awake and alert, despite having had not enough sleep and being beside-myself with tiredness when I'd gone back to bed. As soon as I got up from my perch, however – to make tea, to fetch things, to do anything at all, really – I was exhausted. My chest was heaving, my legs felt like lead and my eyes couldn't have been heavier if they'd entered a Weight Watchers programme and won the prize for world's worst dieter by gaining their own body-weight three times over.

I was not a happy bunny.

By the time K got up I was happily reading away, but ready for some morning physio, which is never fun at the best of times but when you're tired it becomes a peculiar kind of torture – long, drawn out, unpleasant, occasionally painful, sometimes exhausting, often breathless and very, very hot (this morning, anyway). Needless to say I ended in a mildly worse mood than I start – impressive, huh?

I did manage to lever myself into a bath and chill out for a fraction of an hour before throwing some clothes on and getting ready to head off to Oxford, only to be phoned and told that the physio I was supposed to be seeing had broken her tooth and wouldn't be able to see me today, so could I come Wednesday instead? Of course, I said. Why not?

But here's the weird thing: having not gone to Oxford, which I took to be a blessing on account of my overwhelming tiredness anyhow, my body then decided that actually, it was feeling pretty happy and perky. After 5 hours semi-sleep, a 6.30am start, a morning of trial after mood-blackening trial, I found myself suddenly feeling an urge to sit at my keyboard and write – to carry on with my screenplay with which I have been having so many recent tussles. (For "tussles", read: "hit a structural bump which sapped all creativity and forward-momentum and left a big black mark against my 5-page-per-day copy book for the last month or so")

So all afternoon I've been beavering away on my screenplay without so much as a care in the world, pausing only for the occasional break for food, water or the odd episode of Lost (just keeps getting better).

I have no idea what my brain is doing with itself, nor what my body is up to at the moment. My chest feels like it's improving, but my sleep certainly isn't. My mind is lost in a mire of lethargy which saps any mental strength and positivity right out of it, whilst still apparently providing me with enough drip-fed muse to be able to carry on doing the kind of creative writing which is usually the first thing to desert me when I'm feeling rubbish.

Literally nothing about this day is making any sense to me right now. But I guess that's just because I'm tired. Can you tell?

Pootling along nicely

Wednesday 31 October

Up to Oxford today for my mid-IV once-over, during which all signs were pointing to "pretty good". "Good" is obviously a relative term, but compared to last week, where I was perched on the verge of a bit of a downturn, things are doing pretty well.

Lung function is up to 0.75/1.5 from 0.7/1.2, which is a goodly leap (18%/30% from 17%/24%) in the space of a week, my sats are holding steady around the 90% mark on 2l O2 per minute and my exercise tolerance is improving.

Yesterday we took delivery of a brand new exercise bike from the lovely Fitness for Hire, a company who loan out exercise equipment so you can see whether or not you're likely to get into the habit of using it without throwing away a whole heap of dough on something that's just going to sit and gather dust. We've loaned it for 4 weeks for starters and if it doesn't get used, it'll just go back, no hassle.

The theory is, according to the Physios-Who-Know, that working on a bike is easier on the chest/lungs than step-ups with Goliath as the tendency is not to desaturate so quickly. I don't know why that is, or exactly how the process works, but what it basically means is that by using the bike I will be able to do more exercise without getting so out of breath. This, in turn, should mean that I can make my muscles do more work, rather than my lungs stopping me before my muscles really get a work out, and the muscular improvement will serve to improve the flow and use of oxygen around the body, meaning that I require less oxygen to do everyday tasks, which means I get less breathless while doing them.

Theory is all well and good, but we know how my body likes to throw googlies (or curveballs, if you're more comfortable with the American vernacular), so having the option to bail out on the purchase of a hefty piece of equipment is a good option for right now.

I have to say, having had a wee spin on a bike at Oxford today, it certainly looks promising as a less intense form of exercise. Obviously, there are different levels of resistance and speed settings and a whole host of other options, but the great thing about it is that the very basic starting point is easily manageable, giving a lot more leeway in terms of turning things up or down as my chest may dictate from day-to-day. The trouble with step-ups is that they are very set-in-stone – it's a set distance, with a set weight (my body-weight), over a set time. The bike, on the other hand, has myriad ways of making things easier or harder as my body goes through it's yo-yo routine.

Once again – and as usual – we'll wait and see what comes of it. I don't want to get too over-excited at something that's just going to fall by the wayside again, but the promise is there for something with potential.

It's probably a night in front of the TV tonight, maybe catching a flick or something. But it's been a positive day, so I'm not going to moan about a little bit of tiredness at the end of it.

November 2007

It really works!

Thursday 1 November

I haven't been this excited about random developments for ages. I don't think I've actually EVER been this excited about developments relating to fitness-type stuff. But I've just climbed off the shiny new exercise bike sat not 3 feet from this screen and I feel fantastic – this biking lark seems like it might just be the key to breaking the back of this fitness-malarkey.

It's such a bizarre feeling to sit on the bike and be doing real, proper exercise but not to feel completely breathless and deflated by the whole thing – to find a type of fitness that's enjoyable and beneficial without being a real battle of will power to push through the pain/breathlessness barrier.

It appears that the slower slope of desaturisation that I was talking about yesterday is much more significant than I'd first thought and that I can actually go a lot longer on the bike than I'd hoped without gasping for air or feeling like I'm going to keel off it. Rather, I can actually get to a stage where I can really feel the muscles in my legs being worked hard and doing some stretching and improving of their own.

It's indescribable to feel that I've found something which can make the "working" parts of my body feel included in the day-to-day running of life – like their being paid at least a cursory bit of attention rather than being glossed over in the fight to keep the lungs ticking over.

I keep having all sorts of qualifiers about the relation of current treatment/steroids etc. to the improvement in my chest and exercise tolerance and everything else swirling around my head at the moment, but right now I feel so good, so happy, that I don't want to sit here and qualify things.

It's not often these days that I get a chance to just sit and be excited about something going well. And I know that "not-so-good" may be just around the corner – as it is for all of us – so I'm blowed if I'm going to sit here and not let myself enjoy this feeling for tonight.

I've found something I can do physically that doesn't make me 2nd best to a 3-year-old child and much as you may laugh, that's a really, really big thing for me. Tonight, even if it's "for one night only", I'm enjoying it.

Big smiles and hugs to all!

Party!

Saturday 3 November

It's been a while since I had such a straight-up, unabashed, pure-and-simple really good night in with friends. Last night I had one and it was one of the most simplistically wonderful things that I've experienced for a while.

Having decided rather last minute that the best way to combat our household's fear and loathing of fireworks, K and I set about recruiting the usual gang of easily-entertained appendages to join in our frivolities. We also took the opportunity to finally go out and splash a bit of cash on the Scene It board game I've wanted for a while.

The whole evening was really terribly refined, in a loud and rambunctious kind of way – no alcohol, no TV, just a group of friends laughing, chatting and playing games, sometimes all at once, sometimes in a strange mish-mash of the three.

Whatever we were doing, though, it was just lovely to have the guys round and to be enjoying myself without feeling totally exhausted. I'd had quite a quiet day, keeping myself in check and not getting too over-excited about things so that I had the strength to make the most of the evening and it really paid off. The all eventually left around 1am and I was still feeling really good – a bit of a rarity for me.

We got through games of Scene It, Scattegories and Simpson's Monopoly, the last of which having the bizarre novelty of now being a cash-less game. Each player gets a credit card, which is inserted into a little electronic calculator to add or remove money from the account. It's a great idea, but sadly doesn't really work in practice. The novelty wears off after about 5 minutes, by which point you've realised that every transaction takes 5 times as long as it did with cash and that it's now impossible to a) know how much you've got in the bank without having to ask for the machine to check and b) know how much everyone else is stock-piling to help make those cash-rich deals to the hard-up players.

It was just such a great night and we all had a great time. I honestly don't think any of us noticed the lack of alcohol, which goes a long way to proving my long-held belief about having more fun without it than with it. I won't lose myself in an anti-alcohol diatribe here (because you don't want to hear it anyway), but suffice it to say that it wasn't until K pointed out the party's dryness the next day that it even crossed my mind.

Bump

Sunday 4 November

That's the sound made by me hitting yet another low after a nice 48 hours of high.

I've been um-ing and ah-ing over whether or not to drag down the recent positivity of my posts by indulging in my slight rearward step, but on reflection of the last two days I realised that what this blog started out as was a way for me to keep track of the course of my progress up to and hopefully beyond the point I receive my new lungs. It seems entirely counter-productive to gloss-over the bad bits in order to spare what few regular readers I do "entertain" on here from being exposed to more difficulties.

Yesterday was actually a really good day – spent largely in bed/on the sofa doing very little indeed recovering from Friday's grand night in, then sharing a lovely meal with K's 'rents which saw us pass over her Dad's 60th birthday pressie (which is only 6 (and a bit...) months late). Was worth the wait, though – we got a photograph he had taken in Central Park blown up and printed on to canvas for him and it looks amazing.

It wasn't until after they had left that the day slid away from me. Every night I sit at my computer in the study and do my nebs and casually surf around the 'net for the 15-20 minutes it takes, most often taking in other people's blogs and catching up on friends' news.

On Saturday night, I made the mistake (it would appear) of clicking through into Facebook while I was browsing. It was there that I found a new batch of photos a friend had put up of the festivities at another friend's wedding. The happy couple (God bless them, in the most sincere way possible) are friends I used to work with at MK Theatre and have enjoyed many a night out with over the years, both at work and outside.

Clicking through the newly-created photo album (put up by someone who clearly left the party too early if they were awake and/or sober enough to be able to connect their camera to a computer and upload the pics), I was met by face after face of happy, smiling people with whom I've enjoyed countless brilliant nights out over the years I worked at the Theatre and, indeed, since I left.

It struck me suddenly – in that sort of roundhouse punch/kick in the crotch kind of way these things tend to occur to you – that it's been a very, very long time since I was out with all of them. In fact, it's been a very, very long time since any of them would even have thought to bother to ask me to go out with them. Not through any fault or malice on their part, but simply because they know I wouldn't be able to join them.

Sitting looking at happy face after happy face, smiling friend after smiling friend, it slowly dawned on me just how long it's been since I've done anything remotely "normal" for a 25 year-old who claims to work in the theatre industry. I've not been to the theatre, I've not been to the cinema, I've not been out for a drink, I've not even been out for a latte or "done lunch" – it's not just "normal" that I've missed, I've even managed to lose "pretentious" too.

I suppose it's a positive reflection on my state of body/state of mind at the moment that I can sit here after the fact and see inject some humour into it, but it really did hit me quite hard as I flicked through the album. Some kind of intense sense-memory came washing over me and I could hear the voices, the laughter, the banter, the music; I could see the suits, the dresses, the dancing, the staggering, the pretty, the happiness and everything else. I wanted so badly to be back there, to be laughing, singing, drinking, dancing – just being.

When I first started this weblog almost exactly 12 months ago, I truly never would have believed that without my transplant I would still be writing it today, so it is with no little understatement that I suggest it's not a bad thing to be here – sitting comfortably in my desk chair, living with my wonderful girlfriend, having spent an amazing weekend enjoying the company of my friends and both sides of my family – complaining about not "getting out" enough. If there was ever a "meaning" to this blog – a reason, plan or intent behind it – it was to remind myself of the good things in the face of the bad things.

So it is with a deep breath in and a sigh of appreciation that I thank Last Year's Me once again for providing me with a place to come to remind myself that no matter what's going on in my life, my body or my head, things are never as bad as they seem, that there's always a light at the end of the tunnel and that the most important thing in life is to keep on keeping on – Smile Through It.

It's OK, I'm OK

Monday 5 November

So Saturday night was a bit of a bump, but Sunday and Monday have been a much more even keel – I've stayed resolutely on the positivity band-wagon, although I may have slid sideways a couple of times.

Yesterday morning vanished into nothing – a brief wake-up call at 7am to do my morning drugs dose, but the rest disappearing under the covers after another late night.

Shortly after the turn of noon, having stumbled out of bed, K's Dad swung by with the visiting boyfriend of her Hungarian cousin. Actually, technically, I don't think they're cousins, but once you get into the Hungarian side of the family I'm afraid I rather lose track of her clan. I can only just keep track of the English side, but that's because they're inconsiderate enough to have 2 Uncle Peters, which is just foolish if you ask me. I don't see why they couldn't have drawn straws for a name change to help me out just a little.

I digress. T's English was immaculate (handy, considering the state of my Hungarian) and it was really nice to meet him and chat. K was revelling in getting first-hand details of all the goings on with her Hungarian cousins, one of whom is due to have her first child any day now. K was keen for T to let his other half know that being an Aunty is "the best thing in the world". I ventured to point out that I daresay being a Mum might be considered to top it, but I always get shouted down.

They didn't stay long, since K's Dad was taking T off for a

round-the-houses meet-and-greet of the rest of Team H over lunch. I should think he got back to his apartment in London absolutely shattered after getting through the whole gang.

In the evening, we headed over to my 'rents to catch up with them and have a gorgeous roast. I know everyone always says it about theirs, but my Mum does the *best* roast dinners in the whole wide world and last night she even managed to out-do her usual high standards. It was but a whisker short of perfection. (The whisker being Tio's, their lovely little cat, who brought us a wee mouse as a pre-dinner snack).

After dinner we chilled out and played games for a while before K and I headed home as everyone but me had to be up for work in the morning. Not that it means I get a lie in, as I had to be up for my drugs anyway. Sometimes you just can't win.

Today has been a generally un-taxing day. I've not felt 100%, but it's mostly just tiredness, largely caused by a busy weekend and the usual end-of-IV-run lack of decent sleep. Having to be up every 8 hours to do drugs doesn't sound like a bind, but when you figure it means you only ever get around 6 hours of sleep at a given time, it starts to wear you down a fair bit.

I did manage to catch a movie I've been trying to peep for a while now, which actually ended up disappointing me greatly, so I'll not even go into detail here. Suffice it to say I'll not be awaiting the next QT flick as eagerly as I did this one.

Tonight, once K got in from work, apart from nebs and physio, plus another 20 minute bike sesh, we've basically just been in front of the telly finishing off the third season of Lost, which just totally blew us away – it's amazing. If you've never seen it, you absolutely have to go out and get all three seasons in their box sets now and check them out – they're completely compulsive viewing.

Now there's just time for another dose of drugs and a catch-up on some of last night's telly while they go through and it'll be off to bed and start again in the morning. I'm determined to be productive tomorrow. Watch this space.

Cold

Tuesday 6 November

Not much more to say, really. Am feeling utterly deflated that at the end of 2 weeks' IVs which have boosted me rather wonderfully and got me feeling very good and positive, I wake up this morning with puffy, stuffy sinuses and a whisper of a headache, which has spent the day hovering between going away and worsening into full-blown cold.

There's not a lot I can do to keep it from setting in full-blown, I don't think, certainly no more than I'm trying, which is lots of rest with lots of calories and spraying First Defence up my nose like teenage boys spray cologne on a night out. The plus side, I suppose, is that at least I don't smell as bad as they do.

Thinking about it, I suppose I have to take the blame for the onset of the cold, since I did make the mistake of saying yesterday that I wanted to be productive today and get things done. If this blog has proven one thing over the last 12 months, it's that whenever I talk about getting things done, something crops up to get in the way of it. I really should learn just to keep my mouth shut.

Realistically, it's more likely than not that the cold is simply my body's reaction to a frantically busy weekend – it's a long time since I've had 3 nights of "entertainment" in a row and although I rested a lot in the day times, it must still have worn me down.

It's frustrating and – as always – a little scary to be coming down with something, but at least I have the security of knowing that I'm getting it at my very best point physically. I'm just a day from finishing IV's (which will now be extended by another week to cover any knock-on effects from the cold) and still on steroids, which means my appetite is good, my chest is as good as it ever gets and I'm firing on as many cylinders as I've got. If there is ever a "good" time to get a cold when you're aware of the possible consequences to a pair of dodgy blowers, this is it.

So I'm off to get some more physio done, shovel down some more food, suck down some more Lucozade and pray to the Big Guy to keep this one mild. All help appreciated, if you're so inclined.

Worried, relieved.

Wednesday 7 November

It's been a nervous 24 hours here since the cold reared its head and it was made all the worse last night after I spotted a problem with the line into my port through which I give my IV's.

I noticed while I was doing my afternoon dose that the line had gone a little cloudy, but didn't think much of it. By the evening dose, it hadn't cleared up (as sometimes happens) and had a couple of distinct breaks in the cloudiness, which started to concern me slightly.

Anyone with a port-a-cath will tell you how protective they are of them, not least people in my position as the loss of use of a post through breakage or – God forbid – infection is a serious problem: replacing ports is not the kind of thing that can be done on a whim and while it isn't what you'd term "major" surgery, it's certainly more than most doctors would like to be performing on someone with end-stage lung disease.

With all these thoughts running through my head, I took the executive decision to not give my next dose of IV's until I'd been to Oxford to get it looked at and replace the needle and line for a new one.

After a late-night phone call with Mum, we hastily arranged a lunch-time pick up when she finished work (trampling all over any other plans for the day she may have had) and I settled down for the night after pumping another mini-monsoon of First Defence up my nose and downing a handful of Vitamin C caps to try to ward the cold off, too.

For once I slept absolutely beautifully. Without my morning dose of dugs to do, I slept clean through till 10am, when K's alarm woke me. Lucky it did, really, because it didn't wake her, so she'd have been in a spot if it weren't for my eagle-eyed sense of hearing. (Yeah, I know, that confused me, too.) That said, I'm sure she'll jump to defend herself having already been out of bed once to answer the door to a nice delivery man.

A quick call to my team in Oxford and the ever-brilliant Cass opened up a slot for me early in the afternoon. I checked with Mum and we were all good to shoot on over once she'd got her morning at work out of the way.

I got up slowly and rumbled around the house, hesitantly waiting for the cold to hit with full force, but nothing really materialised. My sinuses were much less clogged and though I struggled a little with my physio first thing, I managed to clear a good bit and get my nebs done before Mum arrived. I grabbed some Lucozade for the journey and hopped in the car, leaving K at home for a study session with a college-mate.

Cass looked me over and gave my port a quick once-over and agreed that it didn't seem to be anything too untoward, although she'd never seen anything like it either. She swapped my needle out and re-accessed me, giving it a good flush to check it out and all seemed well. We agreed that although the cold doesn't seem to have taken hold, an extra week on the IVs wasn't going to do any harm. I can't have been there more than 20 minutes before Mum whisked me off again, but it was worth the 3 hour round trip for the piece of mind it gave me.

We got home just before half-three and I connected up my afternoon dose of IVs and hit the sack to recharge my batteries. I woke an hour later feeling really quite energised, hit my nebs and did some physio before dinner.

I think – touch wood – I've managed to ward the cold off, so am hoping that another good night's rest and another day not doing too much should keep me back on the well-wagon and I can look forward to another weekend with family and friends.

Off to catch tonight's episode of Heroes now – we're all addicted and we're only a few weeks from the end of the season! Hooray!

Blog Evolution

Thursday 8 November

I have discovered a new feature on my blog that allows me to change the date stamp on the posts, so I can post an entry for Thursday after typing it up on a Saturday (exactly what I'm doing now). This excites me because a) it means I can technically never miss a day's blogging without feeling like I have to write something hilarious at midnight when I'm straining to keep my eyes awake, b) I can better keep track of all the things I do from day-to-day without having to write a single, enormously long post at the end of the week or such.

Really, the excitement stems from having got lost in re-reading Kevin Smith's diaries, which I used to follow avidly on his website but have now been published in paperback form. What occurred to me as I waded back in to them (alongside memories of their first reading as long ago as 2005) is that part of the reason for creating this blog was not only to try to give myself a kick up the butt when I needed one, but also to have something on which I could look back in a few years time (God willing) and help me to remember what life was like "way back when" in my old life with rubbish lungs.

So I'm hoping to keep a slightly more day-to-day diary of events from here on out, although I'm sure they will still be peppered with the usual random tangents and streams-of-consciousness as all my posts have ever been.

So anyway, Thursday (today… wait, that's weird…) saw me waking, annoyingly, 10 minutes before my alarm went off. I say annoyingly, but actually, thinking about it, it's quite nice to wake up naturally, even if the first impulse on waking to roll over and drift back off to sleep has to be fought off to get up and set the a.m. dose of drugs flowing. Which I manage to do.

I park myself, still slightly dazed, in the chair by the telly and watch something or other while the drugs kick in. By the time they're done, I'm actually nearly awake, which is quite rare for drug-mornings. I stick on the extras disk from Lost Season 3 (which we finished last night) and immerse myself in behind-the-scenes stuff, which always gets my creative-juices flowing.

At 10 I wake K up as we have a visit from our littlest niece and nephew and she just about manages to roll out of bed in time to greet them at the door. They are so excited to get here it's almost magical, and no sooner are they in the living room than they're up on the sofa bouncing their heads off or pulling the contents of the coffee table off onto the floor.

We sit and drink tea with their Mum while they tear the place apart (in a nice way) and we play with anything we can find to play with. Most excitingly, because of the delivery of drugs I had yesterday, we have a big, empty cardboard box to play with, which ends up getting decorated with colouring pencils.

I grab my camera and get some super-cute shots of them as they run around, including some wonderful full-paparazzi-style shots of the little on, hand extended at the camera in "get out of my face" mode.

They leave around lunchtime and I immediately crash out back in bed. I'm pretty impressed that they didn't actually totally exhaust me, but I know for sure that if I don't take the chance to recharge my batteries now, I'm not going to make it through the rest of the day unscathed, and with the hint of a cold still around, I don't want to use all my energy up.

I wake up a couple of hours later and feel strong enough to run K to college, which cheers me up as I'd assumed I would be house-bound most of this week. I drop her off and head home, spending the next hour or so on the 'net checking emails and getting a little lost in Facebook, as is my unfortunate tendency.

K calls in a seriously foul mood (justifiably, after a completely wasted and pointless night at a poor excuse for an educational establishment – shame on you Milton Keynes College) and I run out to pick her up.

We get back to find an old friend of mine from the Theatre in the car park, where she'd been waiting for me to get back (I thought K was going to be out longer, so I'd be around to let her in before I had to shoot off to pick her up, but ended up leaving her parked outside for 20mins while I did the school run). We go upstairs and grab a cuppa while catching up on anything and everything from the last 6-months or so. She has a lot more to share than I do…

In fact, I hadn't seen her since before she went off on a jungle-trek to Thailand in the summer, through which she raised over £7,000 for the CF Trust and nearly died in the process after an unfortunate incident with a bamboo raft and a set of rain-forest rapids. She fills us in on all the details of everything and it sounds like an amazing trip.

What was intended to be a quick cuppa turns into a lengthy evening's nattering, which eventually ends with her taking her leave about 10pm. K and I settle on the sofa while I do my drugs and watch tonight's episode of Studio 60, then hit the sack just before midnight.

Specialists are good

Friday 9 November

I am very much asleep when the alarm goes off this morning and I prize myself out of bed in a slow and careful manner. Drugs duly flowing, I try my hardest to stay awake while they run through, watching some Making of Toy Story DVD as I do.

Once the drugs are done I'm about focused enough to run K into work, but when I get home I take myself straight back to bed for another hour's kip, which is rudely interrupted 45mins in (just when it's about perfect snoozing) by the postman, who can't let himself in again (to the building, that is – he doesn't try to break into our flat of a morning).

I decide it's pointless trying to re-claim my 15 minutes and so head for a bath instead, then check my email quickly before Mum arrives to whisk me over to Oxford for my physio appointment.

My CF team in Oxford have recently reached a deal with the physio department whereby they can cross-pollinate departments – whereas I used to only be able to see chest-specialist physios (who are paid for under the CF-care banner) if I wanted to see any other type of physio, it would have to be a paid-for referral either from my GP (who's in the wrong PCT) or the chest team (who can't afford the extra fees). Charging issues ironed out, however, I am free to go and see a muscular-skeletal physio who is part of the Churchill team up the corridor from my usual clinic.

What a difference a specialist makes. My two regular physios sat in on the session too, eager to learn the basics of what they could do to help me (and others) out with my neck/back problems, all of which stem from the extra work my respiratory muscles are having to do to make up for the cruddy condition of my lungs.

After half and hour's poking, prodding and manipulation, I can already feel a difference, and the physio promises if I can get up there every week she'll find 10 minutes to have another go and keep the main parts mobilized, with the eventual aim that I'll be able to strengthen the muscles back up to pull more weight without so much strain.

After my neck session, I head down to the treatment centre with my regular physio for a regular chest physio session, at which we also do my L-F, which stands back up at a healthy (relatively) 0.8/1.5, which is good to see. Even more astonishingly, my weight has now hit 56kg on the clinic scales, and that's without a thick jumper on. I've NEVER been this heavy before, and it feels like a real achievement.

Back home I feel terrible because K's had a bad day at work and only been home half an hour but all I can do when I walk in the door is fold myself into bed and fall asleep. Rested and recovered after an hour or so, I try to make it up with tea (which is usually a good place to start) and she appears not to harbour any of the kind of grudge I think I would given reversed circumstances. It's times like these that my "frailties" really bug me – it seems such a small thing to ask to be able just to chill and have a cuddle after a bad day, but when I'm tired, especially from travel, I'm really not in a state to do anything. What makes K so wonderful is the fact that no matter what the situation, she never complains at all.

In the evening, an old school friend who's recently moved back over from France pops round and we have a giggle-some night of pizza and board games. We discover, much to our disappointment, that Operation really isn't that difficult if you're any older than about 10. None of us had played it for years, but he'd had it at home and thought it was in marvellously bad taste to bring it round (which we both readily agreed). Naturally, they let me win, since otherwise it would just have been rude.

Another couple of games of Scene It (of which I won neither, let the record show – for those of you who think I must just walk it every time), and B headed off home. My drugs were due later than normal because of bad planning on my part so K headed to bed while I did my last dose, watching some Sky+'d Simpsons and the start of The American President, which I'd recorded a while ago before surfing the 'net for a while during my evening nebs.

I eventually make it to bed about 1.30am, where I read Kevin Smith just long enough to make my eyelids heavy then settle down for the night.

Totalled

Tuesday 13 November

I'm feeling awful at the moment – my cold has hit with a vengeance and is dragging me down big-style. Most irritatingly, it's gone to my throat, which makes clearing all the usual gunk off my chest incredibly hard as a tickly cough makes doing good-quality physio almost impossible.

Coupled with that, obviously, the gunk that is there anyway (which isn't getting cleared) is now getting thicker and heavier and nastier with all the cold bugs in it, too, which is making breathing and life in general incredibly hard. It's basically one great big heap of can't-breathe-very-well, feel-like-crap, need-to-sleep-for-weeks poo.

Of course, me being me, the easiest and most obvious course of action is also the one that my body objects to the most, namely sleeping. Because of all the rubbish on my chest which I'm not clearing, I'm loaded up with stuff which is making breathing hard anyway, but as soon as I try to go anywhere near horizontal (or even just slightly leaned-over) it all starts rumbling around even more and giving me even more problems.

So last night I managed a grand total of about 2 hours sleep and that was taken pretty much because my body literally couldn't keep my eyes open and my brain turned on any more. No matter what position I was in I would be in some form of discomfort, which was either back pain, shoulder pain, chest pain or all three combined with inability to breathe. I tell you something, struggling to breathe on a machine that's suppose to help you breathe is not a pleasant sensation.

So last night wasn't good and this morning wasn't much brighter – what with the distinct lack of rest and still rumbling chest.

I have, however, made it through to the afternoon now and things are brightening up ever so slightly. My biggest problem has been getting comfortable, as whenever my breathing becomes a problem now it causes all sorts of chain-reactions through the rest of my body, specifically back and neck pain which makes sitting in most positions either painful or hard to breathe.

Most annoyingly, it's the positions you would imagine to be the most comfortable that I struggle with the most – sitting on the sofa causes huge neck pain, sitting in bed causes lower-back pain and breathlessness and sitting in the comfy chair in the living room causes one of the two, depending on how I sit.

Ironically, sitting bolt upright in the desk chair at the computer is currently my most chest-friendly position. I've been in front of the screen for a little over 3 hours now and I'm feeling the best I have all day. I suppose there's no excuse for me not being productive, is there? Although my brain isn't entirely switched on at the moment.

Anyway, I thought I'd take the opportunity to catch up on some online diarizing and catching up on the US Writer's Strike, which has got me bizarrely hooked.

I'm hoping a better day, a better throat and some better physio means that I'll be able to get better sleep tonight and things will duly improve tomorrow. The resurgence of the cold has coincided once again with the scheduled end-of-IVs, so I'll be back at Oxford tomorrow but look set to continue into a 4th week of the mega-drugs. Better than ending up feeling even worse and going back on them in a week or two anyway.

The going gets tough

Wednesday 14 November

Today has been, hands down, one of the hardest days I've had in a very long while – harking back really as far as my admission in June, where every day was a challenge.

Luckily, the benefit of hindsight and such tells me that it's not quite that bad – one horrible day in a week can't possibly be as bad as one passable day in a week – but it's only thanks to a little bit of let-up in the relentless onslaught of tiredness, breathlessness and exhaustion that allows me an ounce of philosophy in my outlook.

It started, oddly, not too badly – I woke this morning having had very little sleep but not feeling too bad about it. I clearly had a lot on my chest, but was also managing to get quite a bit off just by being up and about. Early mornings are usually the time when you find out what kind of crap is on your chest, since the very process of getting up and moving around tends to make you cough and splutter, which in turn lets you see a) how productive you are b) how easily it's moving and c) how out-of-breath it makes you when you do.

I was moving stuff pretty easily, although it was exhausting to cough and my throat was still causing problems with getting the big lumps up. (Nice, I know, but this is a full-disclosure blog, so if you don't like it it's not for you, I guess!). Having got my morning dose of drugs out of the way, I crawled back to bed feeling breathless but not too bad.

I woke again around 12.30, later than I'd planned and wanted to. With a 2.30 appointment in Oxford, I'd have to be out of the house in under an hour, so would need to pick and choose the most important elements out of bathing, dressing, eating, doing physio and doing nebs, as well as getting my things together for the Oxford trip (it always involves taking a book as well as my physio-helping device, which all need to be collected into a bag – it may not sound like much but believe me, it was a task-and-a-half today).

I settled on food and nebs being the two most important things, so threw on some clothes in a very slow and deliberate manner and made a sandwich, which I sat and munched before doing a neb and collecting my things, all of which filled the next 45 minutes and made me incredibly, uncomfortably breathless.

At Oxford things didn't improve a whole lot. My nurse changed my port needle, which was fine with the exception of the bioclusive (clear plastic) dressing pulling off a good chunk of surface skin by my under-arm area, which was then healthily swabbed with alcohol prior to the insertion of the new needle. Yes, it smarts.

My physio session was really, really hard work – harder than I've had for a long time. I was breathless, tired and my airways were irritable and not playing ball, the gunk on my chest refusing to be moved around and brought up, so it felt like we weren't really achieving much.

Seeing as I'm now sliding into my 4th week on IVs, the team wanted me to check in with the Doc to see if they wanted to do anything different. I'm loathe to change anything at the moment for several reasons, partially because I believe that once I've kicked the cold the drugs will do their job, but mostly because any change in IVs is likely to mean switching to one that I don't get on with quite so well, which in turn would mean that they'd have to have me in and on the ward for a few days so they could keep an eye on me. I'm not keen on the ward at the best of times, but when I'm not getting a whole lot of sleep at home, it's even less appealing because I know that I won't get any on the ward.

While I was waiting to be fitted into the doc's queue, I had another fantastic session of physio with the wonderful back/neck specialist, who worked me over really well. She did what she calls "mobilizing the joints" followed by "mobilizing the soft tissue". One of the nurses said that the soft-tissue stuff looked like a massage to her, but the physio helpfully pointed out that the big difference was that massages are pleasurable.

Neck attacked, I popped across to the clinic to catch up with the doc, who reluctantly agreed to give the drugs a few days to see if they can kick in after the cold. We agreed that if things are no better by the weekend, then I'll be straight in. If I'm picking up they'll leave me out and check my progress after the weekend and we'll see where we stand.

By this time it was well after 4.30, which meant a slow journey home in the evening traffic. We made an executive decision to take the scenic route, which although dark and not at all scenic, would at least guarantee that we'd be back inside an hour and a half, which is impossible to be sure of if you take the A34.

Back home just after 6 I was completely exhausted, to the level of a childish sense of having no idea what to do with myself. Every single part of me wanted to go to sleep, but I knew if I did I would have no chance at all of getting to sleep. Instead, I sat myself in the study chair to be as comfy as possible and surfed the 'net for a while, before hopping into a bath to try and freshen up a bit.

It worked – to a limited extent – and we then managed to get through our usual Wednesday night where our bestest bud Dazz pops in to catch up on a Sky+'d ep of Entourage (our guilty pleasure) followed by this week's Heroes.

With those out of the way, I didn't have much else to do with myself than dump my exhausted, knackered, buggered old body in the sack and pray for a good night's sleep. And while I was there, I put in a small request to have a better day tomorrow, please, too.

One small step

Thursday 15 November

Well, someone was listening to me last night, because today has, indeed, been a better day so far. That's not to say things are all fine and dandy, or that the picture is yet all rosy, but side-by-side with yesterday, today has been a Good Day.

I managed to get almost straight to sleep last night, sometime after 11pm, which is rare for me these days. Not only that, but I managed to sleep quite solidly, too – no constant waking to switch position or readjust myself. It may have been thanks to having fiddled with Neve and pushed the pressures up ever-so-slightly, or a slightly improvement on the chest front, or simply thanks to complete exhaustion and my body not having any other choice but sleeping it off. My guess would be it was a healthy mix of the three.

Bizarrely, and somewhat annoyingly, I woke up bright-as-a-button(ish) around 5am and couldn't get back to sleep, no matter how hard I tried. I had planned to lay in a bit today and do my morning dose a little later than usual, but given that I was awake anyway, I decided to switch the plans and get up early and get them out of the way, which would have the knock-on effect of allowing me an earlier night tonight.

I got up, got my dose running and sat myself a the computer to surf around and catch up on the over-night writers' strike news, during which time my chest was doing all kinds of weird things, making me breathless one minute and fine the next, and I developed a bit of a killer headache.

By the time my drugs had finished, I decided it'd be a good idea to try to get some physio out of the way before I got myself back to bed, so I did another very uncomfortable session – very hard work again. Having said which, I definitely felt the benefit afterwards, even through it didn't feel like I'd cleared a lot. I did my antibiotic nebs and then took myself to bed around 9am.

Interestingly, for those who keep tabs on this sort of thing, 9am is also the time that the construction workers begin work on resurfacing the road outside the front of where we live. With the sun beating a nice, hot set of rays down on the bedroom window, keeping them shut was out of the question, so keeping the noise out was also not a part of the plan.

As it happened, noisy as they were, I needed sleep more, and I managed to doze on-and-off for another few hours till the early afternoon.

I rolled out of bed feeling much better for the physio and sleep, grabbed a cuppa with K and chatted for a bit, talked to my 'rents to catch them up on over-night progress and then headed back for more physio. It was a much better session than this mornings, and much easier, too, making things look brighter already.

After physio, I got some calories down me and then headed back to bed to chill out with K and watch the first ep of the first season of 24 – a season I've seen but K hasn't and is next on our TV-DVD marathon. I'm amazed at how much I don't remember from the first time it aired, and also at how much of what I do remember they've crammed into the first ep – there must be a whole heap more that I don't remember to come, which is promising.

After chilling in bed for a while, K gets up to do some more revision and I sit and read GQ for a while, before K heads off to college and I do my 3rd physio session of the day. I'm determined to crack the back of this while I can.

Physio out of the way, I jump online for a while and do a bit of Chrimbo shopping (have to bow to the inevitable eventually, I suppose) and look into a couple of other random bits and pieces while the Shepherd's Pie Mum made me yesterday cooks. I sit and eat it while watching the last episode of Extras from the DVD that I'd never got round to seeing, then wash up and get back to the study, going over a couple of old scripts till K gets home.

We watch some programmes from Sky+ and I do some more physio (a really good late-night session, actually), and before I know it my evening drugs are all done and it's time to hit the sack. Things are still very up-and-down, and I suspect they will be for a good few days yet, but today's been a massive improvement on yesterday, and that's a big step forward. Well, at least a little one.

Lost: please find

Monday 19 November

It's closing in on 4am and I find myself sat in the lounge at my parents' house if not quite wide-awake then certainly not sound asleep. Since I finally gave in to my night's chronic lack of slumber just over an hour ago, I've been wondering to myself whether this point marks a new low in my struggle as it has been.

It's extraordinarily tempting to call it that, but putting tiredness and busy-headedness to one side, if I try to clear up the picture a little bit I suppose it's hard to suggest right now that I'm worse off than I was when I was admitted to Oxford back in June.

Certainly, chest-wise, I'm not doing as badly as I was then. Yes, I'm still finding every day a struggle and breathlessness is increasingly a problem throughout the day, rather than being something that tended to isolate itself to certain times or periods that could be identified and focused on. And yes, every night is seemingly harder than more recent times to gather myself and settle down to sleep – the effort of undressing, of washing both myself and my equipment, of simply sitting in bed reading is considerably more noticeable than it was a week or more ago.

On the other hand, I'm not spiking the temperatures I was spiking in June, nor am I confined as I was then to my bed, fighting for breath even at rest and needing the highest flows of oxygen I could muster with my various concentrators to see me to the bathroom and back. I am, on the whole, physically better off than I was back in June, although it is tempting to be blinded to it by the storm of exhaustion that has settled in to my quiet little dwelling.

I can only surmise, then, that if I am physically better off than I was in June then in order to be feeling quite as badly as I do about things at the moment, then my head is very far from in the right place. There is a line of which people often speak between living and existing – an invisible, intangible and yet undeniable line over which the simple matter of getting through the day becomes the be-all and end-all of one's ambitions. I am not entirely sure I have reached such a line yet, but for the first time in a long while it has become more to me than a mark on a road map that I may be approaching. Rather, it is now a hazy, not-so-distant shimmer that presents itself not as far away as one would like or hope it to be.

At the end of last week, K and I made the executive decision to take ourselves back to Chez Parental in order to afford K more time to study for her college finals in a 2 weeks' time and prepare for her uni interview without having to look after me and without me having to worry about whether she was spending too much time on me and not enough on herself (something at which I am incredibly bad at – I spend most of my life worrying that she's worrying too much, which is a vicious circle in itself).

My mood, however, has not taken to the holiday particularly well. I have no idea if it is purely coincidental, or if coming home carries an air of admitting defeat or some other such nonsense, but since settling back in here I have been distinctly more negatively-focused and have noticed the difficulties over-and-above the advantages.

Interestingly, I don't think it's particularly anything about being home, but more a reflection of the general difficulties I'm struggling with physically at the moment. The biggest problem I'm facing is one of discomfort – I find it almost impossible now to be comfortable in any position at all.

Lying down is fine enough, but only if I am truly horizontal, which makes doing anything at all nigh on impossible. From there, there is lying propped up, which stresses my lower back and neck, there is sitting up, as on a sofa, which stresses my neck to the point of causing headaches and my upper back and shoulders causing breathlessness. Sitting bolt-upright in a well-supported armchair is about right, but if the back of the chair is not vertical – like the study chair at home – my neck once again takes the strain if it is not supported or rested back.

When sleeping is a problem, it can at least be countered with good periods of solid rest during the day. But when solid rest is completely unachievable – when it is impossible simply to crash out on the sofa and watch mind-numbing TV or brain-absorbing DVDs – lack of sleep becomes just as debilitating as a lack of breath.

When all of these factors are totted up and combined with headaches, odd, unidentifiable but frequently worrying chest pains, cramps and stomach aches on top of it, life becomes a roller-coaster of moment-to-moment misery through which you ache to enjoy that odd glimpse of sunlight glinting through the clouds.

That's not to say I haven't enjoyed glimpses of golden rays in the last week, nor that the world is entirely shrouded in blackness, but compared to the fights and struggles I've had before, this one certainly feels like it's ramping things up a notch.

I'm not entirely sure what the point of all the above is/will prove to be, other than a manner of half-an-hour's distraction in the early hours of the morning and an outlet for all the mixed up frustrations which are mixing themselves up in the pressure-cooking wash-bowl of my head. The dregs of an active, lively mind are swilling around up there somewhere, drained of colour and vibrancy by the hour of night and relentless, restless energy.

If nothing else, I suspect this will go to show in the weeks to come the extent of any improvement on my part. I can only hope that it marks the nadir of my fortunes and that things are all the way upwards from here. If not, this is going to be a pretty hard place to visit.

EPILOGUE: PART 1

5th time lucky!

Tuesday 20 November

Hi everyone, this is K. I have had permission from Oli to keep you all updated and help provide him with a blog that will cover his progress as he recovers. In case you hadn't caught on yet, Oli has had a transplant!

The call came this evening around 7pm, just as Oli had got in the bath, a bath he had been wanting all day but his lungs were being particularly difficult and he had to wait for them to give him a break.

We all hopped in the car and drove to Harefield, driving in torrential rain that made the journey very interesting as I'm sure the puddles were nearly swimming pool size in places.

Things happened very routinely once we got to Harefield. We know the drill by now, settle into the room, watch Oli have copious amounts of blood taken by the vampire docs, swabs from almost every part of the body, shower and shave with special pink liquid, and then the wait. And more waiting. And more waiting.

The news came at 11pm as Oli was in the shower, he really wasn't having much luck with getting clean today, however this news was the news we have been waiting for for 2 ½ years, the transplant was going ahead and he was due in theatre at 00:15.

The mood in the room was strange, Oli was totally calm, instantly got onto his phone and started letting everyone know. I was absolutely excited, amazed, nervous, scared, every emotion you could possibly imagine, I had it all at once. Whereas I couldn't stop shaking, Oli was so chilled and relaxed – I am still amazed by the strength of character this guy has, he really is one in a million.

The only time he got nervous was when we got to the theatre doors and weren't allowed any further. The goodbyes at the doors were very difficult, it's so hard to reassure someone who is about to have their life changed that everything will be ok. It isn't anything we have experienced before and so words weren't enough. Watching Oli being wheeled down to theatre was the most amazing feeling in the world, good luck Oli – we're here every step of the way…

EPILOGUE: PART 2

Two weeks after my transplant, I sit on my bed in a tangle of wires and bottom out. Not *with* my bottom out, I mean hit the bottom. Rock bottom. The lowest I can ever genuinely remember feeling.

I'd been told by so many people that transplants were this miracle thing, that you woke up from and took an amazing, long, deep breath for the first time you can remember and life just gets better and better.

They were right about one thing: life gets better.

I sit on my bed and I think about everything: the wires attached to me, the indignity of using a commode or – at worst – a bedpan, when my kidneys failed and I was put onto dialysis for a few nights while they recovered. I think about the sheer lack of anything approaching recovery, and I break down.

"No one told me it was going to be this hard," I whisper.

K and my brother are with me and my brother senses his moment to step up.

My brother has always had that knack of knowing exactly what people need at what moment – when to care and cuddle, when to kick some ass. And he sees that I've slipped beyond the care and cuddle phase.

He sits by me on the bed and he speaks slowly and quietly, "You're right, no one did, but do you know what? This is it. This is the worst it gets. This is your rock bottom. You can't get any lower than this, you can't feel any worse, be tied to any more tubes, endure any worse embarrassment. This is it."

Cheers, I think to myself. Really helping.

"You know what that means?" he continues, "Every step you take from here on out is forwards. Every day is a better day than the last. Every week makes you stronger, tougher. You are on the road to beating this simply from the admission that you feel you can't."

*****

Shortly after this episode, he comes back in to see me on a regular visit with something to declare.

He's decided that he and a squad of his men from 42 Commando Royal Marines is going to run the Tresco marathon in April.

Tresco is a tiny island that forms part of the Scilly Isles and, each year, the CF Trust organized what they billed as the World's Smallest Marathon on the same day as the World's Largest Marathon in London.

Not only will 10 of them take time out of their Easter break to do this, but they will all do it wearing full kit and 30lbs backpacks, too. All to raise money for the CF Trust and to raise awareness for organ donation.

But there's a catch, he tells me, "We'll only do it if you come and run the last mile of it with us."

How can you say no to that?

*****

Four months later I find myself standing at the top of the biggest hill in Tresco.

I should point out that Tresco is such a small island that you need to run around it 7-and-a-half times in order to complete a marathon distance. That hill may not look like much, but I'm assured it gets bigger every lap.

I stand looking at my watch as the Marines come into view. They've declared to the organisers that they wanted to finish inside 6 hours, but I know they are secretly hoping to break 5 hours 30 minutes.

Their time as they crest the hill for the final mile is 5:18; my fastest mile in training was 14 minutes. I begin to panic – will I be the reason they miss their target?

I go off like a rocket, trying to make up time for them, but soon tire halfway down the hill and am reduced to walking. I fight to keep my walking pace up, breaking into a run where I can.

I find out later that I'd gone off too fast even for the Marines. From the back of the squad – 25.2 miles into their ordeal in boots, combats and packs – a shout goes up to my bro, "Jesus Christ, boss, he's not gonna keep this up, is he?!"

I slow to a walk, try to run again and slow to a walk. Try to run again. This repeats several times until I see the finish line around the corner. I start to run again, this time at a slower pace that I know I can keep up for the last 200 yards (and that the Marines are far more grateful for).

It feels like the entire island is gathered at the finish.

I see the faces of so many of the CF Trust staff and Patrons, many of whom have become fast friends over the years of my illness and association with them.

I see the faces of the other runners, exhausted and struggling to stay on their feet in some places, but all clapping, cheering and shouting.

As I cross the line, I see my parents, and I see K, and I burst into tears.

Even as I write, I'm almost in tears at the overwhelming emotion of it all.

The previous April, as I contemplated the milestone of my 25th birthday and mourned the loss of a wonderful friend, I could never have imagined being there, in that place, having achieved what I just had.

I hugged K, hugged my parents, hugged my brother and hugged each of the Marines in turn, offering them what felt like paltry thanks for what they had done, not just for the Trust, but for me. I let my tears flow and offered a quiet prayer of thanks to my donor for making it all happen.

My time? 11 minutes 34 seconds.

AFTERWORD

Re-reading these posts as I put the book together, it struck me just how horrendous the wait for transplant was.

It's easy with hindsight to see the happy ending through the trials and even now I struggle to recall the true depths to which I sank, but reading some of the episodes in here I genuinely wonder where I got the strength to continue.

I was incredibly luck to be surrounded by people who loved and supported me, from the wonderful K to my ever-present family, my friends and people I didn't even know who left comments of love and support on these posts.

As I sit here in my lovely, warm, happy marital home (K and I married in summer 2012), I can only think of those who are still waiting for the gift of life and whose very existence hangs in the balance in the same way mine did five years ago.

I always said before my transplant that I wanted six more month: six months of being able to breathe freely, move without pain, run without tiring and play without exhaustion. Six more months with a quality of life I couldn't imagine before my transplant.

I've been given five whole years and who knows how much longer? I've been afforded the time to marry and see my brother marry. I've had the chance to travel all over Europe and the United States. I've grown from being a sickly, dependent young boy to a healthy, independent man.

One of my most vivid memories of the time leading up to

transplant was going to see Casino Royale with my brother. As the end credits rolled with the traditional, "Bond will return...." on the end, I sat and wondered whether I'd be around to see the next one.

Two more Bonds down the line, I'm still here. I may never achieve my childhood ambition of directing one, but it seems a fair trade to be here to watch them.

If this book has touched you in any way, I implore you to seek out your local method of signing the Organ Donor Register in your country. In almost all countries I've worked with or visited, I know the process is super-simple. If you haven't already registered your wishes, get onto Google now and find out how to do it.

And, more than anything, tell your loved ones your decisions. They can still stand in the way of your organs being donated after your death, but studies have shown that familial refusal rates significantly reduce (by up to 75%) if they know what you wanted to happen.

I'm only here to write and release this book because one person and their family saw fit to give me the greatest gift of all. I will never be able to thank them, never have a chance to tell them what this means, but I hope that somewhere up there, they are looking down on me and saying to themselves, "He did OK."

ACKNOWLEDGEMENTS

Enormous thanks to **Kiera** for helping me get the publishing licked into shape and to **Luke** for the wonderful cover design – both of them working for free to help promote organ donation and transplantation.

*****

To my **mum, dad and big bro** I owe a debt of thanks I can never hope to repay for all their love, patience and kindness over the years and for teaching me the true meaning of unconditional love.

To **Auntie Val, Uncle Martin** and the **Grange clan**, **Uncle Malcolm, Auntie Pauline, Uncle Colin** and the many **Phillipses** my love and gratitude for showing me what Uncles and Aunts should be to their nieces and nephews and for being not just cousins but friends.

To **Mike, Sue, Graeme and Norma**, my Godparents all, and the wonderful **Huddie/Kalbraier** families who have guided and supported me and helped shape me into the man I am today

To **Christopher** and **Robert**, for helping me pass on what my Godparents gave me – I would that I could half the person to you that they have been to me.

To the **Halasz** family, my love and endless thanks for welcoming me so readily into the (occasionally manic) fold and giving me the joys of being an Uncle. And to **Jancsi** especially for saying "Yes" on a Budapest balcony.

To my medical teams who, over the years, have kept me well enough to get to transplant and helped me flourish afterwards: Jenny, Nick, Wendy and the **paeds staff at Northampton General**; Lisa, Ali, Leslie, Malcolm, Lou, Cass, Anna, Holly, Jo, Sarah, and the entire **Churchill team in Oxford**; and Martin and his whole **Harefield team** too numerous to mention (but special mention to Janice, the friendliest face of any visit).

Almost lastly, to my wonderful wife **Kati**, who has been with me through the lowest of lows and the highest of highs, who has stuck by me no matter what and who forms the second, better, prettier half of my very being. I will love you to the end.

Finally, to my **donor and your courageous family**. Without you, I wouldn't be here to write this, wouldn't have seen my nieces and nephews grow into wonderful young men and women, wouldn't have been married, seen Hawaii or Italy or Budapest. Without you I would be nothing but a fond memory in the hearts of all those on this page. I hope you can be proud of me.

ABOUT THE AUTHOR

Oli Lewington is a writer, filmmaker and social media specialist. Diagnosed with Cystic Fibrosis – the UK's most common life-threatening genetic disease – at just 18 months, he began his lifelong fight to stay strong, healthy and, ultimately, alive.
He works to raise money and awareness for the CF Trust and organ donation.
He lives to make the most of the new life he's been given and honour the person who gave it to him.
He lives in Northamptonshire with his wife.

11503152R00170

Printed in Great Britain
by Amazon.co.uk, Ltd.,
Marston Gate.